Wickedness

'Mary Midgley may be the most frightening philosopher in the country: the one before whom it is least pleasant to appear a fool.'

The Guardian

'I have now read the book twice, not because it is difficult (on the contrary it reads with the ease and elegance of Bertrand Russell), but because it is so stimulating.'

Brian Masters, The Spectator

'Mrs Midgley has set out to delineate not so much the nature as the sources of wickedness. Though she calls the book a philosophical essay, it is more a contribution to psychology. The book is clearly written, with a refreshing absence of technical jargon, and each chapter is followed by a useful summary of its principal arguments.'

A. J. Ayer, The Listener

Mary
Midgley

Wickedness

A philosophical essay

With a new preface by the author

 London and New York

First published 1984
by Routledge & Kegan Paul

First published in Routledge Classics 2001
by Routledge
11 New Fetter Lane, London EC4P 4EE
29 West 35th Street, New York, NY 10001

Routledge is an imprint of the Taylor & Francis Group

Typeset in Joanna by RefineCatch Limited, Bungay, Suffolk
Printed and bound in Great Britain by
TJ International Ltd, Padstow, Cornwall

British Library Cataloguing in Publication Data
A catalogue record for this book is available from the British Library

Library of Congress Cataloging in Publication Data
A catalog record for this book has been applied for

ISBN 0–415–25551–1 (hbk)
ISBN 0–415–25398–5 (pbk)

CONTENTS

PREFACE TO THE ROUTLEDGE CLASSICS EDITION   vii
PREFACE   xv

1 The Problem of Natural Evil   1
2 Intelligibility and Immoralism   17
3 The Elusiveness of Responsibility   49
4 Understanding Aggression   74
5 Fates, Causes and Free-will   95
6 Selves and Shadows   116
7 The Instigators   136
8 Death-wish   158
9 Evil in Evolution   179

NOTES   208
INDEX   225

PREFACE TO THE ROUTLEDGE CLASSICS EDITION

IS THERE SUCH A THING AS WICKEDNESS?

Wickedness means intentionally doing acts that are wrong. But can this ever happen?

During the past century, wickedness has been made to look somewhat mythical in our part of the world. Many doubts have been raised about whether such a phenomenon can actually occur at all. On the one hand, our increasing knowledge of the variety of cultures has made it seem obscure whether any act can be really and objectively wrong. On the other hand, various scientific systems that describe other forms of causation have undermined the idea of free-will. They have made it hard to see how our intentions can really be the source of our acts.

During that same century, however, the phenomenon we call 'wickedness' has certainly not gone away. Nor has it become any easier to understand; indeed, it presses on us more than ever. For instance, if we think about the Nazi holocaust and other holocausts—for we had better not forget others such as those in

Russia and Cambodia and genocides such as that in Rwanda—questions about the meaning of wickedness weigh heavily on us. They do so, too, when we hear of multiple killers, as in the recent story of Dr Harold Shipman, the Manchester GP who seems to have killed some 300 people while apparently remaining a normal member of society.

WHERE CAN WE SHELVE IT?

It does not seem easy to simplify these cases into any tidy form which we can pack away in pigeon-holes along with the more straightforward parts of our knowledge. It is hard to do this because we inevitably ask *what it is like to be one of these people*—people who, for instance, devise death-camps.

From various scientific quarters we have been told that we should view these people fatalistically, as helpless mechanisms, merely inert tools or vehicles driven by their genes or by their cultures. That would put the issue on the scientific shelf. But if we did this we would have to view ourselves also as tools or vehicles of the same kind. And if we really, seriously believed this—instead of just saying it—it would scarcely be possible for us to get through the day. Life would become impossible, not because our dignity would be offended, but at a much deeper level, because that situation would make all our choices seem meaningless.

Does any other way of simplifying make better sense? Ought we perhaps—as philosophers like Nietzsche and Sartre have suggested—see these people as acting freely, indeed, but as being original moralists, authentically inventing new values which are in principle no less valid than those that are respected elsewhere?

This suggestion proposes an exciting, romantic idea of individual freedom; but again, if consistently followed through, it seems to make ordinary life impossible. If there can be no basis of agreement on these subjects—if each of us wanders alone in a moral vacuum, spinning values out of our own entrails like spiders, making them up somehow out of our own originality, taking nothing from anybody else and passing nothing on to others—then we have ceased to be social creatures altogether. Most of the occupations that interest us must then evaporate, because they are essentially social. They depend on shared values. And we shall certainly then have no shared vocabulary in which to say what we think about actions such as devising death-camps.

PART-TIME SCEPTICISM

Of course these sceptical ideas do not have to be taken to their logical conclusions in this way. Usually they are not so taken. They are merely thrown out in extreme forms, used casually in bits and pieces where they happen to come in handy, and forgotten where they might make difficulties. In fact they are half-truths: one-sided proposals with a useful aspect which needs to be balanced by their other halves and then integrated into a wider framework.

At present, however, not much of this integration is being done. On the whole, these ideas wander about loose in various forms and combinations of immoralism, relativism, subjectivism and determinism—forms which it is often quite difficult to understand and to distinguish. That is why, in this book, I have tried to sort them out and to ask how we can best understand and deal with them.

I have stressed that it is important to see that they are not just perverse aberrations, and to grasp the positive point of these ways of thinking. They arise largely out of two central strands of Enlightenment thought. On the one hand—morally—these scepticisms have flowed from an admirable reaction against the gross abuses that long attended the practices of blame and punishment, and that still do so. On the other hand—in the realm of knowledge—they express a determination to make human conduct as intelligible scientifically as the rest of the physical world.

These are both noble aims, which is why the sceptical views in question have suggested many necessary reforms. But even the noblest aims, if they are pursued in isolation, uncritically, and without regard for other aspects of life, are liable to drag us off to paradoxical conclusions which we ought not to accept.

OUR AMBIVALENT NATURE

Originally, I wrote this book in order to deal with business that I knew was left over from my first book, *Beast and Man*.[1] There, my aim was to stress the benign side of human nature. I wanted to say there that we should not be afraid of our 'animal nature.' We should not deny our continuity with the other social animals out of a groundless fear of degradation. I pointed out that these animals are not embodied vices, not the grotesque stereotypes that our morality has often depicted. They really are our kin. They are like us in much of their emotional life; creatures who share with us many (though of course not all) of the qualities that we most value. So it is wrong to build human self-esteem solely on our difference from them, wrong to make our pride depend on finding a quality that completely 'differentiates us from the beasts.' This kind of attempt to congratulate ourselves on being pure, autonomous intellects, immune from dependence on our earthly inheritance, is unrealistic and it distorts our system of values.

I still think that all this is true and hugely important. But if we

[1] First published in Great Britain by the Harvester Press, 1979. Revised edition with new introduction published by Routledge, London, 1995.

are to accept it honestly we need to notice the darker side of that inheritance as well. We need to grasp clearly how appallingly human beings sometimes behave. And we must see that we cannot always shift responsibility for that behaviour off onto an abstraction called 'culture.' (Culture, after all, is made by people.) There have to be natural motives present in humans which make cruelty and related vices possible.

It surely emerges that our natural motivation is highly ambivalent. It is so rich that it is full of conflicts, which present us constantly with a moral dialectic. On the one hand, our inborn emotional constitution is our only source of ideas about what is good. It is the root of all our wishes. On the other, that constitution does not itself supply a ready-made priority system by which we can arbitrate among those wishes when they clash. And some of those wishes are such that, if followed out on their own, they lead to real disaster.

We are not seraphs, beings who would never have these dangerous wishes and would therefore never have to choose. But neither are we quite like the other social animals. They also have conflicts and choices of this kind, but they seem to make their choices quickly, without a lot of reflection. Our trouble is that we have taken the exciting but dangerous course of opting, during our evolution, to become far more clearly conscious of these choices and far more likely to reflect on them afterwards. That is why we, unlike those animals, absolutely have to find such a priority system. It is why we cannot live without some kind of morality, and why in fact every human culture has one. As Darwin put it, in a discussion which has had far too little attention:

> Man, from the activity of his mental faculties, cannot avoid reflection . . . . Any animal whatever, endowed with well-marked social instincts, would inevitably acquire a moral sense or conscience, as soon as its intellectual powers had become

as well-developed, or anything like as well-developed, as in man.[2]

This point about the relation between morality and our natural feelings is a very complex one, and I went on to investigate it in a later book, *The Ethical Primate*.[3] That book, which deals with the nature of human freedom, is really a sequel to my discussions of moral scepticism in this book. I thought it was necessary to confront this moral scepticism first because, if I did not, my (and Darwin's) somewhat ambitious claims for the importance of morality on the human scene would not sound convincing.

It seemed to me that this kind of scepticism—not in the sense of a readiness to make enquiries, but of a fairly dogmatic profession of disbelief in morality as a whole—was both surprisingly influential at present and also surprisingly obscure. I was particularly struck by the way in which students of philosophy would express quite strong views on some moral question and then, when that question began to get difficult, readily say 'Well, it's all just a matter of your own subjective point of view, isn't it . . .?' I also thought it interesting that they often made remarks like 'But surely it's ALWAYS WRONG to make moral judgments?' without (apparently) noticing that this is itself a moral judgment. I therefore discussed the status of moral judgment at some length both in this book and also in another, slightly simpler one called *Can't We Make Moral Judgments?*[4]

---

[2] *The Descent of Man and Selection in Relation to Sex*, first edition, reprinted by Princeton University Press, Princeton, N.J., 1981, pp. 89 and 71–2.

[3] Routledge, London, 1994.

[4] Bristol Press, Bristol, 1991. This title now belongs to Duckworth Press.

FURTHER READING

I do not think that this topic has become any less important in the ten years that have passed since that book came out. But recently I have encountered several other books which seem to me useful for our understanding of it, and I would like to end this preface by mentioning them. (There must be many others, but I have not made a survey.) The first that I have noticed is *Facing the Extreme: Moral life in the concentration camps* by Tzvetan Todorov.[5] This is a careful study of the moral situation of both prisoners and guards in the German and Russian camps. It shows how much more complex and many-sided that situation was than might have been expected, and it is therefore a good preventive against over-simple views on these matters.

Then there have been a number of books about our primate relatives which have cast new and relevant light on our evolutionary situation. Among them, I have been particularly impressed by *Hierarchy in the Forest: The evolution of egalitarian behaviour* by Christopher Boehm.[6] Boehm traces the similarities and differences between human societies and those of the various great apes, investigating just what changes can have made the evolution of morality possible.

In *Demonic Males: Apes and the origins of human violence,*[7] Richard Wrangham and Dale Peterson discuss the rather alarming facts which have lately become known about the savage behaviour sometimes observed among these primates. Since Jane Goodall first recorded instances of warfare, infanticide and cannibalism among the chimps she studied,[8] many studies of this conduct have appeared. I find it interesting to notice how, in reading

[5] Weidenfeld and Nicolson, London, 1999.

[6] Harvard University Press, Cambridge, Mass., 1999.

[7] Bloomsbury, London, 1997.

[8] In *Through a Window: Thirty years with the chimpanzees of Gombe* (Weidenfeld and Nicolson, London, 1990).

these, one can easily find oneself thinking, 'why, this is terrible; why, they seem to be behaving almost as brutally as human beings sometimes do . . . .'

Further details about these discoveries and their implications can be found in *Beauty and the Beasts: Woman, ape and evolution* by Carol Jahme.[9] This book primarily describes the work of the impressive corps of women primatologists, starting with Jane Goodall, Dian Fossey and Birute Galdikas, who have so greatly increased our understanding of our relatives' lives. But it also contains much information about the creatures themselves which seems to me highly relevant to these important questions about our original emotional constitution.

Was Darwin right? Are we indeed creatures whose evolved nature absolutely requires the development of a morality? Or are we (as Nietzsche used to suggest sometimes, but just as often denied) beings who do not need one and who would get on a great deal better without it? This seems to me an extremely important question, and I hope that readers of this book will help us all to answer it.

Mary Midgley
2001

[9] Virago Press, London, 2000.

PREFACE

The topic of this book has long been on my mind as neglected and needing attention. Steep though it is, I therefore decided to propose it as a subject to the Philosophy Department of Trent University, Peterborough, Ontario, when they did me the honour of inviting me to give their Gilbert Ryle Lectures in 1980. I would like to thank them, and their colleagues at Trent, very warmly, both for accepting this alarming project so sympathetically and for their extremely kind and generous treatment of me during my visit to them. They showed a readiness for serious and helpful discussion which gave me much-needed support and encouragement to continue work on this tangled web of problems.

The four lectures which I then gave have supplied the basis for the first half of this book. A version of the first half of Chapter 6 ('Selves and Shadows') formed a 'Viewpoint' article in the *Times Literary Supplement* for 30 July 1982. I would like to thank the editor and proprietors of the TLS for permission to reprint it, and also an anonymous genius on their staff who supplied the present chapter title, instead of the much duller one which I had suggested for the article.

My family, and my colleagues at Newcastle University, have been endlessly helpful. Their influence is everywhere, but I would particularly like to thank Geoffrey Brown and Michael Bavidge, who read several parts in draft and made many useful suggestions. David Midgley, ploughing a neighbouring philosophical furrow, has been a great support, both with encouragement over difficulties and invaluable suggestions for reading. Prominent among others whom I have pestered, and had essential help from, are Jenny Teichman and Nicholas Dent.

1

THE PROBLEM OF
NATURAL EVIL

What in the midst lay but the Tower itself?
The round squat turret, blind as the fool's heart,
Built of brown stone, without a counterpart
In the whole world. The tempest's mocking elf
Points to the shipman thus the unseen shelf
He strikes on, only when the timbers start.
Robert Browning, 'Childe Roland to the Dark
Tower Came', stanza xxxi

1 LOOKING TOWARDS THE DARKNESS

This book is about the problem of evil, but not quite in the traditional sense, since I see it as our problem, not God's. It is often treated as the problem of why God allows evil. The enquiry then takes the form of a law-court, in which Man, appearing both as judge and accuser, arraigns God and convicts him of mismanaging his responsibilities. We then get a strange drama, in which two robed and wigged figures apparently sit opposite each other exchanging accusations. But this idea seems to me unhelpful. If God is not there, the drama cannot arise. If he is there, he is surely something bigger and more mysterious than a corrupt or stupid official. Either way, we still need to worry about a different and more pressing matter, namely the *immediate* sources of evil—not physical evil, but moral evil or sin—in human affairs. To blame God for making us capable of wrong-doing is beside the point. Since we are capable of it, what we need is to understand it. We ought not to be put off from trying to do this by the fact that Christian thinkers have sometimes been over-obsessed by sin, and have given some confused accounts of it. The phenomenon itself remains very important in spite of all the mistakes that are made about it. People often do treat each other abominably. They sometimes treat themselves abominably too. They constantly cause avoidable suffering. Why does this happen?

There is at present a strong tendency for decent people, especially in the social sciences, to hold that it has no internal causes in human nature—that it is just the result of outside pressures which could be removed. Now obviously there are powerful outside causes. There are physical pains, diseases, economic shortages and dangers—everything that counts as 'natural evil'. There are also cultural factors—bad example, bad teaching, bad organization. But these cultural causes do not solve our problem because we must still ask, how did the bad customs start, how do they spread, and how do they resist counter-conditioning? Can people be merely channels? If they are channels, out of what tap do the bad customs originally flow? And if they are not mere channels, if they contribute something, what is that contribution?

The idea that we must always choose between social and individual causes for human behaviour, and cannot use both, is confused and arbitrary. In calling it arbitrary, I do not of course mean that no reasons have been given for it, but that the reasons given are not, and could not possibly be, good enough to justify so crippling a policy. Causes of different kinds do not compete. They supplement each other. Nothing has one sole cause. And in this case, the inside and outside causes of human behaviour—its individual and social aspects—supplement each other so closely that they make no sense apart. Both must always be considered. It is understandable that embattled champions of the social aspect, such as Marx and Durkheim, were exasperated by earlier neglect of it, and in correcting that bias, slipped into producing its mirror image. Nothing is easier than to acquire the faults of one's opponents. But in the hands of their successors, this habit grew into a disastrous competitive tradition, a hallowed inter-disciplinary vendetta. Social scientists today are beginning to see the disadvantages of this blinkered approach. Now that it has become dominant, these snags are very serious and call for sharp attention.

However great may be the force of the external pressures on people, we still need to understand the way in which those people respond to the pressures. Infection can bring on fever, but only in creatures with a suitable circulatory system. Like fever, spite, resentment, envy, avarice, cruelty, meanness, hatred and the rest are themselves complex states, and they produce complex activities. Outside events may indeed bring them on, but, like other malfunctions, they would not develop if we were not prone to them. Simpler, non-social creatures are not capable of these responses and do not show them. Neither do some defective humans. Emotionally, we are capable of these vices, because we are capable of states opposite to them, namely the virtues, and these virtues would be unreal if they did not have an opposite alternative. The vices are the defects of our qualities. Our nature provides for both. If it did not, we should not be free.

These problems about the psychology of evil cannot be dealt with simply by denying that aggression is innate. In the first place, evil and aggression are not the same thing. Evil is much wider. A great deal of evil is caused by quiet, respectable, unaggressive motives like sloth, fear, avarice and greed. And aggression itself is by no means always bad. (I shall discuss ways of cutting aggression down to its proper size in this controversy in Chapter 4.) In the second place, and more seriously, to approach evil merely by noting its outside causes is to trivialize it. Unless we are willing to grasp imaginatively how it works in the human heart, and particularly in our own hearts, we cannot understand it. The problem of this understanding will occupy us constantly in this book. We have good reason to fear the understanding of evil, because understanding seems to involve some sort of identification. But what we do not understand at all we cannot detect or resist. We have somehow to understand, without accepting, what goes on in the hearts of the wicked. And since human hearts are not made in factories, but grow, this means taking seriously the natural emotional constitution which people are born with, as well as their social conditions. If we confine our attention to outside causes, we are led to think of wickedness as a set of peculiar behaviour-patterns belonging only to people with a distinctive history, people wearing, as it were, black hats like those which identify the villains in cowboy films. But this is fantasy.

In his book *The Anatomy of Human Destructiveness*, Erich Fromm explains his reasons for carefully analysing the motives of some prominent Nazis. Besides the interest of the wider human tendencies which they typify, he says:

> I had still another aim; that of pointing to the main fallacy which prevents people from recognizing potential Hitlers before they have shown their true faces. This fallacy lies in the belief that a thoroughly destructive and evil man must be a devil—and look his part; that he must be devoid of any positive quality; that he must bear the sign of Cain so visibly that everyone can recognize his destructiveness from afar. Such devils

exist, but they are rare.... Much more often the intensely destructive person will show a front of kindliness ... he will speak of his ideals and good intentions. But not only this. There is hardly a man who is utterly devoid of any kindness, of any good intentions. If he were he would be on the verge of insanity, except congenital 'moral idiots'. *Hence, as long as one believes that the evil man wears horns, one will not discover an evil man.*[1]

In order to locate the trouble in time, we need to understand it. And to do this we have to grasp how its patterns are continuous—even though not identical—with ones which appear in our own lives and the lives of those around us. Otherwise our notion of wickedness is unreal.

The choice of examples in this book to avoid that difficulty is an awkward one. The objection to using the Nazis is that mention of them may give the impression that wicked people tend to be foreigners with funny accents, and moreover—since they are already defeated—are not very dangerous. Every other possible example seems, however, equally open either to this distortion or to arguments about whether what they did was really wrong. This last is less likely with the Nazis than with most other cases. I have therefore used them, but have balanced their case by others, many of them drawn from literature and therefore, I hope, more obviously universal. It is particularly necessary to put the Nazis in perspective because they are, in a way, too good an example. It is not often that an influential political movement is as meanly supplied with positive, constructive ideals as they were. We always like to think that our enemies are like this, but it cannot be guaranteed. To become too obsessed with the Nazis can therefore encourage wishful thinking. It can turn out to be yet one more way of missing their successors—who do not need to be spiritually bankrupt to this extent to be genuinely dangerous—and of inflating mere ordinary opponents to Nazi status. This indeed seems repeatedly to have happened since the Second World War when concepts like 'appeasement' have been used to approximate other and quite different cases to the Nazi one—for instance by Anthony Eden in launching the Suez expedition. In general, politically wicked movements are mixed, standing also for some good, however ill-conceived, and those opposing them have to understand that good if their opposition is not to become distorted by a mindless destructive element.

What, then, about contemporary examples? These unfortunately are very hard to use here, because as soon as they are mentioned the pleasure of taking sides about them seems to exercise an almost irresistible fascination, and is bound to distract us from the central enquiry. We all find it much easier to denounce wickedness wholesale than to ask just what it is and how it works. This is, I think, only part of a remarkable general difficulty about facing this enquiry directly and keeping one's mind on it. This has something in common with the obstruction which Mary Douglas notices about dirt:

> We should now force ourselves to focus on dirt. Defined in this way, it appears as a residual category, rejected from our normal scheme of classifications. In trying to focus on it we run against our strongest mental habit.[2]

I have tried to resist this skiving tendency of the mind by many strategies, including another which may look even more startling and evasive, namely, not taking sides about religion. In my view it does not matter, for the purposes of analysing wickedness and its immediate sources, whether any religion is true or not. Neither embracing a religion nor anathematizing all of them will settle the range of questions we are dealing with here. I do not, of course, mean that the religious issue is not important in itself, or that it will make no difference to the way in which we view this matter. But it is not part of our present problem, nor a necessary preliminary for it. In particular, the idea that if once we got rid of religion, all problems of this kind would vanish, seems wild. Whatever may have been its plausibility in the eighteenth century, when it first took the centre of the stage, it is surely just a distraction today. It is, however, one often used by those who do not want to think seriously on this subject, and who prefer a ritual warfare about the existence of God to an atrociously difficult psychological enquiry. Since the useful observations which exist on this matter are scattered broadside across the works of many quite different kinds of writer, regardless of their views on religion and on many other divisive subjects, it seems likely that this warfare cannot help us, and that we had better keep clear of it.

2 POSITIVE AND NEGATIVE

To return, then, to our problem—How can we make our notion of wickedness more realistic? To do this we shall need, I believe, to think of wickedness not primarily as a positive, definite tendency like aggression, whose intrusion into human life needs a special explanation, but rather as negative, as a general kind of failure to live as we are capable of living. It will follow that, in order to understand it, we need primarily to understand our positive capacities. For that, we shall have to take seriously our original constitution, because only so can we understand the things which go wrong with it.

This means recognizing and investigating a whole range of wide natural motives, whose very existence recent liberal theorists have, in the name of decency, often denied—aggression, territoriality, possessiveness, competitiveness, dominance. All are wide, having good aspects as well as bad ones. All are (more or less) concerned with power. The importance of power in human motivation used to be considered a commonplace. Hobbes, Nietzsche, Adler and others have treated it as central. This suggestion is of course wildly over-simple, but it is not just silly. All these power-related motives are important also in the lives of other social animals, and appear there in behaviour which is, on the face of it, sometimes strikingly like much human behaviour. If we accept that we evolved from very similar creatures, it is natural to take these parallels seriously—to conclude, as we certainly would in the case of any other creature we were studying, that, besides the obvious differences, there is a real underlying likeness. The physiology of our glands and nervous system, too, is close enough to that of other primates to lead to their being constantly used as experimental subjects for investigations of it. And common tradition has never hesitated to treat such dangerous motives as natural, and has often been content to call them 'animal instincts'. I shall suggest that the burden of argument lies today on those who reject this obvious and workable way of thinking, not on those who accept it.[3]

The rejectors bring two main charges against it. Both charges are moral rather than theoretical. Both are in themselves very serious; but they really are not relevant to this issue. They are the fear of fatalism and the fear of power-worship. Fatalism seems to loom because people feel that, if we accept these motives as natural at all, we shall be committed to accepting bad conduct as inevitable, and power-worship seems to follow because what seems inevitable may command approval. But this alarming way of thinking is not necessary. There is no need to conceive a wide and complex motive like aggression on the model of a simple drain-pipe, a channel down which energy flows ineluctably to a single outcome—murder. No motive has that simple form. Aggression and fear, sex and curiosity and ambition, are all extremely versatile, containing many possibilities and contributing to many activities. And the relation of motives to value is still more subtle. We do not need to approve of everything we are capable of desiring. It probably is true in a sense that whatever people actually want has *some* value for them, that all wanted things contain a good. But there are so many such goods, and so much possibility of varying arrangements among them, that this cannot commit us to accepting anything as an overall good just because it is in some way wanted. The relation of these many goods must correspond with the relation among the needs of conscious beings, and conflicts can only be resolved in the light of a priority system amongst those needs. What we really want, if we are to understand them, is a full analysis of the complexities of human motivation.

This analysis, however, would be complicated. And many people still tend to feel that what we have here is an entirely simple issue. As they see it, the whole notion that a motive like aggression, which can produce bad conduct, might be natural is merely an unspeakable abomination, a hypothesis which must not even be considered. They often see this idea as identical with the theological doctrine of original sin, and consider that both, equally, just constitute the same bad excuse for fatalism and repression.

But this is to miss the large question. There is a real difficulty in understanding how people, including ourselves, can act as badly as they sometimes do. External causes alone do not fully explain it. And obviously external causes do not save us from fatalism. A social automaton, worked by conditioning, would be no more free than a physiological one worked by glands. What we need is not a different set of causes, but better understanding of the relation between all causes and free-will. Social and economic fatalism may look like a trouble-saver, because it may seem to make the problem of wickedness vanish, leaving only other people's inconvenient conduct, to be cured by conditioning. In this way, by attending only to outside causes, we try to cut out the idea of personal responsibility. If we blame society for every sin, we may hope that there will no longer be any sense in the question 'Whodunnit?' and so no meaning for the concept of blame either. This policy has obvious attractions, especially when we look at the appalling things which have been done in the name of punishment. Certainly the psychology of blame is a problem on its own. Resentment and vindictiveness are fearful dangers here. But when we are not just dealing with blame and punishment, but attempting to understand human conduct generally, we find that this advantage is illusory. The problem hasn't really gone away; we have only turned our backs on it. The difference between deliberate wrongdoing and mere accidental damage is crucial for a hundred purposes. People who are knocked down no doubt suffer pain whether they are knocked down on purpose or not, but the whole meaning of their suffering and the importance it has in their lives are quite different if it was done intentionally. We mind enormously whodunnit and why they dunnit, and whether the action can eventually be justified.

3   IS WICKEDNESS MYTHICAL?

Ought we perhaps not to mind about this? Is our moral concern somehow superstitious and outdated? Have we perhaps even— oddly enough—a moral duty to overcome it? This thought hangs in the air today as a cloud which inhibits us from examining many important questions. It may be best to look at it for a start in a rather crude form. The *Observer* for Sunday 28 February 1983 carried this report:

> ### BRITISH STILL BELIEVE IN SIN, HELL AND THE DEVIL
> Most Britons still believe in the concept of sin and nearly a third believe in hell and the devil, according to the biggest survey of public opinion ever carried out in the West. . . . Belief in sin is highest in Northern Ireland (91 per cent) and lowest in Denmark (29 per cent). . . . Even 15 per cent of atheists believe in sin and 4 per cent in the devil. . . . Most Europeans admit that they sometimes regret having done something wrong. The

> Italians and Danes suffer most from such regrets, the French
> and Belgians least. The rich regret more than the poor. . . . The
> rich are less likely to believe in sin than the poor.

What were these people supposed to be believing? 'Belief in sin'
is not a factual belief, as beliefs in God, hell or the devil certainly
are, whatever else they may involve. 'Sin' seems not to be defined
in a restrictive way as an offence against God, or the minority of
atheists could not have signed up for it. Belief in it can scarcely
be identified with the sense of regret for having done wrong,
since there might surely be people who thought that others
sinned, though they did not think they did so themselves.
Besides, the rich apparently do one but not the other. The word
'still' suggests that this puzzling belief is no longer fashionable.
But this makes it no easier to see what the belief is actually meant
to be, unless it is the simple and obvious one that some actions
are wrong. Is the reporter's idea really that up-to-date people—
including most Danes and even more atheists—have now with-
drawn their objections to all courses of action, including boiling
our friends alive just for the hell of it? This is not very plausible.
What the survey itself really means cannot of course be dis-
covered from this report. But the journalist's wording is an
interesting expression of a jumble of contemporary ideas which
will give us a good deal of trouble. They range from the mere
observation that the *word* sin is no longer fashionable, through a
set of changes in what we count as sins, to some genuine and
confusing reasons for doubt and rejection of certain moral views
which earlier ages could more easily be confident about. At a
popular level, all that is meant is often that sexual activity has
been shown not to be sinful. This does not diminish the number
of sins, because, where a sexual activity is considered justified,
interference with it begins to be blamed. Recognized sins against
liberty therefore multiply in exact proportion as recognized sins
against chastity grow scarcer.

Original sin, however, is of course a different matter. On the face of it, this phrase is contradictory. Sin must, by definition, be deliberate. And our original constitution cannot be deliberate; we did not choose it. I cannot discuss here what theologians have made of this paradox. But many of them seem to give the phrase 'original sin' a quite limited, sensible use, which has percolated into ordinary thought. They use it to indicate what might be called the raw materials of sin—natural impulses which are indeed not sinful in themselves, but which will lead to sin unless we are conscious and critical of them.[4] They are impulses which would not be present in a perfect creature—for instance, the sudden wish to attack an irritating person without delay. This kind of thing can also be described by the wider phrase of my chapter title: it is a 'natural evil'.

Now that phrase too may well seem paradoxical, particularly if we use it to describe human conduct. The phrase 'natural evil' is often used to contrast unavoidable, nonhuman disasters, such as plagues and earthquakes, with 'moral evil' or wickedness, which is deliberate. That is a useful distinction. But it leaves out an area between the two. *Moral evil too must surely have its 'natural history'*—a set of given ways in which it tends to occur in a given species. Not every kind of bad conduct is tempting or even psychologically possible for a given kind of being. There might— for instance—be creatures much less partial than we are, creatures entirely without our strong tendency (which appears even in very small children) to prefer some people to others. Their sins and temptations would be quite different from ours. And within the set of vices which belongs to us, some are much more powerful and dangerous than others. If this is true, it seems to be something which we need to understand. We have to look into these trends, not only for the practical purpose of controlling them, but also for the sake of our self-knowledge, our wholeness, our integrity. As Jung has pointed out, every solid object has its shadow-side.[5] The shadowy parts of the mind are an essential part of its form. To deny one's shadow is to lose solidity, to become something of a phantom. Self-deception about it may increase our confidence, but it surely threatens our wholeness.

4 MEPHISTOPHELES SAYS 'NO'

The notion of these natural, psychological tendencies to evil will, I think, lose some of its strangeness if we are careful to avoid thinking of them primarily as positive tendencies with positive functions, and instead try thinking of them as failures, dysfunctions. Here we stumble over an old dispute about the negativity of evil, one which has suffered, like so many disputes, from being seen as a simple choice between exclusive alternatives, when there are parts of the truth on both sides. The choice is really one between models—patterns of thought which have distinct uses, do not really conflict, but have to be employed in their own proper fields. It has, however, been treated as a matter for fighting, and in the last couple of centuries has been caught up in the general warfare declared between romantic and classical ways of thought. The older notion of evil as negative—which is implicit in much Greek thought, and in the central tradition of Christianity—was marked as classical and shared the general discrediting of classical attitudes. This whole warfare should surely now be seen as a mistaken one, a feud between two essential and complementary sides of life. But its results have been specially disastrous about wrong-doing, because this is a peculiarly difficult subject to think clearly about in any case. Only a very thin set of concepts was left us for handling it, and we are deeply confused about it—which may well account for the blank denial of its existence implied by the reported 'disbelief in sin' just mentioned. The first thing which seems needed here is to recover for use the older, recently neglected, idea of evil as negative—not because it contains the whole truth, but because it does hold an essential part of it.

Apart from its history—which we will consider in a moment—this idea is, on the face of it, natural enough. For instance, people have positive capacities for generosity and courage. They do not need extra capacities for meanness and cowardice as well. To be capable of these virtues is also to be capable of the corresponding vices, just as the possibility of physical strength carries with it that of physical weakness, and can only be understood if we think of that weakness as possible.[6] If we talk of evils natural to our species, we are of course not saying that it is as a whole just 'naturally evil', which is an unintelligible remark. We are drawing attention to particular evils which beset it. And grasping these evils is an absolutely necessary part of grasping its special excellences. Indeed, the notion of the evils comes first. You could hardly have much idea of generosity if you did not grasp the dangers of meanness. A creature with a Paradisal constitution, immune to all temptation, would not have the vices. But it would not have or need the virtues either. Nor would it, in the ordinary sense, have free-will. Evil, in fact, is essentially the absence of good, and cannot be understood on its own. We constantly need the kind of analysis which Bishop Butler gave of selfishness—'The thing to be lamented is, not that men have so great regard to their own good or interest in the present world, for they have not enough; but that they have so little to the good of others.'[7]

If we can use this idea, the existence of inborn tendencies to evil need not puzzle us too much. It only means that our good tendencies are not complete or infallible, that we are not faultless moral automata. But is evil negative? People resist this idea at once because they feel that it plays down the force of evil. Can a negative thing be so strong? Actually it can, and this is not a serious objection. Darkness and cold are negative, and they are strong enough. If we want to dramatize the idea, and see how a purely negative motive works out in action, we can consider the manifesto of Mephistopheles in Goethe's *Faust*. When Faust asks him who he is, he answers,

> The spirit I, that endlessly denies
> And rightly too; for all that comes to birth
> Is fit for overthrow, as nothing worth;
> Wherefore the world were better sterilized;
> Thus all that's here as Evil recognized
> Is gain to me, and downfall, ruin, sin,
> The very element I prosper in.[8]

This destruction is not a means to any positive aim. He is simply anti-life. Whatever is arising, he is against it. His element is mere refusal. Now whatever problems may arise about this diagnosis (and we will look at some of them in a moment) it scarcely shows evil as weak. All earthly good things are vulnerable and need a great deal of help. The power to destroy and to refuse help is not a trifling power.

SUMMARY

The problem of evil is not just a problem about God, but an important and difficult problem about individual human psychology. We need to understand better the natural tendencies which make human wickedness possible. Various contemporary habits of mind make this hard:

(1) There is a notion that both method and morals require human behaviour in general, and particularly wrong-doing, to be explained only by external, social causes. But this is a false antithesis. (i) As far as method goes, we need both social and individual causes. Neither makes sense alone. (ii) Morally, what we need is to avoid fatalism, which is an independent error, no more tied to thought about individuals than about societies.

From this angle, however, the idea of natural sources of wrong-doing has been obscured because it was supposed that any such source would have to be a fairly specific positive tendency, such as aggression. But aggression certainly does not play this role, and it is hard to see what would. It is probably more helpful to use here the traditional notion of evil as *negative*, as a more general rejection and denial of positive capacities. The psychological task is then one of mapping those capacities, understanding what potential gaps and conflicts there are among them, spotting the areas of danger at which failure easily takes place and so grasping more fully the workings of rejection. (This does not have to involve identifying with it. The danger of identifying with a mental process just because we come to understand it exists, but it can be resisted.)

(2) Difficulty, however, still arises about this programme today from a suspicion that the whole problem is imaginary. Officially, people are sceptical now about the very existence of sin or wickedness. When examined, however, this position usually turns out to be an unreal one, resulting from exaggeration of reforming claims. It often means merely that different things are now disapproved of, e.g. repression rather than adultery. (More serious aspects of immoralism will be dealt with in the next chapter.)

The idea of evil as negative does not, of course, imply that it is weak or unreal, any more than darkness or cold. What it does imply is a distinct, original human nature with relatively specific capacities and incapacities, rather than total plasticity and indefiniteness. Unless evil is to be seen as a mere outside enemy, totally external to humanity, it seems necessary to locate some of its sources in the unevenness of this original equipment. But this negative conception has often struck enquirers as insufficiently dramatic. Dualist accounts which make evil an independent force with a distinct existence will be our business in the next chapter.

2

INTELLIGIBILITY AND IMMORALISM

I have not been asked, as I should have been asked, what the name of Zarathustra means in my mouth, the mouth of the first immoralist; for what constitutes the tremendous historical uniqueness of that Persian is just the opposite of this. Zarathustra was the first to consider the fight of good and evil the very wheel in the machinery of things; the transportation of morality into the metaphysical realm, as a force, cause and end in itself, is *his* work. . . . Zarathustra created the most calamitous error, morality; consequently, he must also be the first to recognise it. The self-overcoming of morality, out of truthfulness; the self-overcoming of the moralist into his opposite—into me—that is what the name of Zarathustra means in my mouth.

Nietzsche, *Ecce Homo*, 'Why I am a Destiny', section 4[1]

1 THE DUALIST OPTION

The suspicion that treating evil as negative under-estimates it is a natural one, and it has repeatedly given rise to the opposite view—that evil is a radically distinct force in the world, co-ordinate with good and having nothing in common with it. In the first centuries of the Christian epoch, this dualistic notion was strongly expressed in the rather varied range of creeds which are together called Gnostic,[2] and still more strongly in the Manichaean religion. According to Mani (a Persian sage of the second century AD who developed the views of Zoroaster or Zarathustra) Good and Evil were originally independent powers, eternally co-present but unrelated.[3] Evil, however, had at some point intruded on the sphere of Good, causing a fearful disturbance, in the course of which Evil created the world. That world, having become involved in their conflict, remained a battlefield for these two forces, but one in which its evil creator at present prevailed strongly. (There was hope that Good might eventually win, but this was remote.) Matter itself was therefore essentially bad, physical things were bad, sex and reproduction were bad, and women were almost wholly bad. The only possible course for the human (male) soul was to withdraw completely from worldly affairs in order to reach personal salvation by esoteric devices which might put it in direct touch with the remote Good Principle—a contact which the Gnostics called Gnosis or Knowing. These included rituals, mysterious teachings, contemplation, severe fasting and other abstentions, and also for some sects orgiastic rites—all designed to free the soul from its fatal entanglement in earthly matter.

All this may seem strangely remote from our problems today. But it illustrates the lasting difficulty of thinking clearly about evil, the recurrent tendency to paradox. The impressive thing about the Gnostic and Manichaean approach is its insistence on acknowledging the strength and prevalence of evil in the world, and of the resulting conflicts within ourselves. The unimpressive thing is the startling way in which this attempt ends in a general refusal to acknowledge the world at all—a complete withdrawal from earthly life. The idea of a basically divided world does not provide an atmosphere in which human beings can breathe or act. Nor is it even clear that it is any more realistic than the idea of a basically good one. Accordingly, Christianity set its face against the dualist idea, and the Fathers of the Church argued for the unity and goodness of the world repeatedly against Gnostics and Manichees.[4] They did not of course mean that the world was at present in a good state, or likely to become so. Pessimism about that was common to all sides; sin was agreed to be rife and the end of the physical world seemed likely. All the same (said the Christians) this did not mean that two radically independent systems were at war in it. The devil was, they held, only a fallen angel, a created being lapsed from his original perfection and quite incapable of creating anything. He could only destroy.[5]

What this means—quite aside from its direct religious significance—is something very important about intelligibility. The world, including the internal world of motives, is to be seen as a single system—however vast, however complex and alarming—not as a loose conjunction of two disconnected ones which continually frustrate each other. This is not a piece of wish-fulfilment, designed to support unreal hopes of happiness. It is an essential presupposition for understanding the world at all. It is needed for science as well as for action—needed if all human effort is not to be doomed to equal and incurable futility.[6] In arguing this case, Christian writers faced great difficulties, for the dualist picture exercised a lasting force. On top of its dramatic appeal, it had of course the double advantage of excusing the faults both of God and Man. Manichaean ideas not only cropped up repeatedly in Christian heresies, such as that of the Cathars, but also tinged even the doctrines of those who officially denied them. The strain of misogyny in Christian thought is an interesting instance.[7] For Gnostics and Manichees, women were doubly sinister as providing both a direct temptation to men's involvement in matter through sexual activity, and also a perpetuation of it through childbirth, which continually drew more souls into the material trap. Women stood for continued life on earth, which was something these ascetics wanted stopped, quite as much as Mephistopheles did. Their ideal, like his, was to sterilize it. Official Christian doctrine resisted this view, and Aquinas among others took great trouble to combat it. But unofficial Christian feeling, and the tradition of a celibate clergy, often remained surprisingly Manichaean. More generally, the idea that this world—though created by God—is radically corrupt and has been handed over for a time wholly to the devil, who is now its prince, has extremely sinister possibilities. This idea was popular with the Protestant reformers, and had a very odd effect at times on their doctrines.[8]

2   CAN WE DO WRONG WILLINGLY?

This glance at the strange consequences which people have drawn from the apparently plausible Manichaean alternative may perhaps make us more willing to attend seriously to the ordinary traditional view. We are not directly concerned here with the familiar story of creation by a single good creator—except for its symbolic force—nor with the problems it raises about his responsibility, only with the view of human motives which it implies. Here the central doctrine is perhaps the one which Socrates expressed in a drastic form by saying that nobody does wrong willingly.[9] This obviously does not mean anything so trivial as that evil-doers are ill-informed, or need a better education. It claims that there is a confusion at the root of their thinking—a confusion which is in some sense voluntary and deliberate, therefore responsible, but which yet could not be embraced by anybody who fully understood it. If they really knew what they were doing they could not choose to do it. What this affirms is the unity of all human motivation. It says that, where there are radical moral clashes, involving charges of wickedness, at least one party must be assumed to be wrong. (It does not say which.) It is in fact the manifesto of extreme practical rationalism. It recommends thought as central to morality. At the opposite extreme, a great number of more or less romantic ways of thinking have claimed that, by contrast, thought plays no part here at all—that moral points of view are radically distinct and incommunicable, so that any two sets of principles can clash violently without any confusion having occurred on either side. (Emotivism, existentialism and cultural relativism express in their different ways this pole of the argument.) This has a much more destructive effect than people often think. It does not just mean that some moral problems are so hard that they may never be solved, or that there are always many unsettled disagreements, or that confidently dogmatic people can be wrong. These things after all are also true in science. It means that moral ideas are not in principle common property at all, so that somebody accused of wickedness will not normally have any case to answer, unless—quite by chance—he happens to share the ideas of his accuser. Conflicts within each individual are equally impenetrable to thought. On the whole, as critics have pointed out, this does not seem to be a very clear way of thinking about the moral universe, any more than about the physical one—if only because ideas never are purely private quirks, but are shaped communally by culture and language, and beneath that by our common nature. This is a large issue, to which we must return. But for the psychology of motivation, the effect is more limited and has had less attention.

Here, rationalistic methods have indeed often made trouble, because they have been carried much too far—notably by Plato and the seventeenth-century rationalists from Descartes to Leibniz, who claimed for thought all kinds of functions which really belong to perception or feeling. By treating reason as an alternative to experience, instead of as an aspect or supplement of it, they provoked empiricists to an unnecessary and misleading war.

But besides this, rationalists distorted the psychology of motive itself. It is much easier to declare the unity of all human motivation than it is to fit the whole confusing range and variety of its actual elements onto a single map, or even to draw a map which looks capable of leaving room for all of them. In particular, there are always undignified aspects which it is tempting to leave out altogether. Moralists too easily use the claim that motivation is in principle an intelligible whole as an excuse for restricting it to a narrow and unconvincing range. (The parallel in science is the temptation to cling to elegantly simple theories, rather than admit that they have been premature when awkward facts fail to fit them.)

Thus, the empiricist manifesto, which says 'experience is prior to thought', or—on the question of motives—'reason is the slave of the passions',[10] came into battle against the rationalist one, instead of their being used to supplement and correct each other. This happened in two stages. In the first, the range of motives present was not really questioned, but their emotional component was pointed out as their centre instead of their intellectual one. Thus Hume did a splendid and realistic job of showing how important natural sympathy is in producing a whole range of motives which others had explained as rational calculation.[11] But Hume had still a thoroughly classical view of the human heart. 'The passions' which he discussed were chiefly social ones, and ones which were thoroughly admissible— which fitted the locally accepted map. In the next stage, people like Rousseau, Nietzsche, Freud and Jung made much more serious trouble by pointing out whole seas and continents of motive which either were right off that map, or seemed to be grossly misrepresented on it.

3 THE HOPE OF SIMPLICITY

What was to be done about this? The best course would surely be to conclude that our system of motives really is larger and less simple than Socrates thought, and needs more subtle mapping, but that this need not stop it being still in some sense a unity, an order which is intelligible in so far as it is appropriate to the life of the kind of being which owns it, and which does indeed help us to understand existing moral systems. This seems to be Aristotle's position, and also that of Jung.[12] Nineteenth-century rebuilders, however, tended to be more drastic and more competitive. They saw their new psychological schemes as rivals ousting the old ones completely rather than supplementing them. They often prided themselves on their reductive simplicity. Thus Nietzsche:

> Assuming, finally, that we succeeded in explaining our entire instinctual life as the development and ramification of one basic form of will (of the will to power, as I hold); assuming that one could trace back all the organic functions to this will to power, including the solution of the problem of generation and nutrition (they are one problem)—if this were done, we should be justified in defining *all* effective energy unequivocally as *will to power*.[13]

Freud was equally sure that sternly reductive methods were needed, though his unifying categories were different.[14] Both he and Nietzsche thought it necessary to balance the new range of subtle insights which they contributed by a sharp reduction of others (previously accepted) to crude terms. Both tended to treat this reduction as if it were a matter of method, something made obviously necessary by scientific parsimony.

But this kind of reductiveness is not actually required or justified by parsimony at all. Science cannot require us to simplify complicated facts. The simplifiers' real aim is a moral one. They are attacking humbug. Their guiding idea is that the whole difficulty of understanding bad motives springs from hypocritical mystification, from refusing to be honest. If we would only face the grim truth (say these reducers) the whole matter would become quite straightforward. Now it is true that hypocritical mystification is indeed a chronic plague infesting all these enquiries. This insight—which is an old one[15]—is therefore valuable and constantly needs restating. But its optimistic conclusion about the straightforwardness which will follow is not justified. Even for the most brutally frank speakers, the topic of motives for wrongdoing and of bad motivation generally remains obscure and deeply infested with paradox. It is no easier to talk about without contradicting oneself than such notoriously paradoxical topics as infinity and the ultimate composition of matter. Its logic is not a plain one. Accordingly, vulgar immoralism, which treats the problem as simple, usually turns out to be an impenetrable muddle. Serious, sophisticated immoralism, by contrast, can be enormously valuable, but it is not a single position at all, much less a solid creed, a negative counterpart to morality, which can be preached and make converts. It is a range of critical enquiry, and one which continually changes. It consists of a set of widely varied criticisms of existing moralities, which are themselves various and changing. And these criticisms point in two quite divergent directions. The confident, reductive, theory-building side of immoralism, shown in Nietzsche's programme about the will to power, is flatly opposed to the sceptical side, which laughs at all sweeping theories and points out how little we know. For the reductive kind, Socrates's paradox still holds. Taking the will to power as the one all-explaining basic motive, Nietzsche firmly concludes that nobody ever refuses power willingly, and that those who do refuse it are in the wrong, because they have failed to understand their own basic needs. But from the other, sceptical angle, the whole generalization from which he starts is illicit and unwarranted. To bring these two lines of thought together would call for a great deal of work, and a disappointing curtailment to the claims of both of them.

4 PLURALISM AND ITS PROBLEMS

Perceptive moral philosophers have lately backed the sceptical against the reductive view of this question in various interesting ways. Thus, Peter Strawson calls for a tolerant, liberal society in which 'no ideal endeavours to engross, and determine the character of, the common morality.'[16] What makes this necessary, he says, is not just the need to avoid oppression, or to be fair to varying kinds of people, or to cultivate a seed-bed of new suggestions—arguments on which Mill relied in his *Essay on Liberty*. It is the radical impossibility of ever balancing one ideal against another. 'The region of the ethical is the region where there are truths but no truth. . . .' He gives, as an example, the failure of Bertrand Russell and D. H. Lawrence to understand each other, and concludes that 'the clash was a clash of two irreconcilable views of man; two irreconcilable attitudes. . . . It would be absurd to hope for a reconciliation of the two conflicting attitudes. It is not absurd to desire that both should exist, in conflict.'[17]

Now of course, this is much better than reducing Russell to Lawrence, or Lawrence to Russell, or both of them to an average. But it is still a spectators' model, a cock-fighting model. Is it the best we can do? Reconciliation, after all, does not have to mean reduction. The clash of these two towering egos does nothing to prove that their views were irreconcilable. They would have found it hard to agree on the time of day. Strawson's argument seems to need a discussion of what happens on the occasions when people actually do make progress in understanding each other. Can he show that this progress is always illusory, or that it always results in loss? This would surely be very odd. All our existing attitudes are built up out of such exchanges. We did not form them from our own substance in solitude, as an oyster forms a pearl. (And even oysters must eat.) Our failures in mutual understanding are only noticeable against the background of our modest, incomplete, clumsy but still continuous record of successes. We see that this must be true as soon as we move from the rather remote, spectator's or administrator's point of view, which chiefly interests Strawson, and start to consider conflicts and misunderstandings as they take shape in a single life. For instance, someone who admired both Russell and Lawrence, and was inclined to accept ideas from both of them, could not handle their divergences simply by saying with Strawson that 'the ethical is a region in which there are truths which are incompatible with each other',[18] 'there are truths but no truth' and leaving it at that. That person will have to break these two apparently distinct sets of truths up into their various elements, look for what is central in both, throw out a good deal, and somehow find a reconciliation among the rest so as to use it. For this work, he must assume that both sets operate in the same moral universe for a start—that the two 'views of man' are at some level views about the same thing—namely, human life— and therefore *can* conflict.

It is of course true that, as Strawson puts it, we should not expect to 'systematize these truths into a coherent body of truth' if that means a tidy system like Spinoza's ethical geometry, or even like dialectical materialism when Engels had finished tucking in Marx's loose ends. That kind of demand for order is excessive. But it does not follow that we have to stop trying to find some relation between them. Pluralism is quite right to insist that we must abandon the wild ambitions of unbridled system-builders, but that does not mean it must land us with an irreducible plurality of totally disconnected human aims instead.[19]

5 THE GAMBLING OPTION

Another very interesting sceptical discussion, which usefully supplements Strawson's, is Bernard Williams's account of conflicting aims in his article 'Moral Luck'.[20] His central argument does not deal with luck in our circumstances, nor even in our formative influences ('constitutive luck') but with the element of chance which an irreducible plurality of aims produces, in his view, as we drift helplessly between them. He gives examples of people torn between two ideals—Anna Karenina torn between the claims of her family and the hope of self-fulfilment through love, and Gauguin between similar claims and those of art. Williams says that there is 'no right answer'; a choice can only be justified by success.

Justification itself is therefore a matter of luck. He puts one aspect of this case from a bystander's (Strawsonian) angle, saying, 'The moral spectator has to consider the fact that he has reason to be glad that Gauguin succeeded, and hence that he tried', and speaks of 'our gratitude that morality does not always prevail—that moral values have been treated as one value among others, not as unquestionably supreme'.[21]

What does this mean? The point is, I think, a little obscured by the special—though not new—meaning given to the words *moral* and *morality* here. These words seem to be used narrowly, to refer to personal claims conventionally recognized, as contrasted with the direct demands of an ideal—or perhaps with one's own claims, if we think of Gauguin as serving himself rather than his art, and Anna as serving herself rather than love. One snag about this rather strange narrowed usage of 'morality' is that it easily becomes contemptuous ('Mr Pecksniff was a moral man') and so leads to the situation where a phrase like 'moral arguments for aid to the Third World' is taken to mean 'negligible, unrealistic, hypocritical arguments'. I have discussed this difficulty elsewhere.[22] But it seems to be making worse trouble than this for Williams's position. His idea seems to be that even if, within morality itself, reasoning might be possible and relevant, still, outside it, in this area where raw ideals clash, and the moral ideal is only one of them, thought cannot help us. *There* these are no right answers. Our attempt at moral reasoning fails, and by no accident. As he says of Kant's related enterprise, 'The attempt is so intimate to our notion of morality, that its failure may rather make us consider whether we should not *give up that notion altogether.*' (Italics mine)[23]

Williams's discussion is so rich, and brings together so many different kinds of sceptical argument, that it tends to overwhelm the reader. Its different strands must, however, be kept distinct. In this passage two odd things happen. First, as we have seen, the term 'morality' is used for one of the competing claims, instead of for the whole scene of the conflict. Second, an argument from gratitude is brought in to convince us that, if we support that claim, we must be hypocrites. Thus it is proved that, in this situation, only hypocrites would resort to moral reasoning.

The argument from gratitude, however, is not convincing. In this complicated world, no one can avoid constantly receiving benefits which result from past abuses. To say that we are grateful for these benefits need mean no more than that we welcome them. It does not mean that we endorse all the acts which led to them. Short of suicide, there would be no way of avoiding such benefits, nor would it be very helpful if we determined grimly to receive them but not enjoy them. If, however, we do give a more serious sense to gratitude—if we really think about Gauguin's choice and approve it—then we are taking one moral position among other possible ones. We are saying that art is so important that it can be right to put it above family claims. This is not an undiscussable view. It is one which, in our culture, has been explicitly expressed and defended with a great deal of discussion. It is already internal to our 'morality' in the wider and more natural sense of our thinking about how we ought to live.

Gauguin's problem arises directly out of this discussion and is shaped by it. (A medieval painter could never have had just this dilemma.) The clash is not between raw ideals, unreachable by thought. It arises out of a great deal of previous thought. As with Sartre's famous case of the young man wondering whether he should join the Free French Army or look after his mother,[24] the clash would not be there if a great deal of quite complex moral thinking had not previously been done and accepted. It is, then, always possible that hard, painful reconsideration will show something wrong with that thinking. In this way, some kind of a solution may be found. And in fact this quite often happens.

Is there any reason why we should always decide in advance that we shall not find any solution in this way—why we ought always to treat our dilemmas as intractable? This is, of course, itself a moral question, and there are strong considerations on both sides. In favour of this despairing emphasis there is—as Williams quite rightly points out—the need to correct a kind of idiotic optimism about choice which is rather characteristic of our protected age. We are a good deal inclined to expect that we can always have things both ways, to reject the idea of any real, unavoidable choice of evils. We sometimes support this unrealistic attitude by using the optimistic element in traditional rationalistic thought, and this can make us unfair in judging those who have had such a choice. This is a real corruption of moral judgment. On the other side, however, are the familiar dangers of fatalism, of assuming oneself to be helpless. Fatalism is also an extremely serious contemporary danger, and the idea that thought is useless can do much to reinforce it. (Anna Karenina's fatalistic character makes her a rather unsatisfactory example here. She does not really try to choose at all.) If we look at the matter—as Williams rightly does—as a practical one, from the point of view of the people actually choosing, this anti-fatalistic consideration must surely be very strong. Unless those people assume for a start that there is a right answer to their question 'what should I do?' they cannot ask it at all. No doubt it can turn out that the answer is, 'nothing, you are really helpless', or again—the kind of 'Buridan's ass' case which is perhaps more in Williams's mind, as in Sartre's—'considerations are equally balanced; one evil is not visibly worse than the other.' But these answers ought surely not to be assumed as inevitable in advance. Moreover, the assumption that a better answer can be found is important because it expresses a policy about personal identity—namely, a resolution not to be torn helplessly apart by drifting between unrelated ideals, an insistence on attempting integration.[25] This is surely a legitimate purpose. If not, we need to know why.

The question of responsibility will concern us in Chapters 3 and 5. But as far as plurality of ideals goes, we surely are not always reduced to the position of impartial bystanders, who must either just applaud the co-existence of incompatible aims (with Strawson) or judge between them merely on gambling principles by studying form—by noting the success and failure of those who have backed them—which seems to be the natural conclusion of Williams's proposal. I do not want to travesty either of these arguments. No doubt there are cases where they are appropriate, and no doubt more subtle general interpretations of them are possible. But the sceptical message in both seems to me seriously meant, and likely to be picked up by readers. It is therefore worth stating it flatly in this crude form. To test whether, in this crude form, we could accept it, we need to look at a wide range of examples—not just those specially designed by philosophers to be undecidable. We should consider cases where we would certainly not stay on the fence, such as the Nazi ideal. Or if we need to get third-party considerations out of the way, we could take the case of blind, hide-bound conventionality, or devotion to a religion which we disapprove of. Let the person concerned be someone close to us, or of course, in the limiting case, ourselves. Is it plausible that the best way to deal with this conflict would be to murmur tolerantly, 'Well, well, if it suits you—If you believe in it—If it comes off?'

If this is not plausible, then what these writers are doing surely falls within morality, and is criticism of particular moral attitudes, not a meta-ethical discovery capable of changing our whole notion of what morality is. As we shall see, a great deal of Nietzsche's own criticism has the same limitation.

6 THE USES OF IMMORALISM

Immoralism is a tool-kit, not a base. There is by now plenty of immoralist material around on which this gloomy truth can be checked, and also plenty of puzzled enquiry from even its most sympathetic interpreters. For instance—Machiavelli wrote plainly, but just what did he mean? Isaiah Berlin has collected learned opinions on this matter, from which Machiavelli emerges as at once a campaigning atheist and a devout Catholic, an agonized reformer and a soberly neutral historian, a sharp satirist, interpretable always by opposites, and a literal-minded describer, an entirely modern thinker, and one locked wholly into the ideas of his age.[26] These disagreements certainly do not spring just from lack of courage in the commentators—though they tend to accuse each other of that—nor from lack of good will, but from the real difficulty of seeing how to fit Machiavelli's apparently simple, bald statements to the unsimple world they have to refer to.

In the case of Nietzsche, similar difficulties are partly disguised by his deliberately paradoxical style, by his ostentatiously teasing habits, his insistence that, yes indeed, he does often contradict himself, and is also ready to contradict anybody else who may put their head above the horizon. He combines this prickly, sceptical approach with such unmistakable moral fervour, and with so firm a set of destructive intentions, that readers easily take the paradoxes for a temporary, superficial firework display, behind which a plain, clear immoralist position lies waiting, ready to be revealed to readers with sufficient courage to accept it. But courage is not enough. There is no such plain position. Nietzsche himself lambasts those who suppose him to have one. What he provides is a great deal of first-rate exploring equipment, and a set of suggestions for expeditions in all directions, radiating roughly from the orthodox positions of his day. Those positions, together with some of their predecessors, are the only ones which he rules untenable. He will be committed to nothing else. The term 'immoralist' has no more substantial meaning. Even in his most mature work, the definitions which he actually gives of this term, which he invented, and which he clearly thought important, are disappointingly negative and restricted—

> Fundamentally, my term *immoralist* involves two negations. For one, I negate a type of man that has so far been considered supreme; the good, the benevolent, the beneficent. And then I negate a type of morality that has become prevalent and predominant as morality itself—the morality of decadence, or, more concretely, *Christian* morality . . . morality as vampirism.[27]

But to get morally indignant about one type of morality is not to show a way of getting rid of morality altogether, nor a convincing reason why this is necessary. Apart from his genius, Nietzsche in fact did not differ from the Lutheran pastors who were his forefathers in ceasing to denounce sin, nor in providing a complete, satisfying alternative to their beliefs, but in denouncing different sins and attacking different attitudes. As a moralist, he is essentially and in all his moods *against* something, and to treat him as providing any resting-place is to travesty him.

7 MORAL VACUUMS: THEIR USES AND DRAWBACKS

Nietzsche himself was worried by this negative, destructive tendency in his work. He took Goethe's teaching very seriously, and was determined not to be a Mephistopheles who says only No to life. After his early, nihilistic phase, when he philosophized, as he said, mainly with a hammer, he was flooded by a sense of the need to say yes, and of the difficulty of doing it from the position which he had got into. *Thus Spake Zarathustra* was his first full expression of this need:

> The psychological problem in the type of Zarathustra is how he that says No and *does* No to an unheard-of degree, to everything which one has so far said Yes, can nevertheless be the opposite of a No-saying spirit . . . how he that has the hardest, most terrible insight into reality, that has thought the 'most abysmal idea', nevertheless does not consider it an objection to existence, not even to its eternal recurrence—but rather one reason more for being himself the eternal Yes to all things—[28]

He saw that this was a fearful task, and that the things to which he could say yes must mainly be so distant and general that the hammer would still be his almost invariable tool when confronted with any specific thing or person in the past or present. And there is an obvious risk that this will make the whole task impossible, because our attitudes to what is near us tend to have more reality than those towards the remote, and (as Butler rightly said about the Stoics)[29] it is much easier to destroy ordinary human feeling than to replace it with a loftier, grander, more cosmic substitute. Still, this was Nietzsche's life-long enterprise, and he accepted the need which it imposed on him to be constantly denying most of the things he heard, including things which he himself had previously said. In his sceptical mood, he therefore invoked Heraclitus:

> The affirmation of passing away and *destroying*, which is the decisive feature of a Dionysian philosophy; saying Yes to opposition and war; *becoming*, along with radical repudiation of *being*—all this is more closely related to me than anything else thought to date.[30]

Evidently, this is not the sort of writer who ought to be credited with inventing an easy orthodoxy for the next age.

But that has of course been done. In the usual cock-eyed process attending the digestion of new ideas, Nietzsche's dynamic contradictiousness has served as a source for the kind of static, somnolent, undiscriminating, sceptical tolerance which seems to be expressed by the claim to have stopped believing in sin. Readiness to question everything mutates mysteriously into a pose of equal indifference to all possible answers. Can this be more than pose? That it often is a pose, lasting only till the owner's moral corns happen to be trodden on, is by now a common observation. (The shocked immoralist in Tom Stoppard's play *Professional Foul* is a nice case.) But this is not just an unfair joke by satirists. What else could the undiscriminating position be? It is scarcely possible to vindicate it as a stern attempt to stand by one's moral principles, and remain indifferent in the face of all temptation to do otherwise.

Yet it does seem to be quite widely believed that there exists this clear, plain, immoralist position, unassailable because it says nothing, lying outside all existing moralities and supplying a platform from which to judge them. From this platform they are all to be viewed as equally unnecessary. This places a burden on anybody accepting *any* moral position—that is, essentially, any considered system of priorities—to justify it, to show its necessity to those who (more enlightenedly) have none. Here the sceptical side of immoralism is used in unreal isolation as an all-purpose trouble-saver. General scepticism—not in the sense of an enquiring temper, but of dogmatic universal rejection—

appears arbitrarily as the starting-point of judgment. A procedure like Descartes' systematic doubt, starting in the void, is taken to be the up-to-date treatment for standards, regardless of the crippling faults which that procedure has been found to have in the simpler case of theoretical knowledge. The imaginary critic, standing nowhere, becomes the only one who needs to be considered. This is certainly one way of getting rid of the problem of evil—by simplifying it out of existence. Everything (as they say) becomes subjective.

This popular scepticism is usually quite unconsidered, indeed (as often happens) it is popular just because it cheerfully combines such a wide range of attractive but incompatible views. Bernard Williams therefore does a great service by providing a much more conscious and reflective sceptical argument.[31] Scepticism, he says, really ought to be extended much further in practical, moral thinking than in theoretical thinking. In morals, the very notion of consistency is out of place. Someone faced with a moral dilemma has no answer to look for; whatever he does will inevitably be wrong.

We cannot go into the whole issue about theoretical knowledge here. But we do have to notice some very awkward features of this position. All concepts exist to be used. The concept of knowledge is no exception. The distinction between what we know and what we don't know—between belief resting on good ground and mere guesses—seems not to be less needed for moral thinking than for the theoretical kind, but far more, because there it directly affects action. If we could not think with any sort of method about the relation between our aims, we would have to act at random.

Of course it is true that our thinking is always incomplete, that we need to remember this incompleteness, and that we should avoid over-confidence. But this can scarcely mean that on moral questions nothing is any clearer than anything else. (The need to avoid over-confidence, after all, arises in scientific thinking too.)

Because scepticism about morality is usually conducted so select-ively, with so strong an unconscious bias, its incoherence when it is treated as a general doctrine is often overlooked. The dispute then is not just a verbal one about the use of certain words like knowledge. This is a genuinely neutral activity which has never put people off doing science. It is a much more far-reaching query about whether it is any use at all to try and think when we are dealing with a clash of aims. What concepts do we actually need here? The word knowledge itself may not be very import-ant, though, as Ryle pointed out,[32] it does have its uses. The word truth is also perhaps not central, though we certainly do not want to join jesting Pilate in losing it altogether. There are truths which people die for. Strawson sees the need to preserve the word when he says that there are 'truths but no truth'. The idea of quite distinct, private truths, kept separately by each of us like beetles in boxes,[33] is not however really a possible one. However hard we may sometimes find it to communicate on these mat-ters, we do succeed in doing it a great deal of the time. We are not moral solipsists, and if we were we should not talk of truths at all (nor perhaps of anything else). The really essential concept, however, is consistency. Without this, thought does become impossible. If the clashes which arise when we try to harmonize our aims were simply impenetrable to thought—if confusion here were a doom against which we could not fight—we could never have formed the general moral ideas by which we actually live, and which are taken for granted in all the examples given of supposedly irresoluble conflicts. We should be more helpless in these situations than even the feeblest of us actually is, and should never have managed to build up viable societies.

How does this work in practice? As Jenny Teichman has pointed out,[34] odd results would follow if we applied a genu-inely impartial scepticism to the case of Sartre's student who hesitates between the claims of his mother and those of the Free French Army.

The idea that whatever the student does will somehow be wrong completely blurs a vital difference, the difference between this kind of young man and the entirely different kind of young man who, living in Berlin in 1930, cannot decide between joining the Blackshirts and joining the Brownshirts. There is a very clear sense in which it is quite true to say that whatever this second young man does will be wrong.

And how, she asks, does the matter look if we give the French student some further options, such as poisoning his mother or joining the collaborators? (Or perhaps just sloping off to Marseilles to sell nylons on the black market?) Are all such options just equally wrong with the two already proposed? It becomes clear that Sartre at least is not really applying any general scepticism to moral thought, but merely engaging in that thought like anyone else up to the point where it gets difficult, and then making a virtue of evading the issue. Bystanders can do this; those actually in the fix cannot. Williams too seems in the end to be committed to the spectator's position, a fact which his frequent insistence on the notion of *tragedy* only emphasizes. For Gauguin himself, it would be no help to be told that his situation was tragic and whatever he did would be wrong. Friends—as opposed to spectators or academics aiming to keep out of trouble—would try to look at the problem from the chooser's angle and see what they could point out about it which would help him to a conclusion he could make some sense of. It is of course true that the chooser must not hand over his own *responsibility* to the adviser, nor to any kind of authority. This is one half of Sartre's point, and a very important one. But it does not show at all that no solution is better than any other, nor that the people seeking the best one have no common ground to stand on. They are not doomed always to talk at cross-purposes. If they try, they can make progress in understanding each other.

8 SCEPTICAL DOUBTS FROM THE CLASH OF CULTURES

If we do accept the sceptical approach, we have of course a whole new set of difficulties about the negativity of evil. How do we know which pole is positive and which is negative? The cases of darkness and cold (says the sceptic) are different, they really are objective. Physicists have good reason there for treating heat and light as positive. Wave motions are real, distinct, positive activities which cease in darkness and cold. But is anything like this true of human capacities and the virtues which go with them? Might we not find a tribe tomorrow which counts all our virtues as vices and vice versa? Perhaps this minute these people are praising each other for their meanness and cowardice, while they abuse and punish others for their inexcusable courage and generosity. Might not we ourselves decide tomorrow, freely and existentially, to change over to that system? Or to invent another quite new one, which will also be capable of either polarity?

This idea has its attractions, and of course it is a good corrective for dogmatism. But when you come to work it out, the programme is disappointingly hard. Even the ingenuity of science-fiction writers has not, so far as I know, been able to make anything of it. When we think about praising people for cowardice, it usually turns out that we would be praising them for being prudent or peaceable, and these are quite different things from cowardice. Again, to praise people for meanness would probably mean praising them for prudence, for thrift or for realism, and none of these is actually meanness. This is not just a difficulty about 'emotive meaning' arbitrarily attached to words, but about intelligibility.

Not just anything can intelligibly count as a good quality.[35] And forms of praise are no use if they are not intelligible in this sense—if we cannot understand what people are being praised for. Even new forms of praise, and ones from remote cultures, have to be treated as being intelligible in this way. We expect to be able to find their meaning, if we give them proper attention. When Nietzsche proposed a revaluation of all the values, he did not mean just a random changing round of all the price-tags in the window, nor the systematic adding of a minus sign to each.[36] He meant a coherent new system of priorities. In making this system, it can sometimes be very useful to use terms paradoxically—for instance, to praise people (as he did) by calling them malicious, or perhaps even cowardly or mean. But the point of this ploy is always to show that the polarization needs more thought, that it has been misused, applied to the wrong things, or given the wrong emphasis. Putting this misuse straight can call for great moral changes. But it never calls for the crude technique of reversing the real grounds of praise. I make this sweeping remark fairly confidently because it is now a century since Nietzsche wrote, and neither he nor any other immoralist seems to have resorted to anything like this.

The anthropologists reporting on remote cultures do not do it either. Their news is never simply that a given tribe honours cowardice and despises courage. Anthropologists actually spend their time going to endless trouble in explaining the moral paradoxes which they report—in making us see what the people they study mean by their unexpected forms of praise and abuse. And they have to bring this meaning home to us through polarizations which are not reversed—which are taken as solid ground, shared between our culture and theirs. This assumption of shared moral compass-bearings is what makes it possible for us to praise and learn from other cultures, and also to accept the criticisms which outsiders pass on our own culture. Shared polarization is necessary for all moral thinking, including the thinking of immoralists.

9 BEYOND WHAT GOOD AND WHAT EVIL?

It seems often to be supposed that Nietzsche's programme of
going 'beyond good and evil' showed a way of avoiding all such
polarization. This programme is often strangely misconceived,
most simply and bizarrely as a general rejection of all moral
oppositions, a ruling that distinctions between bad and good
things have become obsolete. It is very remarkable that this view
can be attributed to someone whose burning moral indignation
is his most striking quality. Nietzsche's views on many points
varied considerably with the problems he dealt with, and with
advances in his thinking. But one factor is constant; throughout
his life he denounced abominations, and pointed the way to
distant and demanding ideals. And the general nature of the
things which he saw as ideals and abominations did not greatly
change. He loathed self-deceit, cowardice, complacency, sentimentality, humbug, apathy and inertia, and thought the evils on
which his contemporaries concentrated far less serious than
these relatively neglected ones. For this view he argued strongly.
He did not treat it simply as a private hobby of his own, as a true
subjectivist presumably would. He thought that it could be established, and that the material chiefly needed to establish it was
factual, psychological study of human nature, especially as displayed in relation to morality. About the particular antithesis of
good and evil, his point is actually quite a limited one; it is to
denounce what he calls a 'slave morality'.[37] This is a passive code
based chiefly on fear, concentrated on avoiding 'evil'—that is,
the suffering which might threaten one—and seeing as 'good'
chiefly the absence and prevention of that suffering. He contrasts
this with 'master-morality'—the active code developed among
rulers—which he thinks operates instead with the antithesis
'good versus bad', meaning 'distinguished versus despicable.'
'The distinguished type of being ... creates value. This type
honours everything he knows about himself; his morality is

self-glorification.' The point of the antithesis, for Nietzsche, is to enable him to denounce effectively the elements of slave-morality which he detects, not only in Christianity, but in humanitarian and egalitarian reformers, and in everybody unrealistic enough to suppose that the diminution of suffering is an important aim. What he says is enormously interesting, acute and controversial. Its details are often highly original. But it never attempts to jump off its shadow by abandoning all trad-itional moral polarizations. It depends entirely on using some of these to undermine others; on presupposing a background of some virtues to show up the defects of the rest.

When, therefore, he claims to go right beyond this and abol-ish morality altogether—for instance in the quotation which heads this chapter—he has gone into hyperbole. Often he just means that he rejects the emphasis of contemporary moralists. In that particular quotation, however, he is saying something dif-ferent and perhaps more interesting, something metaphysical. He is attacking the use of a strong religious metaphysic to sup-port morality—'the transposition of morality into the meta-physical realm, as a force, cause and end in itself.' He objects to the idea that the universe dramatizes our conflicts, and still more to the idea that it will resolve them in our favour. These ideas strike him as escapist, anthropocentric falsehoods typical of religious thinking. Besides this general objection to metaphysics invented for reassurance, he has a psychological objection to simple Persian dualism, because he constantly wants to emphasize the entanglement of good human motives with bad ones—the mutual dependence of vice and virtue. 'The greatest evil belongs with the greatest good; this, however, is the creative good.'[38] Like Jung, he wants to correct what he thinks a fatal piece of unrealism in the Christian tradition—the attempt to jump off one's shadow.[39] This is surely a very important insight. But it is still the insight of a moralist. He is telling us our duty. The attack is not really on morality at all.

Nietzsche brings out strongly here an important conflict of interest which besets all moral psychology. For theoretical understanding of the moral scene, we need to emphasize continuity, to see all relevant motives as related, and as falling within an intelligible whole. For practical guidance, however, we need to draw a sharp line between light and dark, up and down, between what are to be viewed as ideals and as abominations. Immoralists do not escape this dilemma, because they too are in the business of denouncing and exalting. In spite of some misleading claims, they do not abandon the enterprise of guidance. Nor do even the changes they can make in it turn out as drastic as is at first hoped, because to make more than quite slight changes is to become unintelligible. And those who want to change the world cannot really afford to do that.

10 THE UNREAL PROBLEM OF WEIGHTLESSNESS

It is not easy, in fact, to give substance to the idea of sceptically rejecting all traditional polarities of value, nor to see what work it would do if it could be formulated. The parallel with the Copernican Revolution may be relevant. It is often suggested that the discovery that the earth was not in the middle of the universe is radically disrupting to human thought, since it shows that there is no 'real' up or down.[40] But this seems unduly dramatic. Whatever use the image of a differently shaped universe may have had in our symbolism, the idea of up and down does not seem to have vanished. Beings such as we, having physical bodies strongly affected by gravitation, can exist only where gravitation allows, and act only in ways to which it is continually relevant. Space-travel provides only a partial and trifling extension of this sphere. Our life is framed for living near the ground. Even our symbolism about value cannot be divorced from this framework. Weight so shapes our lives that what is up is almost bound to count as difficult, arduous, therefore probably good (since why would we be climbing to it otherwise?) and what is *down* is where we fall to—dangerous, swampy, liable to engulf us. Copernicus has not robbed us of our up and down. We have only lost an extra outwork of symbolism which we had built on them. There is no need for vertigo about this. Similarly in our moral universe, basic facts about our physical make-up which many people find too mundane to count as the 'basis' for our more exalted faculties do in fact supply us with our bearings, orient us initially to the world in which we live. They give us our original polarities of value. Without them we could not start to live, so we may as well take them and be grateful. What we do with them afterwards is another story.

Scepticism about these polarities seems, then, to be mostly mistaken melodrama and will not help us. The fixedness of these polarities has been somewhat clumsily expressed by saying that certain norms are innate.[41] The language of this remark needs watching, because of course it will not be true if 'norms' are taken to be the actual detailed standards endorsed by existing cultures. But provided the term is understood widely, just to indicate the general direction of approval, the remark is true and none of us doubts it.

Now if this is right—if the basic polarities are indeed given by our nature and condition—then the sense in which evil is negative grows clearer. To take the case of courage—This concept arises because we are weak, vulnerable, imaginative and subject to fears, and yet fear is not a sufficient guide for us because we value many other things besides safety. In fact, safety is a means to other ends, not an end in itself at all. If, therefore, we always abandoned other pursuits as soon as we saw danger, we should fall apart in confused frustration. That is why, when we see the need for it, we can make an effort to overcome fear. The purpose and the effort mark this as a positive capacity. You cannot give this kind of description of cowardice. To say that, if we see the need for it, we can make an effort to give way to fear is absurd.

Just as in the case of heat and light, a distinctive sort of activity—namely purposive effort—is going on here, which marks off positive from negative on the moral scene, and does so equally for all cultures. But effort only makes sense where its purpose is intelligible. Simply trying to do something difficult is not enough. If, for instance, you try persistently to cut off your own head, this will not qualify you for praise unless that difficult enterprise has a point which other people can see. Our imagination is amazingly fertile in supplying this kind of point. As soon as I mentioned this example the enterprising reader will probably have thought of a point for it—ritual, legal, religious, exhibitionistic, Gilbert-and-Sullivan or whatnot. But if we really did not share a common spectrum of aims with the rest of the human race, we could never supply any point of this kind, and this example would be no more mysterious than any other. We would be equally at a loss whenever we tried to understand any unfamiliar example of human action. And, in fact, we are not at a loss in this way.

11 BRINGING THE QUESTION HOME

What I have been saying here about shared human aims and values is in a way obvious to the point of being boring. In actual life, we take it for granted. But exaggerated scepticism about it has for some time been fashionable among theorists, and it has become hard for us to approach these questions realistically. The word 'wickedness' in the title of this book will certainly have struck many people as odd and suspect. This will partly be because of the relativistic objections which I have just been mentioning—the notion that no act can really be wrong, because standards of wrongness vary infinitely and are entirely relative to culture. I am spending little time on this objection here, because I think it is actually much less serious than others which confront us.[42] It seems to flow largely from an unreal exaggeration of the difference between cultures. That difference cannot possibly justify a general paralysis of the moral faculties. What we are trying to do now is to understand what wickedness is. In order to do that, we do not need to get general agreement first about every borderline case. (Just so, if we were asking what poison is, we would not need to start by settling all disputes about borderline cases of poisons, such as alcohol and valium.) All classifications have borderline cases. But they also have central ones, which provide the best starting-point. If we are inclined to get paralysed here, and to doubt the reality of wickedness, it is probably best to start from cases which are close to us, and which we understand well enough to make doubts about them look unreal. Outrageous acts of our own are one good source of examples. Another is the political scene, where we often identify large-scale criminals with some confidence. (By contrast, doubts in the anthropological cases often turn out to be just a product of their remoteness.) Most of us will have no difficulty in finding examples of such odious acts. In these cases, we shall probably not find that there is much point in questioning the wickedness on the ground that the act *may* not be wrong after all, because some other culture might have standards which would excuse or justify it, or that somebody might shortly invent such a standard. This would not be much of an answer to the charge 'you have—or this politician has—behaved abominably.' The people who committed the acts in question—including ourselves—did not have those alien standards. Instead they had reason, and as far as we can see good reason, to believe that what they are doing was wrong. These acts, therefore, are examples of the phenomenon on which we want to concentrate, namely, actual wickedness.

Scepticism about it has three main forms. First comes the one we have just considered: the idea that no acts are really wrong. Next comes the thought that—though there are wrong acts—nobody actually commits them. And finally comes the thought that—though people do commit them—they never do it on purpose, and so are not responsible. All three ideas will still concern us in the next three chapters.

SUMMARY

The notion of evil as a positive force, totally separate from good, has been attractive because it looks realistic. But this dualistic, Manichaean approach has led to wild paradox and the hatred of life. This is no accident. The topic is really difficult. Though the need for such radically new approaches is constantly felt, each one brings a new set of difficulties and paradoxes. Each needs others to supplement it, and supplies only part of the truth.

The traditional view has its own paradoxes, the central one being probably that strongly expressed by Socrates in his rationalist manifesto—'Nobody does wrong willingly.' This implies a confidence that we all inhabit the same moral universe—that in principle we can understand each other's moral judgments and could therefore, if all went well, reach agreement about them. Moral questions then have a right answer. Thought can help us in the choice of principles on which to act.

Because this kind of claim looks excessively confident, it has provoked equally extreme, romantically individualist claims that thought is simply irrelevant here and these questions have no possible answer. Each individual (or society?) then has its own unique, incommunicable set of problems, and answers them by feeling or decision, not by thought.

Both these extremes are unrealistic. We must think in order to act, and we must understand each other's guiding ideas. The question whether answers 'exist' to our moral questions must therefore be one about method. Just as we are enabled to ask scientific questions by assuming that the world is intelligible enough to supply their answers (though we have no guarantee of this), so we have to treat the range of human motives as in principle unified enough to make communication and agreement possible on the moral issues which actually arise, without wrecking personal identity.

In order to communicate at all—even so far as to acknowledge a disagreement—we have to assume this much uniformity in motives. Rationalists have obscured this obvious truth by claiming much more, and also by neglecting many important but alarming motives. Those who pointed out these neglected motives, such as Nietzsche, saw their activity as subversive of morality—'immoralism'. But they have to choose between two diametrically opposite kinds of subversion which are open to them. The reductive kind substitutes a different, but equally limited theory of motivation for the traditional one. The sceptical kind denies that any such theory is possible. The sceptical line, pursued in isolation, seems to underlie the idea that sin is an exploded myth. If—*per absurdum*—we really could not assume any uniformity in human purposes, and were thus debarred from all generalizing about what might be good for anyone, this might be true. There would then indeed be little sense in morality—or perhaps in anything else. But this is not a clear line of reasoning at all. It seems to owe much of its popularity to being kept for remote cases where particular dogmatic errors need to be resisted. But all of us—like Nietzsche himself— regard some moral issues not as remote but as pressing and serious; we are inside them. When we want to find cases of wickedness, we should concentrate on these. If we do, none of us actually doubts that some things done are wrong.

It is in order to understand these actual cases that we want to use the insights of immoralism. To do so, we shall need to curtail the claims both of its sceptical and reductive wings. Scepticism needs to be genuine enquiry, not dogmatic denial. It is rightly used to point out specific faults in traditional moralities, not to damn them wholesale without examination. As for reduction, it is useful in so far as it means treating motivation as an ordered whole, in principle intelligible. It is misleading where it means exaggerating and over-simplifying that order, to promote a partisan scheme and put its competitors out of business. This merely substitutes one biassed story for another. Accepting intelligibility in principle is not the same thing as enthroning one's own particular scheme as absolute ruler. Immoralists as well as others have to learn to get on with the gloomy truth that this is not a simple enquiry.

3

THE ELUSIVENESS OF RESPONSIBILITY

How troubled men of our time are by this question of judgment (or, as is often said, by people who dare to 'sit in judgment') has emerged in the controversy over the present
book.... Thus, some American literati have professed their
naive belief that temptation and coercion are really the same
thing, that no-one can be asked to resist temptation. (If
someone puts a pistol to your heart and orders you to shoot
your best friend, you *must* shoot him. Or, as it was argued
some years ago in connection with the quiz program scandal
in which a university teacher had hoaxed the public—when so
much money is at stake, who could possibly resist?) The
argument that we cannot judge if we were not present and
involved ourselves seems to convince everyone everywhere,
although it seems obvious that if it were true, neither the
administration of justice nor the writing of history would ever
be possible.

In contrast to these confusions, the reproach of self-
righteousness raised against those who do judge is age-old;
but that does not make it any the more valid.... All German
Jews unanimously have condemned the wave of co-ordination

which passed over the German people in 1933 and from one day to the next turned the Jews into pariahs. Is it conceivable that none of them ever asked himself how many of his own group would have done just the same if only they had been allowed to? *But is their condemnation to-day any the less correct for that reason?*

Hannah Arendt, *Eichmann in Jerusalem*;' (italics mine)

1 THE FEAR OF JUDGING

The uneasiness about judging which Hannah Arendt notes here makes it hard for us to approach our next question. That question is 'How does wickedness work in an individual? Granted that some things—for instance cases of gross exploitation and oppression—actually are wrong, as we have been arguing, do the exploiters and oppressors know what they are doing, or don't they?' To this query the spirit of our age replies, frowning, that the question cannot arise because there is no such thing as individual wickedness, and accordingly there are no people who can be identified as exploiters and oppressors:

About nothing does public opinion everywhere seem to be in happier agreement than that no one has the right to judge someone else. What public opinion permits us to judge and even to condemn are trends, or whole groups of people—in short, something so general that distinctions can no longer be made. . . . This is currently expressed in high-flown assertions that it is 'superficial' to insist on details and to mention individuals, whereas it is the sign of sophistication to speak in generalities according to which all cats are gray and we are all equally guilty. . . .'Undoubtedly there is reason for grave accusations, but the defendant is mankind as a whole.'

(ibid., 297)

Thus public wickedness vanishes into a social problem, as private wickedness does into mental illness. This policy excludes much more than the administration of justice and the writing of history. The knife cuts deeper. It slices off all our power of self-direction. The function of moral judgment in our inner lives is to build up a store of cases approved and disapproved for various reasons—a map by which we can orient ourselves and plot our own course when we have to make decisions. Because we each have to act as individuals, these cases must in the first place be individual ones. Moral judgments on groups and masses have to be secondary, if they can be made at all.[2] Nor can we do what the phrase 'no one has the right to judge someone else' may suggest, and build up our store entirely from verdicts on our own behaviour. Without an immensely wider range of comparisons, self-judgment could never start. When we wonder whether our own conduct is right, we need to be able to ask 'What would I think about this if somebody else did it?' We shall get no answer unless we can call on a range of comparable cases in the past when we actually have judged other people. This does not of course mean stoning them or sending them to jail, merely forming an opinion on what they have done.[3] It is an aspect of treating them with respect as responsible agents.

Equally, approval and disapproval contribute an essential element to our attitudes to all those around us—to our likes and dislikes, our fears and hopes, horror and admiration, respect and contempt for other people. To inhibit these reactions would be to treat them not as people at all, but as some kind of alien impersonal phenomena. Since it is not possible to treat *oneself* in this way, this would produce a bizarre sense of total isolation in the universe. It cannot actually be done.[4] The need to see ourselves and others as on essentially the same moral footing is in fact so deep that nobody gets anywhere near carrying out this policy. What it usually amounts to is a quite local moral campaign directed against the actual process of blaming. Moral judgment is by no means withheld; it is simply directed with exceptional ferocity against those caught blaming and punishing culprits accused of more traditional offences. This carries guidance of a negative kind for occasions when one is confronted with these offences oneself—namely 'Don't blame or punish.' That advice can sometimes be suitable and useful. But it is extremely limited. Most of life does not consist of such occasions, and most moral difficulties call for other principles, with their background of other moral judgments. Another principle which may be seen as flowing from the non-judging attitude might be 'Feel guilt for all evils; you are always involved as part of society.' This, however, seems to reduce guilt to a futile and meaningless reaction. Hannah Arendt comments that 'morally speaking, it is hardly less wrong to feel guilty without having done something specific than it is to feel free of all guilt if one is actually guilty of something.'[5] This makes sense, because guilt is a thought as well as a feeling, and when that thought is specific it has an essential function in continually reshaping our attitudes. To make it universal is to leave little more than the feeling, which can only be indulged as an end in itself.

2 LOSING THE INDIVIDUAL

Obviously, however, the anti-judgment campaign has a serious point, though a much more limited one than its language suggests. Apart from merely attacking *bad* moral judgments, it points to a number of confusions about the notions of judgments and responsibility. Two of them specially concern us here. In both, I think we shall find that the real objection is not to moral judgment as such. It is either to *bad*, distorted moral judgment, or to the absence of some other way of thinking—such as the social or scientific—which is needed to balance and complete it. When these other ways of thinking are absent, and moral judgment is extended on its own to do their work, things naturally go wrong.

But the remedy is not to abolish moral judgment. It is to fit both together. The real trouble lies in the false antitheses which show the moral point of view as a rival to some other, when in fact they supplement each other.

The first and most familiar of these antitheses is the apparent clash between the moral point of view and that of the physical sciences, which gives us such headaches over free-will. We will try to deal with this one in Chapter 5. The second one, which is our chief worry here, is related to it but not quite the same. It is the clash between the corporate point of view and the individual one. Here the trouble is not so much that the social sciences, which take the corporate point of view, assume determinism. They may not even do so. It is that, by studying large-scale events, they place themselves at a distance from which individual behaviour is simply invisible. The reasons for doing this are sound ones. For instance, the old-fashioned view of history as depending on the personal ruminations of rulers was implausible, and it is not possible to replace it by an account of the personal ruminations of everybody. The Marxist conception of history as the play of large-scale economic forces is therefore enormously useful, and there are plenty of other large-scale conceptual schemes which can supplement it.

Trouble only arises when these schemes are taken to compete with and annihilate the individual point of view—to prove it unnecessary by demonstrating that everybody is only the pawn or product of their society. This looks like a causal argument, but it cannot really be one. Causally, it would be just as true that the society was only the product of its past and present members. It is a manifesto, issued on behalf of corporate ways of thinking which are suitable for certain purposes, and designed to extend their empire over other purposes, eliminating all rivals. This imperialism is sometimes seen as a matter of metaphysics, individuals being actually 'less real' than their communities. More often today, however, it is treated as a question of method; the attack is against 'methodological individualism.' This strange language assumes that these are rival methods for a single aim—that one of them must be eliminated if the other is used, like front-wheel or back-wheel drive on a car. But the purposes and interests of different ways of thinking can be totally different. Anatomy does not eliminate physiology, nor history politics.

Large-scale thinking about societies is not an alternative to thinking directly about individuals. Both studies are necessary; each needs its own methods. And within the study of individuals, enquiry about the facts is not an alternative to practical and especially moral thinking, which works out the concepts and principles to be used in action. Moral philosophy investigates these and the conceptual schemes which underlie them and link them to the rest of our conceptual system. Thought, as applied to human life, can therefore be crudely divided like this:

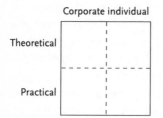

Corporate individual

Theoretical

Practical

But during the last century, when an idealized picture of physical science has obsessed the imagination of the English-speaking world, and come to be taken as the only proper kind of thought, the top left-hand area has increasingly come to look like the only respectable one, because it is the only one which looks like even a bad imitation of the physical sciences. In this alarming situation, interdisciplinary tiffs which already treated neighbouring provinces as rivals and alternatives have made it fatally easy to cut along the dotted lines.

3 AUTONOMY VERSUS CONTINUITY

Moral philosophy, occupied chiefly with matters well down on the right, has been especially threatened. Not surprisingly, it has reacted by producing yet another false antithesis of its own. This is the violent dilemma posed between an individual's autonomy and his or her continuity with the world. Many current ways of thinking tend either to make individuals vanish into their groups, or to reduce them to their physical parts. Both these processes make it seem as if they had no real identity or control, and so to suggest that it does not matter what they do. Against these threats, defenders of autonomy have reacted sharply by painting a very different sort of individuals—purely mental entities, radically isolated, independent, self-creating and alien, perhaps hostile, to everything around them. This extreme picture appears at its clearest in existentialism, in social contract theory, and in a range of educational theories which stress self-expression to the exclusion of what a child receives from the world, though it has many other roots as well.[6]

This inflated notion of autonomy is the mirror-image of Socrates's paradox that 'nobody does wrong willingly.' Socrates eliminated the will, making moral choice seem an entirely intellectual matter. Modern autonomism leaves nothing but the will, a pure, unbiassed power of choice, detached equally from the choosing subject's present characteristics and from all the objects it must choose between. In doing this it far outruns its distant ancestor Kant, more and more limited quotations from whom still appear as its warrant, and who still gets attacked for its excesses.[7] The arrogance of Sartre's remark, 'Man is nothing else but what he makes of himself' is quite alien to Kant.[8] Whatever his mistakes, Kant was always trying seriously to make sense of human life, and therefore to bring its two sides together in the end. By contrast, modern autonomism is embattled, and will have no truck with the opposition.

Both these two extreme views of human agency have a point. Each tells us something important. The nature of the self is so strange and difficult a subject that we have to deal with it by putting unbalanced insights like this together and using them to correct each other. Controversy, however, always tends to make us pit extremes against each other as rivals and force us to choose between them. On a topic so close to our lives, this is very bewildering, and the effect gets worse the subtler and more learned the disputants happen to be. Partisanship combined with great ingenuity is bound to confuse the reader who is not primarily interested in being a lawyer for either side. The large paradoxes which make good weapons of war have to be dismantled, if those of us who are not chiefly interested in fighting want to extract the much smaller nuggets of truth which they contain.

4　ONE-WAY SCEPTICISM

Sartre is often hard to follow for this reason; he is always laying deep mines to blow up enemy positions. And it seems possible that this is also what produces a certain baffling effect in some very subtle attacks on autonomism in the controversy between Bernard Williams and Thomas Nagel about Moral Luck.[9] Both writers draw attention to a wide range of limitations on our individual freedom—distinct ways in which luck can enter into acts and choices for which we would normally expect to hold people (and be held) responsible. Both think that 'the area of genuine agency, and therefore of legitimate moral judgment, seems to shrink under this scrutiny to an extensionless point.'[10] Both wonder—Nagel anxiously, Williams rather triumphantly—whether there is still any place left for it. They treat the issue as one between dogmatic assertion of complete autonomy—which they take to be traditional and comforting— and bold sceptical questioning which is likely in the end to cut it out altogether. (They disagree about the prospects of this, but their area of agreement is what concerns us here.) They present the dispute as one where scepticism has the moral edge; where we *ought* to accept its surprising verdict that morality, or most of it, is illegitimate and the word 'ought' has, one would suppose, almost lost its meaning. (If it did, I am not sure that the word 'luck' would not go with it—but that is another story.)

To justify their approach, we seem to need, first, a reason why only these two extreme positions are considered, and second (if they are), a reason why the burden of proof falls on the side of belief in responsibility. A sceptical temper, just as such, does not make this decision. We can doubt anything, and in choosing what to doubt we must always choose to take some other prem-isses for granted as an undoubted starting-point for our reason-ing. All scepticism—except for the boring kind which is designed only to show cleverness—is therefore propagandist. In the case before us, it would seem just as natural to slice the other way, to develop sceptical doubts about the many excuses by which we limit the area of our responsibility. We could start, for instance, from the many telling objections which Freudian thought has made to the ordinary excuses we use to prove that we are helpless victims of our circumstances. Existentialism too has added to this campaign. These attacks proceed, as much as those from the other side, by questioning common sense beliefs more sharply than is usually done. And they too, as much as their opponents, rely in doing so on extending an opposed set of common sense ideas—the everyday ones which we already use in debunking invalid excuses. Common sense always contains batteries of opposite considerations, loosely organised, which can be used to counteract each other. So there does not seem to be much force in Nagel's insistence that 'the erosion of moral judgment' is irresistible because it 'emerges not as the absurd consequence of an over-simple theory, but as a natural con-sequence of the ordinary idea of moral assessment, when it is applied in view of a more complete and precise account of the facts.'[11] Only one half of the ordinary idea of moral assessment has been used. Normally we use both, and arrive, however clumsily, at conclusions which are always limited and usually tentative—'apparently responsible in this way but not in that, for this and not for that, to this extent but not to that one; more responsible than Pat but less so than Sam,' and so forth.

The ways of thinking by which we thus distinguish between what can and what cannot be helped, and the opinions which we build on them about actions and agents, may be rough and fallible, but they are absolutely essential for human life. Certainly it is of the utmost importance that they should be used rightly and not wrongly. But it seems meaningless to suggest that they ought to stop being used at all. Criticisms of their current usage ought therefore surely always to be as specific, as constructive as possible. They should say in concrete terms what kind of thing is to stop and what kind of thing is to replace it. Academic controversy, however, always tends to give the advantage to the sceptic, and to put the burden of positive suggestions on his opponent. Extremely vague destructive suggestions therefore thrive in it. What is Williams proposing when he says that his sceptical arguments show that we may have to 'give up that notion (our notion of morality) altogether'?[12] Most of his suggestions, like Nietzsche's, seem to be moral ones, reasons—often cogent ones—why we *ought* to view certain things in the world differently. Many are objections to unrealistic optimism. But avoiding that hardly counts to dropping our notion of morality.

At an everyday level, similar sweeping destructiveness is common. Thus Barbara Wootton, after discussing the paradoxes which tend to arise when we try to understand and judge psychopaths, concludes that 'the psychopath may well prove to be the thin end of the wedge which will ultimately shatter the whole idea of moral responsibility.'[13] This seems to ignore the fact that all conceptual schemes run into difficulties and paradoxes when they are used for awkward and unusual cases. We can often extend them to deal with such problems; indeed, this is how we usually develop them. But we can never ensure that the same thing will not happen again with a new range of cases.

Conceptual schemes are not like electric kettles; they do not do a strictly limited job, so they have no guarantee of infallibility. Even with kettles, of course, really careless or malicious use can produce disaster, and this is still more true of conceptual schemes. What seems needed at the moment is that general denunciations of our notions of morality and responsibility, whether at a popular or a philosophical level, should carry explanations which will show, much more clearly than is done at present, where they stand on a scale of specificness which ranges from 'this kettle is no good; they must give us another under guarantee' to 'stop the world and bring me another one.'

Since Nietzsche's day, what tends to happen is that the denunciation is phrased in extremely general terms, while the complaints brought to support it are quite limited, and are actually moral accusations of a familiar kind. Barbara Wootton, for instance, wants a more humane, less vindictive attitude to social offenders, but she has moral reasons for this, and clearly thinks the privileged members of society responsible—in a quite traditional sense—for providing it. Criticisms of this sort are attacks on particular moral misjudgments, not on moral judgment itself. Putting them in a more general, hyperbolical, Nietzschean form certainly gives them dramatic force. But the effect of this move is not what it was in Nietzsche's time. Hypocrisy is not so straightforward today. Many more people now are willing to abandon moral judgment in a quite open and simple way—to drop all attempt at concern for what is happening in the world, and treat all human action as inevitable. Hypocrisy used to be the tribute which vice paid to virtue. Today, some of the vices no longer pay it at all, and the others largely pay in a different coinage, less easily exposed by simple, hyperbolical Nietzschean methods.[14] Indeed it may be that these methods can no longer be used for moral reform.

5 VICE, WEAK WILL AND MADNESS

The last section has been intended to show that the idea of individual wickedness is not an unreal one. If that is right, we come back here to our problem about how this wickedness works, how it is psychologically and logically possible. Do exploiters and oppressors know what they are doing, or not? This question is not easy. Hasty answers to it have supplied further reasons why the use of the term 'wickedness' may seem naive. Aristotle made an interesting distinction between people of weak will, who do wrong against their real wishes and intentions, and vicious people, who do wrong contentedly and with conviction.[15] Philosophers have paid more attention to problems about the first contingent than to those about the second, which is perhaps rather surprising. Certainly weak will is a problem, but it is one with which we are all thoroughly familiar, both from the inside and the outside. And these two views of weakness match reasonably well. We may well be uncertain what is the best way of describing the confused state in which people manage to do things which they admit to be wrong. But the description of this which we accept for our own case is also one which we can apply to other people. With vice, this is not usually so. Contentedly vicious people do not as a rule describe themselves as vicious, nor even think their actions wrong. They tend either to justify them or to reject moral questions as pointless and irrelevant. Exceptions make a curious impression. Ernst Röhm, co-founder with Hitler of the Nazi party (though later murdered by the SS) wrote in his autobiography, 'Since I am an immature and bad man, war appeals to me more than peace.'[16] To understand what he meant by this we seem to need a context—one which will show it perhaps as a real spasm of conscience, perhaps as a passing mood, but perhaps also as some kind of sarcastic joke or way of making a debating point. It cannot have the simple, literal sense that such a remark made about somebody else would have. In general, as Aristotle said, 'vice is unconscious of itself; weakness is not.'[17]

There does not seem to be an inside point of view on vice. And this strengthens the suspicion that perhaps there simply is no such thing, that vice itself is fabulous. That suspicion is most often expressed today by the thought that people who commit appalling acts must necessarily be mad, that is, ill. And although the whole notion of mental illness has come under attack for other reasons, people still tend to regard it as the only possible humane response to this particular problem. A number of very interesting considerations converge to fix this habit of mind. One is, of course, the immense respect in which the medical profession is currently held, the widespread impression that the devoted work of doctors can, given time and resources, deal with every evil. Though there has been some reaction against this faith in recent years, it is still very strong, and doctors who would like to spread a more modest and realistic estimate of their powers find it hard to do so. Apart from the accidental factor that doctors here inherit the magic which is no longer attributed to priests, wish-fulfilment strongly supports this extension of the medical model. Mental disorder itself is terrifying, a vast and indistinct menace which we would be very glad to hand over to an invincible giant-killer. And in their early over-confidence in modern drugs, some psychiatrists did license the public to cast them in this role. But beyond the area of identifiable mental disorder lies another, equally appalling, which has traditionally been viewed as distinct; that of wickedness. Can it, too, be brought under the same benevolent and enlightened empire? Can we hope in this way to make obsolete the whole notion not only of punishment, but of blame, and to apply medical remedies instead?

This suggestion brings out a sharp conflict in our concepts. On the one hand, the idea that wickedness is a form of madness is very natural, because bad conduct is so readily seen as unintelligible. To say 'I simply don't understand how they could act like that' is a quite direct form of condemnation. To say 'What did you mean by it?' is to ask for justification; if no meaning can be shown which will make the act intelligible, then it will be considered wrong. On the other hand, however, madness counts as an excuse. It is assumed that so far as people are mad they cannot help what they do. Extending this medical model to cover the whole area of wickedness would therefore excuse everybody equally, flattening out the whole subtle spectrum of degrees of responsibility, and putting the genuinely unfortunate on the same footing as the sanest and most deliberate criminals. This suggestion makes little sense, if only because the sane ones will not be willing to accept any such diagnosis or treatment any more than many of the deranged, and both equally will often reject another condition which seems naturally to belong to the medical model, namely, the belief that they are suffering from a *misfortune*. Besides, most medical scientists themselves have no expectation of ever being able to extend their skills to cover this range of difficulties, and no wish to be credited with claiming such powers.

6 PHANTOM MORALITIES

In general, then, there are strong objections to viewing all wrongdoers as mad, as well as strong temptations to do it, and for many cases people do not find this explanation plausible. In these cases, however, another strategy often comes into play to make the offence look intelligible. This is to credit the offenders with having a complete morality of their own, which, for them, justifies their actions. This idea leads people to suppose that (for instance) the Nazis must have been original reasoners, with an independent, consistent and well-thought-out ethical theory—a view which their careers and writings do not support at all. As Hannah Arendt points out, at the Nuremburg trials the lack of this much-advertised commodity became painfully obvious. 'The defendants accused and betrayed each other and assured the world that they "had always been against it". . . . Although most of them must have known that they were doomed, not a single one of them had the guts to defend the Nazi ideology.'[18] This was not just from a failure of nerve, though that in itself would be significant in a movement apparently devoted to the military virtues. It was also because there was not really much coherent ideology that could be defended. The only part of it which carried real passionate conviction was emotional and destructive; it was the hatred of the Jews. This always remained constant, but almost every other element varied according to the audience addressed and the political possibilities of the moment. The enemy might be Communism or capitalism, the elite or the rabble, France or Russia or the Weimar government, just as interest dictated at the time. It was therefore hard to say much that was positive and constructive about the aims of the regime. Germany was to expand, but why it would be a good thing that it should do so remained obscure. Hitler has been credited with ideas drawn from Nietzsche, but there seems no reason to suppose that he picked up much more than the flavour of Nietzsche's titles, such as *The Will to Power* and *Beyond Good and Evil*.[19] (Nietzsche himself, of course, violently denounced anti-semitism, and quarrelled mortally with Wagner on the subject. This is one of many cases where he displayed strong, clear, traditional moral indignation, not at all inhibited by the kind of sceptical considerations to which many people today seem to think his kind of reasoning commits them.) Nazism at least is a good case of a moral vacuum.

7 THE PARADOX OF RESPONSIBLE NEGLIGENCE

To return, then, to the general problem—wickedness is not the same thing as madness, nor as a genuine eccentric morality. Both madness and honest eccentric thinking constitute *excuses*. And the notion of an excuse only works if there can be some cases which are not excusable, cases to which it does not apply. The notion of real wickedness is still assumed as a background alternative. Yet that notion is still hard to articulate.

The reason why it is so hard is, I suggest, that we do not take in what it means to say that evil is negative. We are looking for it as something positive, and that positive thing we of course fail to find. If we ask whether exploiters and oppressors know what they are doing, the right answer seems to be that they do *not* know, because they carefully avoid thinking about it—but that they could know, and therefore their deliberate avoidance is a responsible act. In the First World War, when a staff officer was eventually sent out to France to examine the battlefield, he broke down in tears at the sight of it, and exclaimed, 'Have we really been ordering men to advance through all that mud?' This is a simple case of factual ignorance, flowing from negligence. Negligence on that scale however, is not excusable casualness. It is, as we would normally say, criminal. The general recipe for inexcusable acts is neither madness nor a bizarre morality, but a steady refusal to attend both to the consequences of one's actions and to the principles involved.

This is at least a part of what Socrates meant by his paradoxical insight that nobody does wrong willingly. (Socrates, of course, was chiefly interested in the principles rather than the consequences, but as far as the kind of ignorance involved goes the two cases seem similar.) If the wrong-doer really understood what he was doing, Socrates said, he could not possibly do it. This sounds at first like an excuse, like saying that all wrongdoers are misinformed or mad. But Socrates certainly did not mean it as an excuse. He said it as part of his attempt to get people to think more, in order to avoid wickedness. His approach to wickedness was not a remote, third-person one, directed simply to questions about the proper treatment of offenders. It was primarily a first- and second-person enquiry about how each one of us actually goes wrong. He is talking about something fully in our control, something which he takes to be the essence of sin—namely, a deliberate blindness to ideals and principles, a stalling of our moral and intellectual faculties. The balance of positive and negative elements here is complicated and will occupy us again later. But it is perhaps worth glancing here at an example drawn from Hannah Arendt's discussion of Eichmann:

> When I speak of the banality of evil, I do so only on the strictly factual level, pointing to a phenomenon which stared one in the face at the trial. Eichmann was not Iago and not Macbeth, and nothing would have been further from his mind than to determine with Richard III 'to prove a villain.' Except for an extraordinary diligence in looking out for his personal advancement, he had no motives at all. And this diligence in itself was in no way criminal; he certainly would never have murdered his superior in order to inherit his post. He *merely*, to put the matter colloquially, *never realized what he was doing*. It was precisely this lack of imagination which enabled him to sit for months on end facing a German Jew who was conducting the police interrogation, pouring out his heart to the man and explaining again and again how it was that he reached only the rank of lieutenant-colonel in the SS, and that it had not been his fault that he was not promoted. In principle he knew quite well what it was all about, and in his final statement to the court he spoke of the 'revaluation of values' prescribed by the (Nazi) government. He was not stupid. It was sheer thoughtlessness—something by no means identical with

> stupidity—that predisposed him to become one of the greatest
> criminals of that period.[20]

As she says, the administrative complexity of the modern world
makes such cases increasingly common. Bureaucracy tends to
look like 'the rule of nobody', and this obscuring of individual
responsibility is one thing which makes the concept of wickedness seem so hard to apply. But if we fatalistically accept that it
has become impossible, we are falling for propaganda. 'The
essence of totalitarian government, and perhaps the nature of
every bureaucracy, is to make functionaries and mere cogs in the
administrative machinery out of men, and thus to dehumanize
them.'[21] It has not really changed their nature and removed their
responsibility from them. It has certainly made it easier for them
to do wrong, and harder to do right. But there have always been
agencies that would do that, and in all ages much ingenuity has
gone into building them for that very purpose.

8   THE RED HERRING OF INNATE AGGRESSION

What obstacle still blocks the proposal to study the sources of
wickedness in the individual, and in particular its innate
sources? I think the chief trouble is still the idea that, if there is
any such innate source, it must come in the form of a single
positive drive or motive, namely aggression. This idea has constantly loomed in the background of the debate about aggression
which has gone on for some decades now. It has accounted for
the extreme savagery of that debate, and has completely distorted
it. Aggression has been discussed here in a bizarre isolation from
all other motives. It has been treated as if it were the only motive
which could ever lead to large-scale wickedness, and also the
only motive whose innateness might give rise to problems.
Perhaps the most misleading move in this whole twisted controversy has been a mere unfortunate change in a book-title.

Konrad Lorenz's book, whose English translation has the title *On Aggression*, was originally called in German *So-Called Evil*.[22] Its whole point was to distinguish evil from aggression, to combat Freud's views of aggression—which assimilated it to evil—and to show how the confusion between these two topics made it impossible to treat either seriously. Many of those involved in the controversy seem to have ignored this answer to Freud, and in fact only to have read a few parts of the book which dealt with the positive, biological function of aggression. They read these as a simple-minded commercial for war, and the confusion between aggression and evil continued. It still haunts us today.

It has, I am suggesting, two bad effects. On the theoretical side, it hampers us in developing a proper psychology of motive. In general, the study of motives has been trapped in an academic backwater since the time of Freud. Freud asked good questions but often gave them bad answers. And Freud's unlucky weakness for organizing his followers into a church has continued to block the proper development of his ideas. A difficulty about understanding aggression is only one aspect of this general difficulty about understanding motives. But it has been a disastrous one. The veto on talk about innate aggression has been held to ban discussion of the innate aspects of other motives as well. It has therefore denied to the social sciences the use of a whole invaluable tool-kit of concepts, centring on the idea of human nature. This has been a serious loss.

9 THE DIFFICULTY OF BEING REALISTIC

However, bad as this theoretical nuisance is, it probably does less direct harm than the trivialization of wickedness which results from reducing it to aggression. The difficulty about conceiving wickedness realistically is not new. As Socrates' remarks show, the problem is an old one. But it is also still extremely pressing. When we ask why things go as badly as they do in the world, and when we have finished listing the external, physical causes, most of us will have been struck by a thumping residue of human conduct which seems quite unnecessarily bad. We often call this conduct 'mad.' By this we commonly do not mean to give a definite medical diagnosis, pointing to actual mania or brain-damage resulting from lead-poisoning. We mean rather just to throw up our hands, to declare that we don't understand it.

At best, this can come near to a Socratic, negative diagnosis of moral negligence. We may be saying that people, including ourselves, are evidently much less sensible, clear-sighted and enlightened than they make out, that human insight and honesty are weak—that public sanity cannot be relied on to operate mechanically, but needs constant attention. This, I believe, is true, and is a useful attitude. But there is another one, superficially rather like it, which gives a very different diagnosis and shows evil as positive. This is the mood in which we treat wickedness as something quite alien to ourselves, something belonging only to certain lunatics in black hats, the other guys, who are always the cause of the trouble. We may name these guys as a definite group, preferably a remote one, with whom we can have a feud. Or we may leave them unnamed and put the black hat on an abstraction such as Society. The first course will probably lead to more actual shooting; the second will lead to more confusion and bad faith. But in either case there seems to be a fatal element of bad faith, of unreality in this distancing of evil. It seems clear that a great many of the worst acts actually done in the world are committed in the same sort of way in which the battlefields of the First World War were produced—by people who have simply failed to criticize the paths of action lying immediately before them. Exploiters and oppressors, war-makers, executioners and destroyers of forests do not usually wear distinctive black hats, nor horns and hooves. The positive motives which move them may not be bad at all; they are often quite decent ones like prudence, loyalty, self-fulfilment and professional conscientiousness. The appalling element lies in the lack of the other motives which ought to balance these—in particular, of a proper regard for other people and of a proper priority system which would enforce it. That kind of lack cannot be treated as a mere matter of chance. Except in rare psychopaths, we attribute it to the will. The will has steadily said 'No', just as Mephistopheles does. But because 'No' is such a negative thing to say, the mind has often not admitted fully what was happening. The staff officer, when he saw the army struggling in mud, was thunderstruck. Only then did his systematic negligence become clear to him. When it did, he had the grace to be horrified. Once the point was put before him, he could see it. He was capable of remorse, which not everybody is in that situation. Now this capacity for remorse seemed to Aristotle an indication of weak will rather than of vice. But these are surely not sharp alternatives. They are rather ends of a spectrum of clear-headedness about wrong-doing, on which all of us are placed somewhere.

This discussion began with the suggestion that the problems posed by human wickedness cannot be solved by blaming God. It has gone on to suggest further that they cannot be solved by blaming society either, nor by blaming a few selected criminals in black hats, whether in governments or outside them. In fact, to concentrate on blaming anybody will probably spoil our chances of solving them altogether. We want to understand how human conduct goes wrong. Many societies, not only ours, have considered this so grave a problem as to call for a full-scale mythological explanation, parallel to the Fall of Man. Thus, the Greeks held that there had been a descending series of ages, each worse than the last, starting from the Age of Gold, and they had no doubt that the current one was the worst of the series. Hindu thought posits a similar descending series. For the Norsemen, evil forces such as Hela and Loki waged a continual and in the end successful battle against the more or less benign gods. And people constructing mythologies elsewhere have very commonly felt the need to suppose some similar sort of primal conflict, in order to account for the startling moral mixedness of the world.

In our own tradition, since the Enlightenment, such ideas have been strongly rejected. There has been a revulsion, which at root is entirely proper, against the idea that we must resign ourselves to any evil as inevitable. The question about this revulsion is simply: Has it no limits? Are we omnipotent? Can we change ourselves to any degree whatever? If we are not omnipotent—if there are some limits to the change we can make—it seems fairly important to find out what they are. Creatures of limited powers need a priority system, and a realistic map of their own capacities and weaknesses. The sense of omnipotence which expanding technology generated has proved a misleading one, and it has now become clear that technology itself has no tendency to make people behave better, only to distract them more effectively from what they are up to. The notion of psychological omnipotence was itself a myth. Abandoning it does not commit us to fatalistic resignation, but makes realistic attempts at change more possible.

Apart from this general problem of admitting some real evil in the world, there are of course special difficulties about the form which this admission has taken in our own tradition—the ideas of the Fall, the Atonement and Original Sin. This system of thought is strongly inclined to inculcate a chronic undiscriminating sense of guilt, and it revolves round the necessity of punishment. The objections to this emphasis have become clear in the course of endless religious wars and persecutions. The temptation to project one's own anger and hostility on to a punitive God, framed in one's own image, is appallingly dangerous, and the reformers, from Voltaire to Freud, who have pointed out this hazard have surely been justified. But this does not mean that the whole psychological problem has to be abandoned. The discrepancy between human ideals and human conduct is a real one, indicating a great complexity in our nature. It even has its cheering side: why are our ideals usually so much better than our conduct? It calls for serious investigation, rather than for an indignant refusal to recognize its existence. And where the traditional concepts are faulty, it seems to be our business to find better ways of formulating and understanding the problem.

What, however, should they be? At this point the argument of this book encounters a rock, a lump of current controversy, round which it must divide, to reunite later. The natural method of investigation is, to my mind, to study directly the forms of inner conflict involved in temptation—the warring motives that take part in this conflict, especially those which actually tend towards evil—and the relation between this turbulent process and our personal identity. This study, however, involves using a notion of our motives as natural, which has at times been strongly denounced in the social sciences. Though that denunciation is much less confident and unanimous than it used to be, it still seems to need an answer. Moreover, it carries with it a notion that the whole study of motives—as distinct from behaviour—is itself 'unscientific' and disreputable.

These difficulties I shall try to meet in the next two chapters, which can be seen as ways of gaining permission to proceed with the central enquiry. Readers who are not interested in these controversies, and who resent long waits for the examination of passports, can skip this section, moving at once to Chapter 6.

SUMMARY

Was Socrates right? Do wrong-doers know what they are doing, or not?

Today, it is hard to think about this kind of question, because we fear to identify wrong-doing at all; we shrink from judging morally. Such judgment strikes us as presumptuous and self-righteous. Yet these are themselves moral accusations. They can only apply to bad moral judgments. This difficulty, however, looks stronger than it is because it is merged with a quite different one—a suspicion that systematic thought is anyway not possible about individuals, but only about groups. This is a mistake, resulting from overcorrecting an unbalanced concentration on individuals. There is no competition between these two approaches to the study of human life. Both are necessary; each requires the other.

In reaction against this imperialism of corporate thinking, existentialism and several other lines of modern thought have developed an extreme and unrealistic idea of personal autonomy. Reacting in their turn against this, some philosophers have joined social reformers concerned about punishment in suggesting that our whole notion of morality—or of moral responsibility—ought to go. This move widens the gap between champions of autonomy and all those concerned to emphasize our continuity with the world. We surely need to withdraw from both extremes and combine both aspects of the truth.

We ask, then, 'Do exploiters and oppressors know what they are doing, or not?' There is a real difficulty in saying in what sense they do. To cover it, we tend to say that they are mad. This may only mean that we do not understand them. If it also carries an automatic excuse, it is misleading.

Emphasizing the negative element in wickedness may help us here. People avoid thinking about things which would stop them doing what they wish. In some sense, this avoidance is deliberate. The things they avoid thinking about can include general principles—on which Socrates concentrated—and also particular facts. Fixed roles and positions can greatly help this avoidance. The growth of bureaucracy in the modern world therefore makes it easier all the time. But this turning of individuals into cogs is still a temptation, not a doom. We need to resist it, not to reinforce it by philosophic doctrines. General scepticism about the possibility of moral judgment, though it may look like a piece of neutral, formal analysis, cannot fail to act as propaganda in this contest of attitudes. It must make us lose confidence in our power of thinking about moral issues involving individuals—including ourselves. Yet this power is absolutely necessary to us. What we need is not to abandon it, but to clarify it.

When we do return to the enterprise of thinking about individual wrongdoing, especially about its motivation, our worst obstacle is probably still the idea that—if it exists—its only possible motive is innate aggression, conceived as a positive, solitary, irresistible drive. This is a complete mistake. By no means all evil is aggression, nor is all aggression evil (see Chapter 4). To equate them is disastrous. It both blocks enquiry about the wide range of natural motives really involved, and trivializes the concept of wickedness. It makes for an unrealistic notion of the wicked as an alien group. It obscures the extent to which even the most appalling acts can flow from selective negligence.

To grasp this extent is, however, to see how easily things can go wrong in human life—how hard, indeed, it is for them to go right. But this insight does not call for fatalistic resignation. The keener we are to prevent evil, the more we need to be realistic about the difficulties. Many cultures have expressed their sense of these difficulties by myths, painting the world as having something radically wrong with it. In our own culture, this work has been done by the myth of the Fall. Indignant rejection of this myth in recent times has been due to real misuses of it. But the consequences of trying to do without any such notion may not have been fully understood. There really is a deep, pervasive discrepancy between human ideals and human conduct. In order to deal with this, we need to recognize it, not to deny it.

4

UNDERSTANDING AGGRESSION

The tigers of wrath are wiser than the horses of instruction.
Blake

1 NON-AGGRESSIVE WICKEDNESS

In the last two chapters we have seen the need to disentangle the problem of wickedness from that of aggression, in order to get both into their proper perspective. We have opened up the general problem of finding the most realistic way of regarding iniquitous conduct, and exploring in what sense it can be called deliberate. This must lead us presently into some discussion of free-will, and of the difficulties of avoiding fatalism. But in the present chapter we have a smaller, though still very interesting and explosive problem, namely aggression.

For about half-a-century now a rather confused debate has been carried on over the question as to whether human aggression is innate or not. It has generated a lot more heat than light, for the usual reasons. Several questions are being tackled together, and the moral fervour appropriate to only one of them has overflowed into others which do not call for it at all. The issue to which moral fervour actually is appropriate is fatalism. Fatalism is objectionable because it leads to the making of false excuses for accepting avoidable evil, and this really is not only misleading but wicked. But there is nothing fatalistic at all about treating aggression as an innate motive in the way in which this has been done by biologists. In the sense appropriate here, all major human motives are innate, and that fact has nothing alarming about it.[1] Indeed, it is hard to see how life could go on if they were not. The confusion has arisen because people have treated aggression not just as one motive among others, indeed often not as a motive at all, but as more or less equivalent to wicked conduct.

In this chapter, then, we have two points to establish. First, not all wickedness is aggression. Second, not all aggression is wicked. The first point is the simpler, and indeed once you think about it, it may seem obvious. A great deal of the harm done in the world is plainly done from motives which are negative, which stop people from doing things which they ought to do. If, therefore, we are asking about the innateness of bad motives, we have to consider these other motives as well as aggression. For instance, sloth, fear, greed and habit account for an enormous amount of ill-doing. Because people need each other's help so badly, these negative motives can do almost infinite harm.

The example of the staff officer inspecting the front during the First World War makes this clear. He asked, 'Have we really been ordering men to advance through all that mud?' They had, though that was not at all what they thought they were doing. How had they come to do it? If we look into the causes of monstrous human actions like this—or indeed like that whole war—we will usually find great numbers of people, many of them at the highest levels, who seem to have played their part in this passive, unthinking sort of way. Their contribution is mainly negative. That, of course, does not clear them of responsibility, nor does it settle the question what their motives were. There is a real puzzle about how this kind of negative motivation is to be understood both morally and psychologically. I have suggested that we very much need to understand it better. For instance, it is largely in this sort of unthinking way that we in the more prosperous countries of the world are now engaged in starving out the poorer ones. Yet we do not feel like agents. If we are trying to understand how this sort of conduct works, it is surely very misleading to think of it all as aggressive. There are plenty of other ways of going wrong besides the aggressive way. To speak of all injustice as aggression seems to be a distortion of words caused by a mistaken attempt to narrow the problems of evil. A rather similar distortion has been occurring in controversies about the justification of violence.[2] Here notions like 'structural violence' have been coined to describe what is more naturally called simple oppression. The point of this coinage is to prove that oppressed people who revolt violently are only engaging in retribution. This seems a tortuous and misleading way of expressing a justification which can stand perfectly well on its own feet. Injustice and oppression can be *worse* forms of wickedness than violence, but they are still distinct from it. And violence is sometimes the only way of resisting injustice and oppression. When this happens, that necessity is what justifies it. There is no need to distort language by invoking retribution.

The position about aggression is rather similar. Aggression is only one motive among many which can lead to wickedness. Many other motives are normally quite as dangerous and often more so, notably greed. And perhaps every human motive including love, can on occasion be sinister, if it is not properly watched and understood. This point is clear enough, I think, once we grasp that the word 'aggression' really is being used in this controversy as the name of a motive, not of a political act. In its political use, the word means 'unprovoked or unjustified attack.' This does convey a moral judgment, but it says nothing about motives. In that sense, nobody suggests that aggression could be innate. It would be no more sensible to talk of an innate human tendency to make unprovoked or unjustified political attacks than of an innate tendency to rob banks. Natural motives are not that specific. What is meant by innate aggression is a natural tendency to attack others sometimes, which involves an emotional tendency sometimes to get angry with them.

The relation between attacks and anger here may not be familiar: it is very important that we should understand it properly. It is the relation between a kind of act and its typical, sufficient explanatory motive. Examples of this relation are that between eating and hunger, flight and fear, or investigation and curiosity. In all these cases, the acts can be performed for all sorts of reasons other than the one named as appropriate. An ambitious subordinate can very easily eat without hunger, run away without fear and make investigations without curiosity, because these are the acts which his superior requires of him at the time, and his sole hope of rising lies in pleasing this superior. Ambition is then the motive for all these varied acts. This kind of situation is very common even in animal life, and of course still commoner in human life because of the requirements of culture. But it does not follow that acts cease to have motives which are appropriate to them in themselves, motives which would furnish appropriate explanations for them even without a supporting background, because this kind of act is a natural consequence of the feeling in question. The range of acts belonging to a given motive in this way is usually wide, but the principle for limiting it is easily grasped.[3] Thus, hunger explains both eating and making efforts to get food, but for an act to fall into this net we need to see how it could count as that sort of effort. Fear has a wider range of natural, instinctive expressions—not only flight but immobility, cries for help, attempts to protect the young, forming a protective formation, and sometimes counter-attacks. But this does not loosen the intelligible connexion. We understand these different responses as being appropriate to different kinds and degrees of fear, and again, the appropriate one is the one which, even without further background explanation, fits the behaviour and explains it by connecting it with a normal relation to life. Anger is in this way the appropriate motive for attack—not that it must always lead to attack, nor that all attacks are due to it, but that it is the feeling which makes attack intelligible, even without extra background conditions. And the intelligibility is, obviously, not just a vacuous appeal to the notion of some abstract 'attacking force' like a dormitive force, but a reference to the grounds of anger. The robin attacks, not just 'from aggression', but in response to an intrusion on territory which it perceives as a provocation, insult or challenge, and perhaps as a threat to the young. The kind and intensity of the attack varies with the kind of intrusion. But to be capable of this response at all, robins have to have evolved the nervous capacity for feeling angry—a capacity absent in many simpler species. The motive is not just regular outward behaviour; it is also a mood, an affect and a way of perceiving the stimulus as calling not just for one piece of behaviour, but for a whole range of others according to contingencies—a range whose links would be unintelligible if we had not some grasp of the mood.

Ethologists who have used the term 'aggression' to describe the behaviour of animals have done so because they observed, in a wide variety of species, a distinctive range of behaviour, needing to be distinguished from that attributable to other motives— which of course were identified in the same sort of way. This behaviour does not dominate animal life in any species, nor is it designed to kill or destroy. It operates primarily to drive others away on occasion, to provide each individual with the space which it needs for the business of its life. Now if we want to ask whether that emotional tendency extends to the human race, we would naturally do it by asking some such questions as the following: Are human beings naturally capable of anger? Are they to some extent quarrelsome, contentious, irritable, argumentative and peevish? Can they sometimes have too much of each other's company? Do they sometimes make trouble just for the fun of it? Are they liable to lose their tempers and to get resentful if they do not take care to avoid it? Are they prone to thoughts of hatred and revenge? It is much harder to answer 'No' to these questions than to the question 'Are they naturally aggressive?' But they amount to the same thing.[4] Any doubt that remains about answering them can be helped by a bit of science fiction. Suppose that we imagine this issue being investigated by a set of alien beings, who themselves genuinely do not have any angry motivation at all, and who therefore look with a cold and puzzled eye on all the excitement involved in anger. Is it likely that they will report (to the Galactic Federation or whoever else has sent them) that inhabitants of this planet are free from any natural tendency to anger as themselves? It scarcely seems likely.

It will be useful to put by for future use the thought of these totally and genuinely non-aggressive creatures—or Nongs for short. They will, I think, supply a useful contrast and throw light on various aspects of our problem. For the moment, our point is simply that aggression is only one of many possible bad motives, that it supplies only one ingredient in bad conduct. If, therefore, we think the question of its innateness important, then we certainly need to enquire also whether other dangerous motives are innate. This will mean enquiring about the possible innate elements in all motives, dangerous or otherwise. For instance, sexual motivation obviously has a strong innate element, and this is not usually thought to be incompatible with human dignity and freedom. But the case closest to aggression, and therefore the most useful one to examine, is probably fear.

2 THE PARALLEL OF FEAR

Suppose, then, that we put the question as to whether fear is innate. Fear is a useful parallel to aggression for several reasons. (1) Fear, like aggression, does unquestionably produce sin. Sheer cowardice, even without any other faults, can produce one of the most worthless lives imaginable. And, by inhibiting helpful action, it can also immensely harm other people. (2) As is well known, fear is 'natural' in the sense of having plain, substantial physiological causes. The nervous and glandular changes it involves are very marked. They can easily be studied, and are in general quite similar for human beings and for other comparable species. So is much of the outward behaviour which fear produces, such as shrinking and running away. But nobody thinks that we are therefore doomed to uncontrollable cowardice, still less that we must positively praise it. In the first place, the physical system for fear is no isolated machine, but is just a small part of our whole emotional system. Even on a simple mechanistic way of thinking, it no more needs to prevail than a brake needs to in a car.

What, however, about value? Does our capacity for fear commit us to praising and honouring it, or can we despise it? Fear aims at security; is that good or bad?

No one, probably, will feel like giving a simple answer to that question. There are various kinds of danger; some things ought to be feared and others ought not. Somebody who was altogether without fear would be as incapable of managing his life as somebody who could not feel pain. (This was Siegfried's problem.) And somebody who does not fear hurting others is a psychopath. Fear of a special kind enters into respect, which is an absolutely necessary kind of response for the recognition of any kind of value—('The fear of the Lord is the beginning of wisdom . . .'). Rashness is, in general, as real a fault as cowardice. In short, if somebody presses the crude question whether fear is a good or a bad thing, we can only give an indirect answer—an answer which may look evasive, but is absolutely necessary in dealing with such a crude question. As Aristotle suggested, we need a mean.[5] Fear is all right in moderation. There should be neither too much nor too little of it. And this moderate level is not just an arithmetical mean, halfway between extreme rashness and extreme cowardice. It involves fearing the *right* things, not the wrong ones, and fearing them as much as, not more than, their nature calls for. It involves understanding what are suitable objects for fear, and what kind of fear is suitable for them. And so forth.

This kind of balanced answer is in fact much more substantial and less evasive than it looks. It would be evasive if it did not suggest a context for deciding on 'the right level.' But it does. It refers us to the context of a whole human life, and sends us for the details to investigate how the various parts of that life are lived and how they fit together. (This includes, of course, understanding the culture.) It rightly refuses to judge the weight to be given to one element in the priority system without considering the shape of the whole. It tells us to reject as inadequate any simple moral rule about fear, such as the rule that 'nobody ought ever to run away in battle' or that 'anyone is a fool who risks his skin for an ideal.' Certainly there are problems about how to evaluate total ways of life, problems which we must take seriously. They are the sort of problems which we must study if we want to judge the simple moral rules, and also if we want to understand the whole relation between motives and values. To indicate them is not to evade them; they must be considered separately. If we are to get guidance about values from our nature, it will have to be from that nature taken as a whole, not from the presence or absence in it of a particular motive.

Both fear and anger (I am suggesting) are necessary motives, and necessary elements even in a good life, because they are responses to evil, and there are always some evils which ought to be feared, and some which ought to be attacked. If this is right, the essential thing is not to get rid of these motives, but to direct them rightly. Now this position may seem weak, because it assumes that the evils themselves will still remain. Should we then treat fear too, as people have treated aggression, as simply a removable evil, an accidental consequence of bad societies, a state of mind which ought to be entirely swept away? This thought seems to be expressed in the phrase 'Freedom from Fear'—one of the Four Freedoms declared as ideals at the end of the Second World War. Fear might in fact be compared to pain, as an unpleasant experience which we should be better without. Yet people born without the capacity to feel pain do not live long or happily. Pain and fear, equally, are not just bad experiences. They are indications of something *wrong*, and necessary responses to it. So is anger. If we wanted to do without these states, we would need, not just a world where nothing goes wrong, but one where nothing is ever in danger of going wrong. A world where nothing goes wrong is a Utopia. But Utopias only work because they are carefully organized to prevent evils. This means that the people running them must be continually governed by certain well-directed fears. A world where nothing could possibly go wrong would presumably be some sort of heaven. But the idea of it is not very clear, nor, I think, very useful.

The trouble is that action as human beings know it does not seem to be possible except in a context of constant choice between better and worse possibilities. And for action to seem worth while, that choice has to engage us. The difference between better and worse must therefore be a real and serious one. The worse must sometimes count as really bad. And while pure intellects, or Nongs, might perhaps make their choices by just registering values calmly and changing course without any excitement, we are emotional creatures, which can act only when we are moved. The quickened pulse is an essential part of our endeavours. If we are to be capable of hope and desire, we must also be capable of fear.

We have been occupied so far with the first half of our programme—with pointing out that aggression is not the only motive which can lead to serious wickedness, nor the only dangerous motive which can have innate roots. I have illustrated this from the parallel case of fear. That illustration has already led us to our second enterprise—to remarking that, in spite of their dangers, neither of these motives is essentially bad. Both of them would still be necessary in any life we could possibly conceive of. They are responses to evil, and we are not going to run out of evils. Nor need we expect to run out of them in order to undertake social change. The reasons for wanting change lie in certain iniquitous and appalling conditions of life as it is. We can see the need to change these, and the sort of changes which would improve them, without positing that we could make life perfect. Thoughts of an earthly heaven may sometimes be helpful, but what usually fuels reform is the sight and anticipation of earthly hells. In fact, science-fiction speculations about the possible behaviour of perfect human beings are usually rather harmful, because they distort our approach to problems which actually lie before us. The point of talking about (for instance) 'freedom from fear' as an ideal, is to make us concentrate on certain gross, unnecessary, removable dangers, and insist on removing them. That is what the people who coined the slogan had in mind. They did not mean that human life should really be organized in such a way as to exclude fear of any kind. Suppose now that we ask whether, in a Utopia, that exclusion of all fear would be a proper aim? We may find reason to doubt it. This is partly because, as I have suggested, precautions would still be necessary. But it is also for reasons which are rooted more directly in our own emotional constitution, and which might not apply to pure intellects or to Nongs. The occurrence of some fear is a normal part of human life. Even physiologically, a fear-free existence for humans is scarcely conceivable. Children's play involves the constant, subtle use of fear to heighten the tensions. It seems designed as an inoculation for an essential aspect of human experience. Adults too naturally want some excitement; it seems essential for a healthy life. Without real danger people get bored. They gamble, they fall into depression, they go mountain-climbing, they pick quarrels. The reviving flood of adrenalin seems at times to be a necessary stimulant.

3 THE HARMLESSNESS OF A PHYSICAL BASIS

This tendency to get bored by security and to look for excitement by seeking danger is such a familiar feature of human life that nobody questions it. People inquiring into such things as the causes of juvenile delinquency or of other violent behaviour simply mention this kind of boredom as an explanation. And it is an explanation, because we all recognize that we too are capable of responding to boredom in the same sort of way. But that explanation only works because we assume that everyone has a strong natural taste for excitement, and that fear is the simplest source of excitement available. Now this taste, and this resort to fear, depend physically on our adrenalin system. They are therefore innate. Nobody, however, sees this fact as calling for fatalism. Nobody launches academic controversies about the innateness of fear. Everybody finds it obvious that we are not committed to pursuing this taste merely by possessing it. We are intelligent beings, who can weigh the real dangers involved in an enterprise against the pleasures of risk-taking. We are not forced to take risks simply because we have the nervous capacity for enjoying them, any more than we are forced to do mathematics simply by our cerebral capacity for calculation. Both these capacities do exercise their attraction on us, and both can carry us away if we are not aware of their dangers.

Gamblers who construct elaborate systems are carried away

both by the love of mathematics and the love of danger. But they don't need to be. The innate taste for excitement explains some extraordinary and destructive conduct. But in responsible beings it does not excuse it, because it is not an overwhelming or irresistible motive. Accordingly, nobody sees the innateness of fear as justifying fatalism.

On the face of things, aggression seems to call for much the same treatment. The motive of anger—the wish to attack—seems to be just one of many motives to which we are prone, but which need not overwhelm us. It seems to arise naturally in us in a wide variety of situations, some of them suitable, others not, and it is apparently our business to discriminate and control it where necessary. If this is right, a good human being is not expected to be a bloodless intellect, or a Nong, naturally incapable of anger. Instead he or she is expected to be one who can feel it strongly and act on it on occasion, but who yet manages to direct it only to its proper ends. This view is particularly hard to reject if we accept a similar account of fear, because physiologically these two emotions are very closely linked. They are in fact aspects of the same physical system. Adrenalin works to prepare the body for fight or flight: both outcomes have the same glandular basis.

Moreover, the physiology of anger is also quite closely related to that of sex. Now in the case of sex probably no one will hesitate to accept an innate physical basis for emotion. We rightly don't think of this as compromising our freedom, as limiting our emotional life, but as extending it. There might be beings, such as Nongs, whose reproductive life was carried on with no excitement at all, but we are not like them. We have a whole nervous and glandular apparatus devoted to the business, and its effect is not to turn us into machines, but to enrich our emotional and social life enormously. Again, if we ask a similar question about our aesthetic sensibilities, it seems clear that these, too, must have an inherited physical basis. Our brain must

have a natural leaning to certain modes of imaginative symbol-
izing, and our senses must dispose us to react to certain kinds of
form and rhythm. These capacities, however, are not a clog or a
fetter on our aesthetic life, instead, they are the basic apparatus
which makes it possible. (Nongs, again, might have no such
responsiveness at all. Bad luck; no natural susceptibility, no
Beethoven.)

The reason why people have not been willing to think of
aggression in the same way as these other motives is, of course,
that they have seen that it was dangerous, and apparently have
not thought of other motives as being dangerous at all. I have
been pointing out that plenty of other motives are dangerous,
and in fact that any motive can be dangerous if it gets out of
control. Parental love can be extremely dangerous, and so can the
love of mathematics. Curiosity is also dangerous. Sheer uncritical
force of habit, persisting when circumstances change, can be as
dangerous as anything. Fear, along with its offshoot the love of
excitement, is profoundly dangerous, and we had better not
under-estimate its effect in politics. A great deal of international
ill-feeling, and also much persecution of minorities, seems to
flow from irrational fear of the unknown—fear of groups which
are seen as threatening because of their strangeness. And, as
newspaper proprietors well know, there is nothing like fear for
selling papers. Murder, too, seems to be a crime which is commonly motivated by fear, and often fear of a quite obsessive,
irrational kind. Murderous situations are often like the one
which is so well shown in the second half of *Macbeth*, where
Macbeth tells himself that he is already well protected by the
witches' prophecies, but still says 'But yet we'll make assurance
double sure', and murders MacDuff's family—an act which in
fact destroys him. Obsessive fear blinds people to the effects of
provocation. There seems to be a strong element of this motivation in cold-war thinking. It is a great deal more dangerous than
straight aggression.

4 DISTINGUISHING AGGRESSION FROM DESTRUCTIVENESS

How, then, is aggression different from these other motives? It may seem to be different in being a tendency which does not just happen to be destructive, but which has destruction as its aim—in being itself a mere wish to destroy. This, however, is a misleading idea. It is indeed the way in which Freud conceived of aggression. He thought of it as the death-wish turned outward—as a mere general urge to wreck and kill. But later investigations have not supported this strange suggestion, either in human life or elsewhere. In other animals, no such vast, sweeping motives as either the inward or the outward death-wish have been found at work. What has been found is a far more limited, specific, easily satisfied set of tendencies to become irritated by certain sorts of intrusion, and to attack intruders to the extent of driving them off. Only where strong competition develops and both sides hold their ground does this develop into fighting, and only where fighting is exceptionally persistent does it kill. Most commonly a much simpler, less sensational solution is provided by one side's running away. Most attacks among social animals are therefore soon over and do little harm. They serve in general to settle disputes, to space out individuals, not to kill them, and do not as a rule seriously interrupt social life. Certainly there can be injury and sometimes death. But aggressive tendencies of this moderate kind do not answer to the essentially diabolical formula of a truly wicked motive, the interest in destruction for its own sake. When Mephistopheles tells Faust that he is the spirit which always denies, he is expressing something very different from a sharp, impulsive, wish to attack. That 'always' gives quite another colour to the business. Destruction as a policy is not just aggression. It is hatred. This is not a single, natural motive, but a considered attitude, in the end, a way of life. It represents a decision, not an original distinct motive. We will come back to this crucial difference in Chapter 8.

This difference between aggression and true, destructive hatred is very important. To grasp it clearly, it may be worth looking at an example—namely, the psychology of argument. In arguing, people certainly feel that they are in conflict. They may very well get angry, unless they make an effort to avoid it, and they certainly want to attack. But they don't normally wish each other dead, or even damaged. A really destructive approach in argument is an unsuitable element; when it is present, the argument proper cannot proceed. None the less, argument does involve aggression. However scrupulously it may be conducted, territory is in dispute, and it is remarkable how continually the military metaphors of attack and defence are used. This happens even in academic controversy, where the size and difficulty of the problems is well known. Granted that difficulty, one might have expected less talk of winning battles, since on difficult questions it is obvious that the truth may not belong to either party yet. It might be better to use less military language here, and to talk more of exploration, of paths to be found and land not yet surveyed. This does happen to some extent. But it constantly yields to talk of rival forces demolishing each other's positions, of bastions crumbling and citadels falling and all the rest of it. The language is that of battlefields, or at best of law-courts. It is highly aggressive, and it does not misrepresent the spirit of argument. Argument does involve attack, and unless the disputants make an effort to control themselves, there will sometimes be anger. All this, however, is perfectly compatible with good humour, and can go on between people who are excellent friends, and mean to continue so. Disputants do not in general hate their opponents or wish them dead. They simply want them out of the way—that is, in the context of argument, they want them silenced. That silencing will satisfy them. There can be genuine anger, but that anger alone will never produce hatred.

For hatred to arise, strong resentment and some fear must usually be added to anger. Perhaps it is also necessary that the hated person should come to symbolize an element in life which, in general, the hater dreads and wants to kill. The result is an extremely complex phenomenon, in which the original aggression is only a single ingredient.

I have used this example because it lies conveniently to hand in our investigation of this debate—which has from time to time been conducted with a great deal of anger—and because it may serve to give us a rather more realistic view of how aggressive motives actually work. Getting angry in controversy is certainly not the same thing as feeling destructive. In principle, it is a matter of feeling moved to assert and defend the truth. But of course it can very easily get combined with other feelings in a way which makes it far less respectable. When anger is entangled with personal vanity, with crude quarrelsomeness and the desire to dominate, things can get very bad. And when we add to this mix a whole range of fears associated with loss of status, they get worse still. If, still further, we drop into the brew some strong symbolism projected on to the opponent, it may indeed turn into actual personal hatred and a wish to destroy. But the original aggression was still only one element of this. I certainly do not want to deny that it was a dangerous element. But in order to attend to its dangers, we need to understand it, and a first step to that understanding is distinguishing it from the surrounding scenery. I am inclined to think that a very important aspect of its danger is in fact this same quarrelsomeness in controversy which has led the human race to squander its intellectual resources disgracefully by its obsession with disputes. Clever and articulate people spend a lot of their time reproducing the conditions of the Tower of Babel, shouting at each other instead of trying to co-operate.

5 THE FUNCTIONS OF AGGRESSION

Undoubtedly, we need to understand the dangers of our innate aggressive tendencies, just as we do those of our motives. But we can scarcely do this unless we also understand their positive functions. If we think of aggression as Freud did, as a pure wish for destruction, it is hard to see any positive function for it, and its occurrence, if it did occur, would be a monstrous evolutionary puzzle. But is anger like this? Is it something which it would be a good thing to get rid of entirely? Ought we to proclaim 'freedom from anger' as a fifth freedom, and aim to eliminate all conflict from human life? Should we view quarrelling as merely an artificial corruption, flowing from removable faults in social organization? Is it something which in a properly organized Utopia would simply not occur?

To decide about this, we have to consider realistically the part which mild, controlled aggression actually plays in human social life. As with fear, it is probably best to start here by looking at the behaviour of small children. At this simple, primitive end of the spectrum, simulated attack is a marked and essential part of play. This is not because children are full of hatred and destruction. It is because the sense of otherness, the contact with genuinely distinct personalities around them, fascinates them, and it is best conveyed by mild collision. Laughter and other distancing devices safeguard the proceedings—but the wish to collide, to invade another's world, is a real one. Without that contact, each child would be isolated. Each needs the direct physical clash, the practical conviction that others as well as himself are capable both of feeling pain and of returning it. Surprising though it may be, that interaction lies at the root of sympathy. The young of other social animals play in the same mildly aggressive way, and derive the same sort of bond-forming effects from it.

Besides play, however, children also need at times more serious clashes. Real disputes, properly expressed and resolved, seem essential for their emotional unfolding. In this way they begin to get a fuller sense of the independent reality of others. They find that there is somebody at the other end. They learn to control their own anger, to understand it and to reason themselves out of it. A quarrel which is worked through and made up can be profoundly bond-forming. But they need to feel anger before they can control it and to learn that it can sometimes be justified. They learn the difference between justified and unjustified anger, and come to accept that justified anger in others can be the consequence of one's own bad conduct. What they learn is thus not to eliminate anger and attack from their lives, but to use these things rightly. And in adults, right up to the level of saints and heroes, this is an essential skill. Mild, occasional anger is a necessary part of all social relations, and serious anger gives us, as I have suggested, a necessary range of responses to evil. Our linked capacities for fear and anger—for fight and flight—form a positive organ to be used, not a malfunction. This no more commits us to misusing it than our having feet commits us to kicking people.

These positive functions for aggression, both in childhood and in adult life, do not seem to be confined to our culture. They are found everywhere. The evidence which has been brought forward recently for the existence of cultures which are in some ways 'non-aggressive' is interesting, but it is not a kind which could throw doubt on the presence of innate human aggression as one motive among others. Much of it is directed simply to the question of war. Undoubtedly here are peoples who do not recognize war as an institution, and this fact is of enormous interest and importance. It answers any crude theorist who claims that to make war is 'only human nature' and therefore an uncontrollable tendency. But this is not the point of our present enquiry.

A much bolder claim which has been made for some of these anthropological studies is that they show ways of life in which even private aggression does not arise, in which no tendency to anger or quarrelling is shown. The claim is a startling one, and it is hard to see how the evidence can be stretched to support it. For instance, Ruth Benedict described many ways in which the Zuni Indians discouraged and penalized aggressive conduct, and even the feeling of anger.[6] But this is so far from showing the absence of aggressive tendencies that it is incompatible with it. One could scarcely discourage and oppose a tendency which was not present. Similarly, Eibl-Eibesfeldt describes how, among the Bushmen, who also discourage aggression, children still display it, wrestling and quarrelling in a style familiar to us from our own children.[7] He adds that they do not hit each other with weapons, nor do the adults encourage their aggression. Instead, at times they try to calm it down. Thus, although the aggression is spontaneous, it is pliable, and the policy of suppression does to some extent succeed. This is what we need to know, and (again) it is enough to supply us with an answer to the crude theorist who might say that personal quarrels too are 'only human nature', and that therefore no attempt to bring them under cultural control can ever succeed. There is clearly an immense difference between Bushman life and the life of peoples who institutionalize quarrelling as one of their central interests. But attempts to elevate this difference to a Utopian extent, to show these less quarrelsome peoples as friction-free, paradisal beings are clearly unjustified. Anthropologists themselves have gone to some trouble lately to correct this idealization. Even the absence of raiding among the Bushmen and Pygmies, on which much stress has been laid, turns out to be a recent change; when there were more of them, and less interference from governments, they appear to have raided their neighbours at intervals like so many other self-respecting peoples, including ourselves.[8] Their admirable conduct is focussed, in a familiar manner, on those nearest to them, and even there they are not immune from temptation to transgress; they find peacefulness difficult. It is surely important to recognize this in order to give them due credit for their impressive achievements. They are not societies of Nongs, beings in whom anger could never arise. They are people very much like ourselves, who are prone to it, but they seem to make a more determined and successful effort than we do to minimize it and bring it under control. Their anti-aggressive (rather than non-aggressive) cultures are of enormous interest and can have a great deal to teach us. But it seems important not to cheapen their enterprise by over-simplifying it—by treating it as easier and less impressive than it actually is.

SUMMARY

Not all wickedness is aggressive. Much of it has quite different motivation.

Aggression as a motive—which is quite distinct from aggression as a political act—is only sinister when it is out of control. Other motives out of control are also sinister. As a motive, 'aggression' means a tendency to attack—typically, though not necessarily, from anger. It therefore presupposes the capacity for anger. It is a limited tendency. It is found in many kinds of animal, and is not, in any of them, a mere general tendency to kill or destroy. Instead, it operates within limits, apparently serving as a mechanism for spacing out individuals and ordering them in a way which makes their life possible. Human beings clearly share this capacity for anger, and a good deal of the limiting structure which guides its use.

Is it innate? Well, is fear innate? Fear too produces vice. It too involves a neural mechanism—indeed a related neural mechanism. This does not make fear irresistible. It is only part of our being. Nor does it make fear wholly bad. It is good or bad according to context.

Both fear and anger are necessary motives, because both (like pain) are appropriate responses to evil. We do not need to get rid of either, but to direct them properly. We are not called on to plan for a heaven where there are no evils, nor perhaps even for a Utopia where they are kept permanently at bay, but for a world where they occur. This can call for both fear and anger.

Perhaps, too, even where evils really are absent, human beings need excitement, which apparently involves some fear. They certainly need sexual emotion. Both have a clear physical basis. In general, nobody finds this sinister. Nor should they. Is aggression different? People suppose it to be more dangerous than fear, but this may well be a mistake. Nor is aggression—as Freud thought—essentially destructive. For instance, disputes are aggressive, but they are not attempts to destroy one's opponent. And children's play, which has a strong element of controlled aggression, is certainly not destructive. There are not (as used to be supposed) any non-aggressive human societies. Opposition is an essential element in human life: aggression is part of the emotional equipment for making it work. Societies which keep it within reasonable bounds (unlike our own) are doing something much harder and more interesting than merely never feeling it in the first place.

5

FATES, CAUSES AND FREE-WILL

'Tis all a Chequer-board of Nights and Days
Where Destiny with Men for Pieces plays;
Hither and thither moves, and mates, and slays,
And one by one back in the Closet lays.

Rubáiyát of Omar Khayyam, translated by
Edward Fitzgerald

1 THE MENACE OF FATALISM

With such vast, central topics as free-will, where many problems
tangle together, safety depends on dealing with one element at a
time, starting with the ones which our immediate problem
raises. At present we are attempting the understanding of bad
conduct. How do people—how do we ourselves—contrive to
behave as badly as we do? This is only one side—a neglected
one—of the question how we manage to behave well. I have
been suggesting that every capacity for virtue can be expected to
carry with it a corresponding capacity for vice, that vice is simply the reverse of virtue, our refusal to use our most important

capacities. The understanding of those capacities is therefore the key to both phenomena. This calls for a good deal of empirical—as well as conceptual—investigation of just what these capacities are, and at what points they are naturally most liable to fail. It calls for a study of our innate constitution.

This view conflicts with one widely proclaimed for some time in the social sciences, namely that we are blank paper at birth and have no constitution at all. Wickedness is then entirely the product of our society. This view is most often expressed as the denial of a single innate motive, aggression. But it calls for a much wider basis, the denial of all innate causes for human conduct. That is our business now.

The denial of innate causes is phrased as a defence of free-will against determinism, which is here described, rather oddly, as 'genetic determinism' or 'biological determinism.'[1] I call this phrasing odd because determinism seems to be a presupposition of the sciences generally, not of those sciences in particular. I believe we shall find that the reference to determinism is actually a red herring. The real objection is to fatalism, which is something quite different.

To state this difference crudely—fatalism is the superstitious acceptance of unnecessary evil, based on a false belief in human impotence to do anything about it. As a practice, it means taking no steps to cure that evil. As a temper, it is the tendency to take up false beliefs in order to excuse inaction. Determinism, on the other hand, is simply the modest assumption of that degree of regularity in nature which is necessary for science, and is as necessary for the social sciences as for the physical ones. (I shall use the word here in this very general sense, without entering at all into the controversies about just how this regularity is best described, and how complete it can be expected to be, which divide philosophers of science.) Determinism has no direct relevance to conduct, and there is no deterministic temper, apart from the scientific one. Determinism is of course often taken to be incompatible with a belief in free-will. But it seems possible that this idea springs from a superstitious over-inflation of both concepts, particularly of determinism. A melodramatic tendency to personify physical forces and other scientific entities can represent them as demons driving us, rather than humble general facts about the world, which is all they have a right to be seen as. This produces fatalism, which certainly is incompatible with a belief in free-will, since it teaches that we are helpless in the hands of these superhuman beings. The temptation to think in this animistic way is much stronger than is sometimes noticed, and deserves careful attention.

I have suggested that our concentration on the question of whom to blame for our troubles hinders our attempts to understand them. This is, in fact, a serious nuisance. We shall find, I think, that the idea of blame is deeply entwined with our whole notion of explanation, and that it is this connexion which gives rise to fatalism. We easily view causes as hostile beings. This is clear from some remarkable facts about the history of the language we use when we speak about it. The word 'cause' does not, as you might expect, mean originally an earlier event, nor yet an explanation. It originally means in Latin simply 'blame' or 'lawsuit'. The same is true of the Greek word which corresponds to it, *aitia*.

This linguistic fact is not as odd as it may seem. In the first place, misfortune calls for explanation more strongly than ordinary prosperity. People tend to take the course of nature for granted when it goes right. It is when it goes wrong that they are forced to find out about its workings. So causal enquiry naturally arises as 'fault-finding' in the engineer's sense. And this easily turns into fault-finding in the personal sense—into asking who is to blame. Causal enquiry is personalized, partly for the good reason that human conduct is often easier to bring under control than natural forces, and is to that extent better worth knowing about. But another, much more troublesome factor comes in as well. We are strongly inclined to think personally even when we are not actually dealing with persons, to dramatize all our relations with the world. Even people who sternly resist this tendency over good fortune often find it almost irresistible in disaster. The idea of a malignant fate or demon is much harder to root out than that of a good God. Thus Housman's defeated revolutionaries call down curses on 'whatever brute and black-guard made the world' as if it were obvious that such a being must exist. And 'Nature, red in tooth and claw' is continually being placed in the dock.

Now there is a great difference between explaining one's troubles by blaming the will of a malignant being, and explaining them by a natural law. Natural laws certainly cannot be shifted, but, once understood, they can often be used. A farmer who comes to understand the workings of the river which sometimes floods his fields, instead of thinking that a demon is in charge, may still not be able to stop the floods, but he does get better warning, and he may in time learn to control the damage. At least he can change his planting habits so as to avoid disaster. But the will of a powerful and malignant being cannot be deflected in this way. It will get you whatever you do. True fatalism characteristically shows human effort as useless, indeed, self-defeating. This comes out very clearly in the story of Oedipus. Here disaster is repeatedly foretold, but all the efforts which anybody makes to avoid it are futile; they only bring on ruin the sooner. Serious belief in this sort of fate would completely paralyse action.

The word 'fatalism' can of course be used to describe many less extreme resigned attitudes, some of them quite rational. In very bad situations, where human effort actually can make no difference, resignation is appropriate enough. Thus, we all do right to be resigned to eventually dying. And someone (for instance a soldier) who is surrounded by great and unpredict-able dangers may do right not to attempt much precaution, but instead to think in terms of getting on with with his business and waiting for 'the bullet with his name on it.' He needs to concentrate on what he can still achieve, and to do this he must dismiss from his mind the precautions which are no longer useful. But the fantasy about the name written on the bullet is significant. The idea of impersonal danger is not just unwelcome, it is deeply foreign to our imagination. We have real difficulty in accepting it.

The most extraordinary case of this personal approach is perhaps the dramatizing of chance itself into a force or deity. Properly speaking, chance is not a positive thing at all. It is just a name for our ignorance of causes. But even quite sophisticated people do seem to think of it as a being with a purpose. Such a person lately said to me that the Darwinian theory of evolution was intolerable 'because it showed chance as ruling the universe instead of God.' Now the reference to chance in Darwinian theory ought in fact only to mean that there is a great deal which we don't know about the origin of species. No being which could possibly stand in competition with God is involved in that admission. What my friend said was, however, thoroughly excusable in the light of the personal language into which people constantly fall when they talk about chance—'playthings of chance', 'blind chance' and all the rest of it. As a character in Webster puts it, on finding that he has carelessly murdered the wrong person

> We are merely the stars' tennis-balls, struck and bandied
> Which way please them.[2]

I shall use the word 'fatalism' here to mean not reasonable, limited resignation, but this superstitious irrational abandonment of effort, based on the feeling that the opposing force is alive and will get you whatever you do. It is of course a very old attitude, particularly common over such things as disease. Now this sort of fatalism is as different from determinism as night is from day. Determinism, which is a relatively modest view dating from about the seventeenth century, is the belief in natural regularity which makes modern science possible. It says simply that we should view events as connected in an intelligible way, and occurring according to laws. This means that, given suitable evidence, they could be predicted in advance. It is not a belief in any supernatural beings who will force them to occur as they do. The word 'determine' does not mean 'force'. It means 'make known', as when mathematicians say that any three points determine a circle. Similarly, the term 'force of nature' does not describe a powerful being in the background, occupied in compulsion. If we speak of the force of gravitation, we simply mean the way in which things regularly move. This way of thinking does not treat human effort as a special case, and does not at all suggest that it must be useless. The farmer who uses his increased understanding of water movement to build dams and control the floods is not defying the force of gravitation but using it. He is not doomed to find, like Oedipus, that his efforts must always rebound uselessly on his own head. In so far as he really does understand the laws involved, he can genuinely change the outcome. He is—we will say—one of the first people to farm beside the Nile. When he learns to harvest before the flood and plant after it, he has succeeded in changing, not just his own fortunes, but the world. By accepting certain limits, by understanding what was not possible, he has made other things possible which before could never have been so.

2 THE LIMITED ROLE OF PREDICTION IN THOUGHT

This willingness to accept certain limits as given is the seed of determinism. It is at least as old as humanity. But only in the seventeenth century was it extended into an explicit general assumption of the regularity of nature. That extension, which has made modern science possible, has now become a central part of our culture. It scarcely makes sense for anyone today to talk of rejecting it unless he also means to reject most of science. What we need to do is to grasp its limitations, and in particular to notice the limited area in which it operates. Even within science, there can be areas, such as quantum mechanics, which are non-deterministic. And a great deal of our most essential thinking is not, and ought not to be, any part of physical science at all. It is practical, evaluative, creative, historical, legal, symbolic, contemplative or the like. This range of thinking is 'scientific' only in the general sense that it is capable of method, that it can be organized and is subject to standards. It is not concerned with finding general theoretical laws of how the world runs and basing predictions on them. It has other work. For instance, in practical thinking, we are wondering *what to do*. We are certainly not trying to make predictions about our own future conduct. We use predictions only as a part of our raw material. Practical thinking is an art, not a science, though it uses the sciences. And that art is the province of free-will.

We shall return shortly to the question whether prediction clashes with free-will—whether, for instance, our farmer, by doing what an intelligent person might be expected to do in his circumstances, has put himself in the position of Oedipus, of becoming a mere slave to destiny. (I don't myself think so.) But it is worth noticing first how little scientific determinism need actually commit us to. It does not have to be a view about the world at all. It need be no more than a piece of advice on how to conduct science. The world might really be quite irregular—subject from time to time to uncaused events—without destroying determinism. If it was like that, we would still have to work on the assumption that it was regular, because no other assumption would yield us any results at all. We would sometimes go wrong, but that would be better than never going right. We do not therefore have to have the metaphysical certainty, which the seventeenth-century rationalists thought they had, of universal order, to have reason to do science in the way in which it has been done so far. Determinism need not make any of the bold assumptions about the universe which fatalism makes. Determinism can be purely pragmatic and operational. And if we want to avoid superstitiously inflating natural forces into fates, perhaps we had better keep it so.

There are, of course, big philosophical problems here about the status of rationalism, about our right to attribute order to the world. We can scarcely touch on them here. Both scientists and philosophers, I think, now agree that the claims of the seventeenth-century rationalists were too bold. We do not have a proof that the world is perfectly orderly. Nor do we need it for science. I suggest that we follow Kant's general line here, and take it that we do need to assume some kind of order if we are to think at all and that this need is itself enough to justify the assumption. We can add to it Konrad Lorenz's point that it would be very odd evolutionarily if we had evolved with a set of cognitive faculties totally out of tune with the world we are a part of—so that the set of laws which we naturally assume is likely to be a fairly suitable set.[3] This covers our theoretical thinking, and therefore determinism. For practical thinking, as Kant said, we need a somewhat different set of laws. But as they have a different function, they do not conflict with the theoretical set, but supplement them.[4] We must look into this further in a moment. But first, there is a rather smaller but still troublesome point to mention.

Besides any real philosophical difficulties which arise about determinism, there remains a lurking emotional one. This is the entanglement between the scientific issue and an older dispute about God. Real trouble about free-will first arose in the controversy about God's foreknowledge between St Augustine and Pelagius in the fifth century AD. If God knows all that we are going to do, can we freely choose to do it? Pelagius thought not, and was therefore willing to say that God might not know everything. But Augustine replied that God must know everything. Augustine won the dispute, and the church was committed to the more difficult view of free-will. It is more difficult because, on top of the problem which scientific knowledge raises, God's knowledge is that of a creator, and it shows him as somehow responsible. He made us, and if he knows what we are going to do, it rather looks as if he is really doing it. Thus, unless a good deal of care is taken, we are liable to get the picture which Calvin sometimes presented, of a clockmaker who designs, builds and winds a clock, and then punishes it for striking.

We cannot really discuss this problem here. There are certainly ways of avoiding the crudity—notably by putting God outside time. But what matters for our present purposes is that this issue of responsibility is extremely compelling to the imagination. Once introduced, it tends to dominate all discussions of free-will. Accordingly, when the focus shifted from God's fore-knowledge to science, the supernatural figure in the background was not properly exorcized and removed from the controversy as he ought to have been. The language in which determinism is promoted continually goes beyond saying what it needs to say, which is simply that science is possible. It constantly represents human effort as an unreal cause. It shows people as helpless pawns and puppets in the grip of all sorts of non-human entities which act as puppet-masters—Nature, Entropy, Evolution, History, personified laws and forces of all kinds (notably economic ones), and most recently the selfish gene.[5] Writers whose point is really just to show us some general fact about the world are led on with astonishing ease, by way of saying that we cannot change this general fact, to treating it as if it were itself an agent manipulating human beings, and as if all real human agency had been absorbed into it. We need always to demythologize this sort of writing. Without it, determinism ought to be a modest assumption about the possibility of knowledge, which will do us little harm.

3 THE CONTINUITY BETWEEN THE PHYSICAL AND SOCIAL SCIENCES

In general, today, it usually is taken as harmless so far as the physical sciences go. Objection is raised only when we come to the social sciences. But to drop determinism at this point is an impossible move, calling for a total divorce between mind and body. It is true that there is an interface between the physical and social sciences at the nerves and brain, and this is what has caused the alarm about 'genetic' or 'biological determinism.' But *the barrier against determinism cannot possibly be erected there*. The social sciences, after all, are already real sciences. They too make predictions, which have to be taken seriously. The people whose acts they predict are not robots, but ordinary free people like ourselves. The threat of determinism, if it is a threat, arises already at its full strength within the social sciences.

How much of a threat is it? Does conduct cease to be free merely by being predictable? It is not obvious why it should, provided that the prediction rests on the right sort of grounds—namely, on there being good reason to act in that way. Our farmer used his head and did what could have been expected of an intelligent and resolute man, given his problem. People who predict his act do not, therefore, show his independence as a sham, which they would if they predicted successfully that, after a lot of enterprising talk, he would in fact sit around and complain that somebody else ought to have tackled this flood problem. The action is a free action, and it does not cease to be so merely because some wily bystander manages to predict it. The opposite of freedom is not predictability but slavery of various kinds, whether to an outside master or to inner impediments such as sloth or habit, which inhibit rational activity. If there are no such inhibitions, we call the choice free, regardless of whether somebody could predict it. It is in fact quite easy to be unpredictable, if you don't mind acting crazily. But freedom does not require craziness. Nor does it require omnipotence. We are not put off calling an act free by the presence of outside difficulties. The problems created by the flood are a necessary setting for the action just mentioned, not an obstacle to its freedom. They could be a great deal harder and more sinister without affecting its nature as a free and rational choice. The free approach, as opposed to the habit-bound, unthinking one, is not marked by an absence of outside difficulties, but by a resolution to understand and conquer these difficulties. And among them (as we normally consider the question) there will be a number of psychological factors as well as the physical ones. The farmer and his colleagues must reckon with their own and each other's quirks, gifts and tempers, with their various strengths and weaknesses, and with the effect to be expected on these from various strains and opportunities, as well as with the soil and the floods. They need to assume some regularity in the mental as well as in the physical universe.

4 THE IRRELEVANCE OF RANDOMNESS

How much psychological regularity, however, should we assume? This is a vast question. It may be best to approach it by asking first how much regularity we actually do assume as things are. I shall outline what I think we do expect, and then consider whether we ought to change our habits.

As things are, I suggest that we expect about the same degree of regularity in psychological matters as we do in physical ones. Both over things and people we do expect some order. We expect experience to be some use to us, to serve as some sort of guide. Both about things and people, we know that we shall make mistakes and get surprises. But in general we attribute the mistakes to our own ignorance rather than to real discontinuities in the world. A person whose house suddenly blows up usually concludes that there was something there which he did not know about, not that explosions obey no laws. And if, out of the blue, a friend suddenly pulls a gun on him, he is likely to draw the same sort of conclusion. Neither misfortune makes him decide that determinism was just a mistake, and that these events are actually random. And if he did think that in the case of the friend, he would not be thinking that the action was due to free-will. Whatever else free-will may be, it is not randomness. Somebody who may act at any time in a way which has no roots in his previous life is not free, but disordered. To be unpredictable, not only to other people but to oneself, is to have lost all control over one's destiny. That is a condition as far from freedom as rolling helplessly downhill.

In a normal person, we expect that changes, however sudden and drastic, will flow out of pre-existing motives and will preserve some sort of continuity. Even a sudden conversion, if it is to be real and effective, must belong to, and have the consent of, the previous personality. That is what distinguishes it from possession by an alien spirit. Personal identity must at some level be preserved. This means that both the changing person and those around him could, if they really understood the signs, to some extent predict the change. Our common failure to do this shows merely our enormous chronic ignorance and inattention, rather than a real discontinuity in the changing self.

This, I suggest, is our usual view of the matter. There seems no reason to think that we actually conceive our mental life as less continuous, more broken-up, and therefore less intelligible than the physical world. I think we conceive it simply as much more complex and mysterious, so that there are naturally many breaks in our perception of it. Does this assumption of continuity conflict with freedom? Again, it does not seem obvious why it should. What conflicts with freedom is over-confidence in crude, narrow psychological theories. This leads people to rule out perfectly possible and desirable changes as impossible. It leads them to treat local bad habits as if they were universal laws. But then, just the same thing happens with crude physical theories. The mistake does not seem to lie in supposing that there is enough order present to make theorizing possible, but in theorizing badly.

The views about human nature which have provoked people to reject the notion of such a nature altogether have usually been of this negative and restrictive kind—the kind which tends to suggest that good and enterprising conduct is impossible. This tendency grows out of an element in everyday thought which perhaps deserves attention. This is the habit of assuming that truth is always nastier and duller than appearance—the habit which leads people to speak of 'illusions' as if they were always pleasing. Terms like 'knowledge of human nature' and 'knowledge of the world' tend to be used in a distorted way to cover only disagreeable and disappointing discoveries, usually those concerned with discrepancies between ideals and practice. The suggestion is that no one could be misled by forming too bad an opinion of his fellow-being—that nobody ever has disagreeable illusions. Psychological discovery is conceived as only working one way—as showing unbreakable moral limitations and discouraging effort.

But of course the assumption that psychological generalization would be bound to work like this is itself a piece of the same cheap cynicism which it seems designed to counter. People often surprise each other by unpredictable good conduct, and that fact is bound to emerge from any honest psychological enquiry. Our positive capacities and aspirations, our gifts and affections are as much a part of human nature as our weaknesses. It is true that for Nietzsche and Freud, as for the bar-parlour moralist, psychological enquiry did often seem to centre on tearing up the floorboards to find where the bad smells were coming from. Certain forms of endemic human self-deception do make that emphasis often necessary, and at the end of the last century there seems to have been a particular need for it. But it only makes sense against a background of wide understanding, a context in which the rest of the house is examined as well. (Jung is often useful in restoring this balance.) As I have pointed out, the discrepancy between ideals and practice has two sides to it; it is of great interest that ideals are so much *better* than practice. We would be astonished to find a human society in which there were no such ideals, in which everybody was perfectly satisfied with current practice. And even Freud and Nietzsche, of course, were not actually only interested in bad smells, but in foundations, in the sources of our strength.

The notion that we could dispense altogether with the concept of human nature is fashionable but it is not, I think, actually an intelligible one at all. It would involve a depth of scepticism, a deliberate ignorance which its proponents do not seem to have noticed. And that general ignorance would not in fact do the work for which it is proposed. Reformers, from Marx onward, who have somewhat rhetorically suggested dropping the notion of human nature do not really want general scepticism. What they want is to get rid of certain quite limited mistaken views about human nature, in particular, views about its resistance to historical change. They do of course want to say that human nature is more malleable than conservatives suppose. But to say this is not to stop having a view about it. (Someone who argues that iron is more malleable than had been supposed is not denying that iron has a nature.) Revolutionary theory involves having views about how people will feel and behave when certain strains and pressures are removed. And if it makes any use of concepts like *dehumanization*, it presupposes a set of natural tendencies which will then be released to shape the human future. If people were really natureless, were mere indefinite lumps of dough moulded entirely by historical forces, we could have no notion at all of what they would be like or how they would feel in any other culture or epoch than our own. Marx was well aware of the ruinous effect this would have on any attempt at a general theory of history. In the first volume of *Capital*, arguing against what he takes to be Bentham's position, he remarks,

> To know what is useful for a dog, one must study dog nature . . . . Applying this to man, he that would criticize all human acts, movements, relations etc. by the principle of utility, must first deal with human nature in general, and then with human nature modified in each historical epoch.[6]

Moreover, of course, if the individuals were really taken to be mere passive dough, the notion of the historical forces which would be needed to do the moulding is liable to become a wild and superstitious one, an example of the fatalistic thinking I mentioned earlier. Historical enquiry about natureless beings themselves would become impossible. Only by personifying the historical forces and conceiving them as purposive demons shaping the future do theorists get the impression that they can understand what natureless beings would do in an unfamiliar situation—or what they did do in the past.

Hume, pointing out the need for a notion of human nature, describes very well the sceptical predicament which we should be in without it:

> Were there no uniformity in human actions, and were every experiment which we could form of this kind irregular and anomalous, it were impossible to collect any general observations concerning mankind; and no experience, however accurately digested by reflection, would ever serve any purpose.[7]

Now our situation may be bad, but it is not that bad. History and anthropology, not to mention the other social sciences, do teach us something. They are not substitutes for an understanding of natural psychology; they depend on it and presuppose it. There is no competition between these various disciplines; they are all parts of our apparatus for understanding that very complex thing, the behaviour of our species.

In this chapter we have been mainly occupied so far in saying that determinism is not fatalism, and that science does not threaten free-will. It seems important to say this, because the sciences are so prominent and useful a part of our culture that we do not want to get into a conflict with them unless we really need to. But it is of course equally important to say that they are not the whole of our culture, nor even the whole of our thinking.

A great deal of our thinking is practical. It is not aimed at establishing facts, but at deciding what to do. It does not aim at prediction at all. When someone is wrestling with a practical problem, what he wants is a course of action. Bystanders who watch him and make predictions about which answer he will come up with are not contributing to his search; they may actually hinder it. When I mentioned the bystander who might successfully predict that the Nile farmer would find the right way of planting, it may have struck you that there was something a bit odd about that picture. If this bystander knows already what the right method is, why doesn't he say so? Co-operation, not prediction, is usually the proper business for bystanders in this situation. Large practical problems commonly need communal solutions. And until they get them, there are often no answers on hand at all. So the idea of predicting which answer will be chosen scarcely arises. My example of discovering how to plant beside the Nile was of course a deliberately simple one. The aim here is simple and obvious, no other aims conflict with it, and the means for achieving it are at hand. This problem, in fact, is nearly solved already. But practical problems are often far more complex than this, and call for creative efforts of quite a different order. To solve them, somebody may have to invent the wheel, or the Buddhist religion, a new kind of music, the theorem of Pythagoras, or the principle of representative government. People who stand by and try to make predictions about this sort of thing are going to look pretty silly.

Now does this strong creative element in practical thinking conflict with determinism? It does not seem so, because determinism is simply irrelevant to it. Here again, it is important to notice how little determinism promised us. (As with those Delphic oracles which misled Oedipus, we need to look closely at the small print.) Determinism, as I have expressed it, says that we should assume that events are connected in an intelligible way and occur according to laws. Therefore, given suitable evidence, they can be predicted in advance. The key clause is 'given suitable evidence.' What would be suitable evidence for predicting the theorem which Pythagoras is just about to invent? If we had a comprehensive account of the state of his nerves and brain, and all the laws governing them, could we predict his next move? Determinism says that in principle we could. And perhaps it is right. But obviously, in saying this, the deterministic demon (if there were one) would be laughing quite as hollowly as the Delphic oracle laughed at Oedipus. In the first place, we could not possibly have all that evidence, and any attempt to get it would kill our subject before he ever makes his mathematical discovery. But besides this, and much more interestingly, *even if we could make the physical prediction* we would still not be able to read off the theorem from it, unless we also had a complete account of the relation between brain-states and thought. But if we had that, we would already have a complete description of Pythagoras' thoughts, as well as of his brain-states. And this is what we should have to use to discover the theorem, because accounts of brain-states simply do not mention matters like triangles and hypotenuses at all. In trying to predict thought, we should have to use existing thought as our only possible starting-point. And in order to do this, we should have to drop the attempt at prediction and start instead to work out the problem for ourselves. Given all Pythagoras' data, we might even come up with his solution. But this would be quite a different feat from predicting that *he* would come up with it, and a much more interesting one. In this way, we would have become colleagues in his enterprise, instead of mere predictors. If we had stuck only to the physical data, we would have made no headway with his problem at all.

There is a certain misleading picture which often crops up at this point, and which I think is in the minds of people who object particularly to 'biological determinism.' It shows physical particles as forcing thought to work in their way. It treats the patterns of the thought itself as somehow illusory and unreal, mere façades covering the genuinely effective movements of the neurones. This epiphenomenalist metaphysic is obscure and unnecessary. I think its appeal is again that of fatalism. The neurones or what-not are being treated as alien beings forcing the mind to do their will. This is idle because they are not agents and determining is not forcing. Mind and body are two interdependent aspects of a person; neither forces the other. The determining is mutual. Physical activities are predicted on mental evidence just as often as the other way round. The mental pattern is not a cheap substitute for the physical one. It is often itself exactly what we need to know. There is nothing unreal about it. If we want to understand thought, we must study it on its own terms. This means that, in all but the simplest cases, we have to co-operate in it as fellow-thinkers, not just stand by and predict it. This need becomes more obvious the more creative the thought gets.

Pythagoras, of course, is not an extreme case here since he did start from a given problem. But how would someone set about predicting Dickens's novels, or Descartes's philosophy? The social sciences are no more able to do this kind of thing than the physical ones. Works like this are not events to be predicted at all, but patterns of thought, and indeed of life, only to be understood by following them out and living through them. And the creativity which is so striking in these large-scale achievements is also present on a small scale in the actions of every human being. It is not possible to predict just how any one of us will react to a given surprise, to a particular loss, bereavement, challenge or provocation. We do all kinds of unexpected things, and in doing them we continually change society. Yet our 'all kinds of things' do fall within certain patterns, and the social sciences are not wasting their time when they add them all up deterministically, to build some sort of statistical laws and predictions. Psychology, in fact is an art as well as a science. It is, like medicine or archaeology, an art which uses many sciences. It need not fear academic contamination if it freely uses evidence from the physical sciences as part of its raw material. Nor need anyone anxious to reform society suppose that the existence of a definite human nature, predictable within wide limits, will act as a fate, making that reform impossible.

SUMMARY

It is fatalism—the superstitious acceptance of unnecessary evils as inevitable—not determinism, which can menace our freedom. Determinism is, or should be, only a pragmatic assumption of order, made for the sake of doing science. Our tendency to dramatize such notions into threats, and to personify physical forces and entities, is natural but misleading. ('Determine' here does not mean 'force' but 'make known.') We need determinism (in this wide, untechnical sense) in order to generalize and make predictions. But much of our ordered thought is not generalizing or predicting at all. Practical thinking, for instance, is the art of thinking what to do. (Arts are not sciences.) It is certainly not an attempt to predict our own conduct, but to frame it. There need be no conflict between these different kinds of thinking. Prediction does not compete with deliberation, and cannot subvert it (Kant).

This point is made harder to grasp by the legacy of disputes about God's foreknowledge and its relation to free-will. These encourage the tendency to elevate ordinary physical forces into deities. Theories of history, including Marxism and Social Darwinism, easily fall into this superstitious language and way of thinking.

Alarmed by these apparent threats to freedom, social scientists have tried to protect us by confining determinism to the physical world, and denouncing all explanation of human qualities by physical causes as 'biological determinism.' Determinism, how-ever, can hardly be fenced off in this way. The result is not only a strange divorce between mind and body, but a crippling threat to the generalizations and predictions which the social sciences themselves need to make. It is better to see that predictability itself is not really dangerous.

Provided that the grounds of prediction are appropriate ones, being predictable does not threaten anyone's freedom. Reliabil-ity and action-in-character are perfectly compatible with human dignity; indeed they are needed for it. Randomness would not be freedom. What makes predictions offensive is grounding them on mechanisms which bypass conscious choice, in a way which leaves the agent helpless and deceived (Oedipus). Nor is the recognition of physical conditions as setting the scene for choice offensive. Background causes and conditions remain distinct from the choice itself. The reductive, fatalistic elements in some sweeping theories of motive—notably Freud's—have caused reasonable alarm. But they are only dangerous if they get out of balance.

Accordingly, the notion of human nature is not dangerously fatalistic, but a necessary background for our understanding of motives. Marx and others who have claimed to get rid of it do not do so consistently. The infinite adaptability which is sometimes claimed for human behaviour is not found, and if it were would make history and the social sciences impossible.

Determinism, then, is not fatalism and does not threaten free-will. Nor, however, is science the whole of our thinking. Practical thought is non-predictive, and is often creative. Creativity does not conflict with determinism provided that determinism remains as modest and pragmatic as it ought to be. The 'epiphenomenalist' drama which depicts the brain as *forcing* thought into alien patterns is a mere fantasy. Rather, brains are the soil in which thoughts grow. To explain thought, mental evidence is usually far more important than physical. Psychology needs both kinds, which supplement each other on equal terms and do not compete.

6

SELVES AND SHADOWS

1 THE PROBLEM OF SELF-DECEPTION

We come back now to our original problem—the attempt to make wickedness understandable—absolved, if all has gone well, from various objections to the whole project, and equipped with some concepts which may help us. The problem, however, can still look an uncommonly awkward one. A cartoon of Edward Kliban's may suggest why.[1] It shows a cheerful mechanic, tools upraised in triumph, pointing to the open bonnet of a car and telling the owner with satisfaction, 'Well, *there's* your problem.' Inside the car there is nothing but a huge, prickly monster, crouched together in a sinister manner and baring its huge teeth in a knowing grin. The owner knows what's wrong now. But what is he going to do about it?

I have been suggesting that the wrong kind of approach to the problem of wickedness does make it look very much like this. Evil, considered as something positive, would indeed have to be an alien being, a demon which had taken possession. The only possible kind of treatment would then be to cast it out somehow from the possessed person. (That feat is indeed often expected, not only of witch-doctors and exorcists, but also of educators, of psychiatrists and of psycho-analysts.) This casting-out will not get far unless it is somehow replanned to take account of the fact that evil traits are not just something alien. In one sense they are simply qualities of the person who owns them, though in another they are indeed something extraneous which has attacked him. This duality is a most puzzling feature of our mental life, and a continual practical as well as theoretical problem. We try to avoid 'owning' our bad motives, not just from vanity (though that is important) but because we feel that to own or acknowledge is to accept. We dread exposure to the hidden force whose power we sense. Our official idea of ourselves has no room for it. It therefore does not seem merely humiliating and depressing (as our known faults do), but alien, inhuman and menacing to an indefinite degree. When this sense of menace gets severe, it is almost certain to get projected on to the outside world, supplying fuel for those irrational fears and hatreds which play so central a part in human destructiveness.

In what may be called contentedly wicked people—and in all of us so far as we are contentedly wicked—this process is far gone, and may involve no more conflict in the inner life than in the front shown to the world. It is the fact that no conflict is visible that makes this kind of case so opaque. But this need not force us either to assume a special alternative morality at work, or to give up the attempt at understanding altogether. Instead, we can approach this kind of case by way of the much less opaque ones where conflict is still visibly raging. Hard though this is, it seems necessary to attempt it since self-deception, in spite of its chronic obscurity, is a topic which we badly need to understand. Bishop Butler, at the end of his discussion of it, cries out suddenly:

> And, if people will be wicked, they had better of the two be so from the common vicious passions without such refinements, than from this deep and calm source of delusion, which undermines the whole principle of good, darkens that light, that *candle of the Lord within*, which is to direct our steps, and corrupts conscience, which is the guide of life.[2]

Does this mean that there are two quite separate alternatives, self-deception and vice? It seems not. Butler apparently takes 'the common vicious passions' to be something conscious and acknowledged. But the more fully conscious they are, the nearer their owners come to what Aristotle called weakness, rather than vice.[3] They suffer spasms of (say) furious or covetous action alternating with fits of repentance. People who are weak in this sense are supposed still to keep so clear an intellectual grasp of the situation that they judge their own acts impartially, as they would other people's. This seems rather strange. The disadvantages of oscillating violently in this way are obvious, and in fact if we find people who seem to do it we tend to look for an explanation in some oscillation of their physical state. Without this extra factor, it is hard to see how the oscillator's clarity of vision can really be maintained. Some self-deception seems absolutely necessary, first so that he can have some kind of a story to tell himself during his vicious fits, but also, and more deeply, because the whole process of oscillation is going to need some justification of its own, and it will be uncommonly difficult to find an honest one. The question why one is behaving alternatively like two quite different people is one that cannot fail to arise. The answer 'I just happen to be two people' has never been found to be very satisfactory. Butler's point, then, seems sound, but it is a matter of degree, not a complete dichotomy. The more chronic, continuous and well-established is the self-deception, the deeper and more pernicious the vice. But some self-deception is probably needed if actions are to be called vicious at all.

2 INNER DIALOGUE AND DUALITY

I am suggesting that self-deception arises because we see motives which are in fact our own as alien to us and refuse to acknowledge them. This is not an isolated event, but is one possible outcome of a very common and pervasive inner dialogue, in which aspects of the personality appear to exchange views as if they were separate people. We are used to this interchange between alternating moods or viewpoints. (If we were not, we should probably find it much harder to disown some of them, because it would be harder to separate them from our official selves in the first place.) This inner dialogue is, I believe, the source of drama. Good plays and stories do not just show clashes between distinct individuals, externally related. They show ones which take place within us as well as outside. However black the villains, however strange the character-parts, we need to feel something within us respond to them. Drama helps inner conflict by crystallizing it. It can, of course, be used to help self-deception by externalizing villainy, but it can also help self-knowledge by showing up the participants clearly. Properly used, it always helps us to avoid that dangerous thing, an over-simple view of personal identity.

There is a great deal more to the problem of personal identity than meets the eye, or gets mentioned in current philosophical discussions. This connexion with inner conflict and the problem of evil, in particular, seems to have had very little academic attention of late. It is, however, very important, on account of the existence of shadows. In this century, academic philosophy, as much as psychology, has been reluctant to pay much attention to the shadow-side of human motivation. It has not occupied itself with the agonizing question 'Can it really have been I who did that?' or with the genuine clash of reasons for answering yes or no to it. Nor has it dealt much with the still more startling division of the self into two or more embattled factions which marks the process of temptation. If we want to find a way into these problems, we had therefore better turn to those who have seriously and methodically considered them. Setting aside the religious traditions for a moment—because we are not sure how much of their conceptual equipment we shall want to accept—we are left, therefore, with works of imagination, and particularly of imaginative literature.

There is absolutely no shortage of shadows here. Resisting the urge to plunge in and round them all up, I shall deliberately start with a rather simple and schematic specimen, namely *The Strange Case of Dr Jekyll and Mr Hyde*. Critics have sometimes treated this story as a lightweight, but I think they are mistaken. Any crash course on evil must acknowledge a great debt to the Scots, and the debt to Stevenson here seems to be quite an important part of it. It is worth while, if one has not taken it very seriously, having another look.

What Stevenson brings out is the negativity of Hyde's character. Evil, in spite of its magnificent pretensions, turns out to be mostly a vacuum. That does not make it less frightening, but more so. Like darkness and cold, it destroys but it cannot replace. The thought is an old one, but we may have regarded it simply as a platitude. In the story, however, Hyde's first appearance shows it sharply:

> Street after street and all the folks asleep. . . . All at once I saw two figures; one a little man who was stumping along eastwards at a good walk, and the other a girl of maybe eight or ten who was running as hard as she was able down a cross street. Well sir, the two ran into one another naturally enough at the corner; and then came the horrible part of the thing; for the man trampled calmly over the child's body and left her screaming on the ground. It sounds nothing to hear, but it was hellish to see.[4]

What makes it so is not deliberate cruelty, but callousness—the total absence of a normal human response. David Hume (a Scot of a different kind) asked, 'Would any man, who is walking along, tread as willingly on another's gouty toes, whom he has no quarrel with, as on the hard flint and pavement?'[5] Well, here is that man, and his total blindness to any feeling but his own is central to his character. As Jekyll puts it, when he is eventually driven to attempt a choice between his two lives:

> Hyde was indifferent to Jekyll, or but remembered him as the mountain bandit remembers the cavern in which he conceals himself from pursuit. Jekyll had more than a father's interest (because he shared Hyde's pleasures); Hyde had more than a son's indifference.[6]

This is why, although Hyde had

> a soul boiling with causeless hatreds, and a body that seemed not strong enough to contain the raging energies of life, [Jekyll]. . . thought of Hyde, for all his energy of life, as of something not only hellish but inorganic. This was the shocking thing; that the slime of the pit seemed to utter cries and voices; that what was dead and had no shape, should usurp the offices of life.[7]

This fearful limitation is, of course, the reason why he cannot choose to settle for Hyde, but must continue the doomed effort to be Jekyll. He notes it again, as he draws his memoirs to a close:

> Should the throes of change take me in the act of writing this, Hyde will tear it in pieces; but if some time shall have elapsed after I have laid it by, his wonderful selfishness and circumscription to the moment will probably save it again from the action of his ape-like spite.[8]

Hyde, appalling though he is, is no princely Lucifer; he is meanly sub-human. Mention of the 'ape' here has its usual negative point. Symbolic animals stand merely for the absence of certain human powers and feelings, even though in real life animals may share these. Most animals in fact avoid trampling others under-foot, as has been noticed with annoyance when people have wanted to make horses or elephants do it. In the animal king-dom, Hyde is something special. But his specialness does not consist in a new, exciting, positive motivation. It is an emotional crippling, a partial death of his faculties.

3 SHADOW-SHEDDING

What has produced this crippling? It resulted in fact from a rather casual miscalculation on the part of Jekyll. (This casual-ness is, I think, what stops some people taking the story ser-iously. But the story is surely about the casualness, rather than being an expression of it.) Jekyll found, early in life, that his ambition was in conflict with his taste for dissipation, and decided to try and separate these two motives so that each could pursue its interests without hindrance from the other. He therefore accepted, and still defends to the end, the proposi-tion that 'man is not truly one, but truly two. I say two, because the state of my own knowledge does not pass beyond this point... [but perhaps] man will be ultimately known for a mere polity of multifarious, incongruous and independent deni-zens.'[9] But of course he does not accept this idea seriously and literally as requiring a full separation, with an impartial distribution of chances to the multifarious denizens on a time-sharing basis. He sees it simply as providing a splendid disguise, which will allow the old Jekyll his fun while protecting his reputation and his complacency. (This is where the casualness comes in.)

'I do not think I ever met Mr Hyde?' asked Utterson. 'Oh dear no sir. He never *dines* here,' replied the butler.

'Indeed, we see very little of him on this side of the house; he mostly comes and goes by the laboratory.'[10]

And again, as Jekyll puts it, 'The moment I choose, I can be rid of Mr Hyde. I give you my hand upon that.'[11] This was his whole plan for the relationship. His 'discovery' of duality therefore means merely something which others have tried out before him, namely, the hypothesis that *it doesn't matter what you do with your shadow.* Peter Schlemihl sold his shadow to the devil, never supposing that he would need it.[12] He soon found out his mistake. Dorian Gray let his picture absorb the effects of his iniquities, supposing that he could ignore it, but it got him in the end. The dismissed shadow in Hans Andersen's story came back after many years, having grown a new body, though a thin one. It was embarrassingly obsequious at first, but rapidly grew more and more domineering, and reduced its former owner to the status of its shadow. When he tried to resist, it killed him. It is well known that you can't be too careful about these things. But the project of shadow-immunity which throws most light on our present subject is another Scottish one, James Hogg's novel, *The Confessions of a Justified Sinner.*[13]

This is an altogether deeper affair. The sinner, Robert Wringhim, has accepted with his whole heart the doctrine of justification by faith alone. He then becomes convinced of his own salvation, and thus believes himself to be henceforward incapable of sin. Going out to give thanks to God for this state of affairs, he is stopped by a mysterious stranger, his exact double. This person deflects him from his purpose by flattering words. ('I am come to be a humble disciple of yours; to be initiated into the true way of true salvation by conversing with you, and perhaps of being assisted by your prayers').[14] Instead of joining Wringhim in thanking God, he points out to him that he is now a highly exceptional and privileged person, incapable of sin, and therefore free to commit every possible kind of action without blame. Are there not, therefore, remarkable acts to which he is called? Wringhim, who already believes most of those around him to be worthless enemies of the Lord, predestined to damnation, has no defence against the suggestion that it is his duty to kill many of them, including his own family. And this, in spite of his timidity and some other natural objections, he is finally led on to do.

The ingenious use of Calvin's doctrine thus provides Wringhim's shadow-self with a quite exceptionally wide scope for exemption from responsibility. Dorian Gray's exemption covered only his appearance. Jekyll's, even in his most prosperous days, covered only the exploits of Hyde. His own life had still to be lived normally on its previous lines. But Wringhim (or the devil who counsels him) has so arranged things that his whole active life is to be immune from judgment and from serious consequences.

Two points emerge. One, that the price of this playground is high. Freed from consequences and from judgment, action altogether loses its meaning. Wringhim is very mad indeed. Two, that what he pays this price for is, again, something utterly squalid and negative. Certainly he is able to satisfy briefly his resentment against those who have not appreciated him, but this is hardly an aim proportioned to the tremendous metaphysical pretensions of the original scheme. His heroic acts are only a string of spiteful murders without any public or political point. The fate of all souls being in any case fixed, it is not even clear why cutting off the wicked in their prime should have the slightest value. It is a mean, unimpressive and disappointing enterprise, judged against the glittering hints dropped by the mysterious stranger, to whom Wringhim, in spite of his new-found importance and freedom, soon finds himself enslaved. Trying to get a hold on events, he asks the stranger for his name:

'I have no parents save one, whom I do not acknowledge', said he proudly. 'Therefore pray drop that subject, for it is a disagreeable one. I am a being of a very peculiar temper, for, though I have servants and subjects more than I can number, yet, to gratify a certain whim, I have left them and retired to this city, and, for all the society which it contains, you see I have attached myself only to you. This is a secret ... pray let it remain one, and say not another word about the matter.'

It immediately struck me that this was no other than the Czar of Russia. . . . I had henceforward great and mighty hopes of high preferment as a defender and avenger of the oppressed Christian church, under the influence of this great potentate.[15]

Vanity is the key to Wringhim's enslavement. And it plays a central part also in that of Jekyll, who is throughout happy to sacrifice the whole integrity of his being for the sake of his spotless reputation. Vanity comes upon him at a fatal juncture, when he has for a time renounced Hyde, and been living as himself but has finally weakened and indulged, in his own person, in a night on the tiles. Next morning

the Regent's Park was full of winter chirrupings and sweet with spring odours. I sat in the sun on a bench, the animal within me licking the chops of memory, the spiritual side a little drowsed, promising subsequent penitence, but not yet moved to begin. After all, I reflected, I was like my neighbours; and then I smiled, comparing myself with other men, comparing my active good-will with the lazy cruelty of their neglect. And at the very moment of that vainglorious thought, a qualm came over me, a horrid nausea and the most deadly shuddering. . . . I was once more Edward Hyde.[16]

The trouble is not, of course, that vanity is the worst of the vices. It is just that it is the one which makes admitting all the others unbearable, and so leads to the shadow-shedding project. And the reason why this project is doomed is because, as Jung sensibly points out, shadows have a function:

> Painful though it is, this [unwelcome self-knowledge] is in itself a gain—for what is inferior or even worthless belongs to me as my shadow and gives me substance and mass. How can I be substantial if I fail to cast a shadow? I must have a dark side also if I am to be whole; and inasmuch as I become conscious of my shadow I also remember that I am a human being like any other.[17]

The acknowledged shadow may be terrible enough. But it is the unacknowledged one which is the real killer.

Of course Stevenson's story is somewhat crude and schematic. But by being so it gets past our defences and makes us pay some attention to its topic. Jekyll was partly right: we *are* each not only one but also many. Might not this fact deserve a little more philosophic attention? Some of us have to hold a meeting every time we want to do something only slightly difficult, in order to find the self who is capable of undertaking it. We often fail, and have to make do with an understudy who is plainly not up to the job. We spend a lot of time and ingenuity on developing ways of organizing the inner crowd, securing consent among it, and arranging for it to act as a whole. Literature shows that the condition is not rare. Others, of course, obviously do not feel like this at all, hear such descriptions with amazement, and are inclined to regard those who give them as dotty. There is not, however, the sort of difference between the conduct of those aware of constant internal debate and that of other people which would justify writing this awareness off as an aberration. When real difficulties arise, everybody becomes conscious of it, and has what is recognizably the same sort of trouble. There are then actually advantages in being used to it. Someone who has never felt gravely divided before is likely to be more bewildered than a habitual splitter. Most people, too, probably would recognize that serious troubles do give rise to such conflicts, that rather more of them go on than are sometimes noticed, and that, through the process of temptation, they do have an important bearing on wickedness. But just how does this connexion work? Can inner conflicts explain major crimes?

4 THE POWER OF PROJECTION

The difficulty for thought here is this. We feel that motives ought to be adequate for the actions they produce. In the case of good actions they often are so; indeed, it is common to find that the people who did something good were trying to do much more than they achieved. The frustration of really good schemes by outside difficulties is a commonplace. But in the case of evil actions this is much less clear. When we look for someone who conceived them we often cannot find him at all; when we can, we often find a number of culprits with no clear connexion with each other, none of whom was apparently trying to do what actually resulted. In such cases, we are inclined to retire baffled, give up the search for causes rooted in human motivation, and fall back on other sorts of explanation, such as the economic. But this is clearly not very satisfactory, since the human conduct in question—for instance, that of launching the First World War, and of carrying it on in the way that was in fact followed—is not a rational response to the economic factors. Although a few people profited from it, the damage which it did was so enormous, and the chance for any individual of immunity from that damage so small, that Hobbesian calculators of enlightened self-interest would not have been led to take such action. For instance, even the most selfish of politicians and generals did not want to lose their sons, nor to risk their careers in the chaos that follows defeat. The rational aims they were pursuing could have been followed up by methods which did not involve these dangers. And anyway most of those involved were not simply and clear-headed selfish; they thought they were doing their duty. We have therefore to look for diffused human motives, not clearly recognized, which blind people to their own interests as well as to other people's, and incline them to see as their duty actions which, if they viewed them impartially, they would consider wrong.

What makes these motives hard to see is the very same fact which gives them their force—namely, their immense diffusion. The habitual, half-conscious, apparently mild hostility of one people towards another is as little noticed, consciously, as the air they breathe. It also resembles that air in being a vital factor in their lives, and in the fact that a slight shift in its quality can make enormous changes. Yet it differs from it in being something for which they are, at root, responsible. To take the crudest case at once, it is what makes war possible. And a very interesting and significant point about the way in which it does so is its versatility—the ease with which it can be shifted from one opponent to another. Orwell's caricature in 1984, where a political speaker in the middle of a speech changes fulminations directed against one enemy into ones directed against another, in response to a slip handed up to him showing that the High Command has changed its policy, contains a truth with which history has made us familiar, but whose oddness we need to notice. Alliances are changed far more easily than one might expect, and hostility is even more easily redirected. This is connected with another striking feature, the ease with which improbable charges are believed against anyone designated as an enemy, the invention of further charges when real data fail, and the general unreality with which enemy thought-processes are imagined. We need to notice again how contrary this habit of mind is to rational prudence. If one has enemies, it is surely of the first importance to discover their real intentions, to study them carefully, and assess realistically the dangers which they actually pose. No real enemy is unlimitedly hostile. All have particular aims, and between such aims compromise is nearly always possible. Certainly some enemies are more threatening, some conflicts of interest harder to reconcile than others. But this only makes it all the more important to discover realistically which sort one is facing at the moment.

When we consider people's frequent failure to do this, and the extraordinary flourishing of violent hostility where no real threat is posed at all, we are (as far as I can see) forced to look for an explanation within. People who seriously believe that they are being attacked when they are not, and who attribute hostile planning groundlessly to their supposed attackers, have to be projecting their own unrecognized bad motives onto the world around them. For instance, the suspicion of witchcraft is a very common form for this projection, found in many cultures. The more convinced we are that witchcraft does not actually take place, the more necessary it surely is to account for this belief in terms of projection. In our own culture, the story of witch-hunting is a very remarkable one, since the early church actively discouraged it, and laid down rules which made the practice very difficult. In order to let loose the witch-hunting movement which was rife between the fifteenth and seventeenth centuries, it was necessary for those who saw witchcraft everywhere to break through established custom and reverse many ecclesiastical rulings.[18] This and many similar cases show how shallow it would be to attribute these beliefs merely to chance tradition and primitive ignorance of causes. Other obvious cases are anti-semitism and persecution of religious minorities. When we turn to disputes between nations things are, of course, often more complicated, since real conflicts of interests, and real threats, may be involved as well as irrational hostility. But when we look at these apparently more solid causes, complications appear. How rational is resentment? When one country has previously attacked another—for instance in the case of France and Germany after the war of 1870—what follows? It is natural for the invaded party to fear that it will happen again, to want its provinces back, and in fact want revenge. But intense concentration of these aims is certainly not the best way to secure, in the end, harmonious relations with the neighbour. And those harmonious relations provide the only possible hope of arbitrating the conflict of interest effectively.

Even in the most reasonable kinds of dispute, uncontrolled, chronic hostility is a liability, not an asset, and this, again, gives us further grounds to suppose that it takes its rise in irrelevant, projected motives, not just in the specific, apparent causes of the outward dispute. Specific grievances wear out; the unchanging-ness of group hostilities marks them as fraudulent. They are not responses to real external dangers, but fantasies. We erect a glass at the border of our own group, and see our own anger reflected against the darkness behind it. Where we know a good deal about neighbouring groups, the darkness is not complete and the projection is imperfect. If we want to maintain it, we may then have to do quite a lot of arguing. But the more unfamiliar that group is, the deeper the darkness becomes. The illusion can then grow wholly convincing. This is the point at which even people who know perfectly well that the so-called *Protocols of the Elders of Zion* were deliberately forged by the Czarist police still find no difficulty in accepting them as evidence.[19] The dark vision is too vivid to be doubted; its force is its warrant. What we see out there is indeed real enough; it is our own viciousness, and it strikes us with quite appropriate terror. And by an unlucky chance, while it remains projected, there is no way to weaken or destroy it. Persecution and punishment of those to whom it is attributed do not soften it at all; indeed, to the persecutors' alarm, they often seem to intensify it. Hence the strange insatiability of persecution, the way in which suspicion seems to grow by being fed, and security never comes nearer.

5 COMPLICITY BETWEEN LEADERS AND LED

This account of course raises many questions which we have still to deal with, notably about the origin of the projected feelings in the first place. But it has one great asset which, as it seems to me, makes some form of it a necessary move. This is that it resolves the difficulty about finding an adequate motive. The joint repressed aggression of a whole populace makes up a very powerful motive for communal crimes, such as pogroms, witch-hunts or gratuitous wars. It is a cause suitable to such effects. By invoking it, we can avoid a very odd and unconvincing feature of those explanations which ignore it, namely, that they divide populations sharply into a few guilty instigators and a majority of amazingly passive dupes or fools. Unless we think that a particular population is weak and foolish on all subjects, we must surely find it odd that they become so as soon as some particular feared or persecuted group comes in question. The picture of innocent passivity is not convincing because it is too selective. We know very well that not every kind of political leader, and not every kind of cause, finds this kind of uncritical passive obedience. And if the picture of the passive herd is suspect, that of the wholly active, creative instigator, stamping his personality at will upon this wax, is still more so. Mass leaders must use the causes they can find. Konrad Heiden, in his life of Hitler, stresses the incoherence and vacillation of his policies, the random, opportunistic way in which he picked up his ideas, largely according to their saleability:

> Rather than a means of directing the mass mind, propaganda is a technique for riding with the masses. It is not a machine to make wind, but a sail to catch the wind. . . . The more passionately Hitler harps on the value of personality, the more clearly he reveals his nostalgia for something that is lacking. . . . Yes, he knows this mass world, he knows how to guide it by

> 'compliance'. . . . He did not have a plan and act accordingly;
> he acted, and out of his actions a plan arose.[20]

Influential psychopaths and related types, in fact, get their power not from originality, but from a perception of just what unacknowledged motives lie waiting to be exploited, and just what aspects of the world currently provide a suitable patch of darkness on to which they can be projected. In order to catch the wind, they must (if Heiden is right) be without any specific, positive motivation of their own which might distract them from taking up and using skilfully whatever has most popular appeal at the time. Many aspiring Caesars have come to grief here; they had too much individual character. They did not see the sharpness of the dilemma. To gain great popular power, you must either be a genuinely creative genius, able to communicate new ideas very widely, or you must manage to give a great multitude permission for things which it already wants, but for which nobody else is currently prepared to give that permission. In order to find these things, and to handle skilfully the process of permitting the unthinkable, absolute concentration on the main chance is required, and this seems only possible to those without serious, positive aims of their own. There is therefore a sense, and not a trivial one, in which such demagogues are themselves the tools of their supporters. This becomes disturbingly plain in causes where they eventually lose their influence and are cast aside to end their days in obscurity, like Titus Oates and Senator Joe McCarthy. It then becomes a mystery, even to many of those who followed them, how they can ever have had such power. The only place where solutions to this mystery can be sought for seems to be the unconscious motivation of those who allowed themselves to be deceived.

All this does not, of course, mean that the difference between instigators and dupes is not a real one, only that it is a good deal less simple than we often suppose. Instigators are not wholly active nor dupes wholly passive. And many people, of course, fill both roles, adding a good deal on their own account to the suggestions they receive. The problem of understanding the instigators, however, still remains. And it may well seem to present particular difficulties for the notion which we have been considering, that evil is essentially negative. That notion is of course particularly easy to apply in the sort of cases we have looked at in this chapter—cases of conflict, resulting in weakness and self-deception. When we consider the strategies by which people who do not officially choose to be wicked still manage to do so while quieting their consciences and denying their shadows, a diagnosis which focuses on what they fail to do may seem plausible enough, or at least not surprising. And we have seen that it is possible for people in this situation to commit an immense proportion of the evil which is actually done in the world—a proportion which the impersonal complication of modern society may be continually raising. The harm that can be done by not thinking is literally immeasurable. All the same, there do still have to be some people to make the suggestions. No movement consists solely of followers. Might there still be a need for a different, entirely positive notion of evil there?

SUMMARY

We come back to the problem of making wickedness understandable, after considering the objections that it (a) does not exist, and (b) has no real roots in us, being an external phenomenon induced by culture. This last view belongs to a group of ideas about evil, many of them quite old, which treat it as something quite foreign to us, external and therefore a positive force (demonic possession). This approach necessarily obstructs the understanding which we need for dealing with it. But it springs from a real problem. Evil is in one sense part of ourselves; in another it is not. 'Owning' bad motives can indeed lead to fatalism about them. But disowning them can conceal their presence in us. We then tend to project them on to the outside world and attribute them to others.

Complete cases of this self-deception are rare and obscure, but partial ones, where conflict rages, are common and can be studied. The inner dialogue surrounding them finds natural expression in drama. Inner conflict is a normal, more or less constant feature of our personal identity. Our characters are constituted largely by the way we handle it. Transactions between people's official selves and their 'shadows'—the aspects of their personalities which they try to reject—have not lately had much philosophic attention, but are often very shrewdly treated by imaginative writers. One example is Dr Jekyll and Mr Hyde. This story brings out, more subtly than is often noticed, the negative aspect of evil. Jekyll has not so much 'become two people' as ceased to be anybody. He has become hollow, losing his centre, from refusing to acknowledge his shadow-side. Another example is Confessions of a Justified Sinner. Wringhim's ambitious vanity, taking him over, leaves him in the end no core to his personality—even no real motives except an obscure and quite impersonal terror. By denying and projecting his shadow, he has disintegrated altogether. ('Losing one's shadow' is how Peter Schlemihl puts it.)

These are stories about the loss of direction which results from denying one's shadow and its accompanying conflicts. If we find them convincing, they surely throw light on the familiar puzzle of finding adequate motives for bad actions—the puzzle which leads to calling them 'mad'. Communal projection of unacknowledged shadows is a possible cause—and seems the only plausible cause—for the strong element of fantasy in our hostility to outgroups (witchcraft, heresy-hunting, anti-semitism). Wild, paranoiac accusations seem hard to explain in any other way. The idea that a few wily leaders may have imposed this whole condition on an entirely passive mob of supporters is not plausible. The supporters must themselves be active. The leaders can only take them where they will go, and this particular direction is one which has succeeded too often to be a matter of chance. Leaders and led must surely be in collusion. Shared, half-conscious projected shadow-motivation supplies the steam.

If this (not very surprising) view is right, we can see the point of saying that evil in the supporters is negative. Their trouble lies in their *failure* to do something universally necessary. They have failed to acknowledge, and to deal with, powerful motives which are in origin their own, but which, through projection, are officially now no part of their personalities. What they do is, of course, positive action, but it proceeds, in a strange but familiar way, from a vacuum. By their own responsibility, they have let themselves become passive instruments of evil. Simply by not thinking, they can do immeasurable harm (Eichmann).

This diagnosis, however, cannot extend so simply to the leaders. What should we say about them? They will occupy us in the next chapter.

7

THE INSTIGATORS

1 THE SOURCES OF SPLENDOUR

What, then, shall we say about the grandeur of evil? Have we forgotten Milton's Satan?

>   He, above the rest
> In shape and gesture proudly eminent,
> Stood like a tower. His form had not yet lost
> All her original brightness, nor appeared
> Less than Archangel ruined, and the excess
> Of glory obscured . . .
>   Darkened so, yet shone
> Above them all the archangel; but his face
> Deep scars of thunder had intrenched, and care
> Sat on his faded cheek, but under brows
> Of dauntless courage, and considerate pride,
> Waiting revenge. Cruel his eye, but cast
> Signs of remorse and passion, to behold

> The fellows of his crime, the followers rather
> (Far other once beheld in bliss), condemned
> For ever now to have their lot in pain—
> Millions of spirits for his fault amerced
> Of Heaven, and from eternal splendours flung
> For his revolt—yet faithful how they stood,
> Their glory withered.[1]

What is Milton doing here? Very plainly, he is not painting a figure of complete and unqualified evil. He is showing us a tragedy, whose chief figure has—as tragedy demands—every kind of quality except the one kind whose absence must ruin it. What brings Satan down is pride, the inability to tolerate anyone above him. This fault stands out all the more clearly because he still has all his native power and intelligence, and also a whole range of virtues—courage, resolution, enterprise, loyalty, even compunction and self-sacrifice in his willingness to volunteer for the dangerous mission to earth. Milton goes out of his way to explain that all this is only to be expected:

> For the general safety he despised
> His own, for neither do the spirits damned
> Lose all their virtue; lest bad men should boast
> Their specious deeds on earth, which glory excites,
> Or close ambition varnished o'er with zeal. . . .
> O shame to men! Devil with devil damned
> Firm concord holds; men only disagree
> Of creatures rational. . . .[2]

These fallen spirits, in short, are not mere abstractions, personified vices in a morality play. They are shown as complex beings like ourselves, free and subject to temptation, and capable at times of resisting it. Though they play out their parts on a far vaster stage, their struggles have the same general form as ours. They are ones into which we can enter. Barring the difference of scale, Satan's role is comparable to that of a human instigator. He is in fact the arch-instigator of all time, having just carried off to ruin a third of the heavenly host, and—merely from spite—he is about to lure the human race to wreck its happiness as well. He could scarcely have done all this if he had not kept much of his original quality untarnished. Its corruption has not been instantaneous. And though all that he says to his followers is steadily bold and defiant, once he is alone his soliloquy shows that he is torn with doubt and inner conflict:

> Me miserable! which way shall I fly
> Infinite wrath and infinite despair?
> Which way I fly is Hell; myself am Hell;
> And, in the lowest deep, a lower deep
> Still threatening to devour me opens wide,
> To which the Hell I suffer seems a Heaven.
> O then at last relent! Is there no place
> Left for repentance, none for pardon left?
> None left but by submission; and that word
> Disdain forbids me, and my dread of shame.
> Among the Spirits beneath.[3]

This is not the most heroic of motives, but it is the first which occurs to him, and it seems to be the one which makes submission impossible.

2 THE MEANING OF REVERSAL

All this is worth going into because it forms the background for some words which are often quoted on their own to give a misleadingly simple impression of Satan's stand, namely 'evil be thou my good.' They occur near the end of the soliloquy just quoted; when Satan has decided that God would anyway never forgive him:

> So farewell hope, and with hope farewell fear.
> Farewell remorse! All good to me is lost;
> Evil, be thou my good: *by thee at least*
> *Divided empire with Heaven's King I hold*,
> By thee, and more than half perhaps will reign,
> As Man ere long, and this new world shall know.[4]

The point is not that evil has been suddenly perceived to have a greater value than good, nor that an existential decision can confer that value on it, but simply—as the italicized words show—that it looks as if it might provide an empire independent of, and corresponding to, that of God. The same point was made earlier:

> To do ought good never will be our task,
> But ever to do ill our sole delight,
> *As being the contrary of his high will*
> *Whom we resist.*[5]

Their purposes, in fact, are parasitical on God's. They do not know what they want to do till they find that it will compete with him and displease him. This motivation is not magnificent; it is mean. Pride is not really a sublime motive, though it graps at sublimity. Proud people avoid certain crude and common forms of meanness, but fall into others which are in the end more appalling. Emotionally and dramatically, crime does not pay; what is odious is odious, and remains so even on Milton's magnificent stage and with all the starry properties of the cosmos. As the novelist William Styron puts it in *Sophie's Choice* in discussing the dreary memoirs of the Nazi official Rudolf Höss,

> Within these confessions it will be discovered that we have really no acquaintance with true evil; the evil portrayed in most novels and plays and movies is mediocre if not spurious, a shoddy concoction generally made up of violence, fantasy, neurotic terror and melodrama.
>
> The 'imaginary evil'—again to quote Simone Weil—'is romantic and varied, while real evil is gloomy, monotonous, barren, boring.'[6]

Milton himself takes care to bring this out again and again by touches which emphasize the contemptible motivation, and by never hinting at any larger, reforming purpose which might seem adequate to redeem it. But, like a good dramatist, he also shows the counterbalancing virtues, qualities which make Satan not only a whole character, but one so impressive that we feel the real tragedy of his corruption.

All this, of course, is so far only a point about dramatic effect, about magnetism. It does nothing to settle the much larger question whether essentially, in real life, crime can pay—the question which is the central issue in Plato's *Republic*: at the deepest level, can injustice profit us? Of that question, our whole present enquiry is only a small province. But there is a certain simple way of treating remarks like 'evil be thou my good' which may seem to settle that large question at once. This is the belief that any judgment about values made with the eyes open has a dignity proportional to its boldness and comprehensiveness, and that there is no way in which such judgments can be compared other than in this dignity, since for all other purposes they are entirely separate and uncommensurable. Satan's judgment looks about as sweeping as one can get, and may therefore seem to be a clear winner. Yet the sweepingness is illusory, as it usually is with such apparently vast pronouncements. To understand them, we need to read into them some much less ambitious, more specific interpretation. We are so well practised at doing this that we supply the meaning without hesitation, and commonly without being aware that it was needed. As Elizabeth Anscombe points out, it is never intelligible to praise something if you cannot say what is the good of it, unless that thing is one of the final, basic human needs which provide an explanation for the praise of anything else. What, then is so good about evil?

> If the answer to this question at some stage is 'The good of it is that it's bad' this need not be unintelligible; one can go on to say 'And what's the good of it's being bad?' to which the answer might be condemnation of good as impotent, slavish and inglorious. Then the good of making evil my good is my intact liberty in the unsubmissiveness of my will.[7]

Satan, in fact, is intelligible because he is not original at all in his views on liberty; he sees it as a good just as everybody else does, and uses the notion of its being good to praise it. That notion has not vanished into its opposite by some startling logical trick in the inversion of opposites. Opposites have not, indeed, been inverted; the war-cry merely exalts one good—liberty—over all others with which it may conflict. And the sense which liberty has here is that rather melancholy one which it has sometimes been found to have in human politics; namely, liberty to rule others, to have one's own kingdom.[8] It is only his own freedom which interests him. At the other end of the scale, impotence and slavery are still evils, which is just what they were before. Satan's value-judgment is not the magnificent start of a totally new game. It is a familiar move in the old one, a move which still leaves room for the questions which occur to him, such as 'Is your dignity really more important than your entire happiness, along with that of all your followers? and if so, why?' Answers to such questions are not read off by each individual from his personal and conclusive formula. They are worked out painfully again and again by all of us in a shared situation, where similar clashes arise for all, and no compromise is finally satisfactory. Neither dignity nor liberty can be erected into a supreme value, settling all conflicts. That would give a morality every bit as naive as the conventional one it is designed to replace. And tragedy cannot subsist with a naive morality. For tragedy, the moral as well as the physical force on both sides must be felt; there must be real loss, whatever the outcome. We make nonsense of *Paradise Lost* if we insist on thinking of Satan as simply a noble liberator or an unfairly oppressed individualist.

Yet today we are drawn to think in this way, and this distorting tendency illustrates our whole problem about the understanding of evil. We find it hard to hold before our minds both Satan's genuine grandeur and his fault. Since the Romantic Movement, the idea has grown that perhaps the fault itself is the real source of the grandeur, that its sheer magnitude makes it intrinsically splendid. I have just met this suggestion with the prosaic, non-Romantic reply that most of the grandeur actually depends on the familiar good qualities which still remain—notably on virtues such as courage—and the rest on the mere scale of the conflict, which is not of Satan's creating. If one constructs a morality in which courage and independence are the only significant virtues, it is certainly possible to consider Satan as a straightforward hero. But this is to destroy the tragedy. Its central paradox would then vanish, and its hero would simply be noble, persecuted and unfortunate. We would get no light from him on the psychology of wickedness, because the idea of wickedness itself would then have vanished from the world and only bad faith would remain. We have seen the difficulties of this kind of view, and we now notice how it would wreck the drama. If we abdicate the right to judge between motives—if we refuse to put ourselves in the place of a dramatic character and ask whether he ought to have let them move him—we lose all concern about his choice, and can learn nothing from it. The story of Satan is there so that we can understand his motives, not so that we can honourably refrain from thinking about them on the grounds that we are in no position to judge him. His motives are of great interest. They should not be assumed to be those of liberators like Garibaldi, on the one hand, nor of honest individualists like Nietzsche, on the other. Instead, they are the kind of motives which are adequate for the instigation of a great crime, though not (as we have seen) for actually committing it, since great crimes demand many hands and therefore many motives. Their centre is the violent hatred and rejection of all that seems to be superior to oneself, and their familiar names are pride and envy.

3 THE EMPTY CENTRE

These motives are negative in that they are essentially destructive. They are of course positive in being strong. The daemonic force of those people who are able to lead multitudes to appalling acts is real; the thesis of this book never questions that. It is still, however, negative in two closely related senses—because its aim really is destruction, and because there goes with it a lack of other interests and motives, an emptiness at the core of the individual, which apparently accounts for the peculiar force with which the chosen, purely destructive aim is pursued. It really does not seem to be a matter of wanting something destroyed because it stands in the way of some other aim, but of pursuing other aims because they allow opportunities for destruction. Thus, all accounts of Hitler's activities agree about the centrality of his obsession with anti-semitism, and this was expressed repeatedly in a way which endangered other apparently essential aims. For instance, even towards the end of the war, when Germany was in real danger, transports taking Jews to the extermination camps were still given priority over urgently needed supplies for the army, and subject governments in the conquered territories were continually urged to anti-semitic activities rather than to those which might be relevant to the war-effort.[9]

This motivation is so extraordinary that people have difficulty in believing in it, or, if they admit its existence, in accepting that it could be powerful enough to produce the acts which appear to flow from it. We must consider this whole question in the next chapter. It may help, however, to approach it by way of a rather fuller discussion here of what constitutes an adequate motive. Hannah Arendt's remarks about Eichmann are of great interest here:

> Eichmann was not Iago and not Macbeth, and nothing would have been further from his mind than to determine with Richard III 'to prove a villain.' Except for an extraordinary diligence in looking out for his personal advancement, he had no motives at all.[10]

4 THE CASE OF IAGO

But as it happens, Iago too has been held to lack motive. Coleridge described his soliloquy as 'the motive-hunting of motiveless malignity',[11] and many other critics have joined the motive-hunt and tried to bring it to a better conclusion. The difference between the two cases is very interesting. The point about Eichmann is of course not the absence of any motive, but the difficulty of finding one which distinguishes his career clearly from that of an ordinary unimaginative official. He himself admits no such motive. He has plenty of commonplace motives, centring around prudence, ambition and loyalty, but they seem only appropriate to the details of his career. What he lacks—at least on the obvious, conscious level—is any motive appropriate to the whole of what he has done. Yet unless he could in some way see it as a whole, all the rest lacks sense, and people who work hard normally do have a more general motive, a framework within which the rest does make sense.

With Iago the trouble is different. For destroying Othello he has a suitable motive; spite or malice. But the provocation which gives rise to this malice is so weak that people find it hard to believe that it can supply a motive strong enough to explain his conduct. In general, the motives of followers such as Eichmann do not seem to explain properly the direction they take, while the motives of instigators like Iago explain the direction, but not the lengths to which they are prepared to go. To explain the followers' behaviour, therefore, we often invoke obedience, a kind of passive motivation in which these people are supposed to let others choose their direction for them. I have suggested that this is superficial and overlooks the choice of a leader. The supposed working of obedience is too selective; we are not equally open to every kind of command. Reformers do not find tools so easily. Turning to the other side, however, what shall we say about the instigators? Is their motivation unintelligible? If so, where is the gap in it? And what kind of addition would fill that gap? To approach this question, it will be worth while to look at Iago in rather more detail.

What sort of explanation do we need? If we are looking merely for causes, in the sense of earlier events, we can go back in time and tell the story. Iago applied to be Othello's lieutenant. Othello, however, gave the post to Cassio, making Iago merely his ensign (or 'ancient'). In this minor position, both of them treated him civilly enough, but entirely as a subordinate.

> —I prythee, good Iago,
> Go to the bay and disembark my coffers—
> —The lieutenant must be saved before the ensign—[12]

and so on. Enquirers, however, already know these things, just as they already know that Iago is a forceful man. What they still need, in order to make sense of the matter, is something that links the two—something that connects the force of Iago's character with the project of destruction, by showing how facts like those just mentioned can be seen as a *reason* for destroying several lives. For unless these facts were viewed as reasons, they could not become causes. This still unknown factor is a general motive. We can find two such motives, his pride and envy. These motives are not extra events or series of events. Nor are they exactly forces—certainly not as gravitation is a force. Pride and envy are structural factors in people's lives, principles of assembly on which they organize experience, and principles of interpretation by which they understand it. A morbidly proud person reads everything that the people around him do as an answer to the single question 'Do they honour him enough?' If this is his central motive, that is his basic rule, the plan of his life. And in that case the honour he is looking for is something enormously higher than any of them could possibly give. This is because it has to take the place of all other motives, a point which will be very important to us.

It may seem surprising to speak in these rather intellectual terms of pride or envy, since they certainly are, among other things, feelings. But feelings are not just formless floods of emotion that wash over us. They are lasting attitudes; they have a logic, a structure of their own. And when we name a feeling as a motive, we certainly do not mean that it washed over someone and 'moved' him to action as a stone might be moved by a flood, or indeed a dog by a wasp sting. Caution, prudence and thrift are motives, just as much as the passions; they often lead to inaction, but again, not in the same way as a magnetic force holding something down. The formula of envy, so to speak, is 'Why has he got it when I haven't?' Similarly the formula of thrift is something like 'How can we do it more cheaply?' and the formula of caution is 'What further danger is there?' No doubt each kind of question does have a range of feelings which characteristically goes with it, and which may sometimes cause it to be asked. But the feeling alone is not the motive. Feelings are things which may happen to anybody, but to have a motive is to envisage a policy. Each motive has a cognitive structure which commits people to asking questions like 'What risk does it carry?' or 'What does it cost?' And where we do not grasp this structure, naming earlier events as causes will not give us an explanation, even where these events come (as causes are supposed to) in constant conjunction. Suppose, for example, that someone admits that he has murdered a total stranger, and when asked for his motive says, 'I just thought he would look better without his head.' If he says no more, it is a motiveless crime, which does not mean that anybody doubts his word. He has named a precipitating cause, but not a motive. Even if he convinces us that he really did have that feeling, that it was very strong, and in fact determined his action, that he has had it before, and has always killed, or tried to kill, in consequence, these may be interesting and important facts about him, but they do not explain his act. At best they give quite incomplete causal explanations, by linking an isolated act with an isolated feeling, as people ignorant of electricity may link lightning with thunder. But they do not give the special sort of explanation which a motive gives.

If, however, we name envy, we do have that sort of explanation. And it does not turn on constant conjunction at all. It can group together an immensely wide range of actions which may have nothing outward, nothing behavioural in common. They just share the single relational feature that they gratify some frustrated wish of a person who is angry that others have been put before him. Certainly we can state that feature in a causal form— 'such things madden him.' But to know what 'such things' are, we have to use the key, which is his plan of life, his principle of interpretation.

5 WHAT MAKES MOTIVES ADEQUATE

This is why understanding motives is possible, and also why it is so difficult. We cannot do it just by outward regularities; we have to put ourselves in other people's shoes, in order to follow their principle of interpretation and see what questions arise for them. Since not everybody finds this equally easy, failures are notorious. We are bad at interpreting motives which we do not fully share. Thus the motivation of people hopelessly in love can be really mysterious to those who have never got near having such an experience. And as the whole logic of Iago's thought depends on asking first the questions which arise from pride and envy, people who would not dream of thinking in this way have real difficulty in following it. Those who surround him are mostly not fools, but they are all notably unenvious, and are absorbed in their own concerns. This is why no one suspects him. On the other hand, they are all in a general way capable of envy. And it is a crucial point about motives that they arise from universal human needs. The kind of explanation which they give works by connecting an action with such a need. It works only because that need is present in all of us. We are all capable of using the key, though we often fail to do so because of minor differences, and because we are too preoccupied. This is quite different from an attempt to understand magnetism or capillary attraction, where no such key is needed. We do not have to follow the reasoning of a magnet, or a liquid creeping along a tube.

The same is true of pride. Pride is intelligible because the longing to be honoured, to be important to others, is universal, and we are all sometimes tempted to gratify it at other people's expense. Naming a motive is not just naming a habit, however widespread. It is accounting for its appeal. And this can only be done if we too respond to it. It is no good, for instance, explaining the appeal of bullfighting by positing a tauromachic drive present in Mediterranean peoples, nor by merely proving that it is an ancient custom. We can only do it by mentioning tastes whose roots are present in all of us—cruelty, the love of spectacle, the attraction of risk, the admiration of skill. Similarly, the washing compulsive's motivation cannot be made intelligible to the rest of us merely by statistics showing that there are plenty like him. The most that this will do is to make us more willing to attempt an imaginative identification, by giving more prospect of success. To succeed, we have to understand the sort of importance which purity has for him—by relating it to the moderate, but natural, interest in cleanliness which the rest of us share, and thereby to the wider surrounding interests which make up our structure of needs.

For of course there must be a structure. Needs come as a set. They are intelligible only in the context of a whole way of life, which is in the first place that of a given species, and in the second that of a certain culture. This is the background presupposed when we speak of a given motive as adequate or inadequate. (If we were dealing with alien beings, we could make no guess at what would be an adequate motive.) Iago's motive strikes people as inadequate, as not fully explaining his actions, so Coleridge speaks of it as motiveless malignity. On the face of it this seems odd; why should one motive demand another? If we have been thinking of a motive as an 'efficient cause', a pusher, we seem to be asking what pushed the pusher, and setting up an infinite regress. Motives, however, are not pushers; as we have said, they are cognitive contexts. Why does our first context need another, an outer framework to supplement it? Because the background of a more or less normal life is always assumed, and people generally relate their whole set of motives in some sort of a system, however rough, however unsatisfactory. The outer framework is a rough arrangement of other motives in the background, a general pattern of life which brings the motive we are dealing with forward and makes it the dominant one in this particular action. But might all this be irrelevant? Might this particular person simply happen to have no other motives except envy? Might his sole need be to be always better off than other people?

6 OBSESSION AND MONOMANIA

In common life, we do not usually expect monomania. We expect the ordinary spread of motives, and if some seem to be missing, we most naturally assume that they are repressed and unconscious. This is not a new idea, invented by modern theorists. Euripides expressed it plainly in the *Bacchae* and *Hippolytus*. Bad motives, in particular, have always been supplied readily to fill out the picture of those who claimed only to have good ones, and inconsistencies of conduct can usually be found to justify such speculations. But awkward and surprising cases remain, and have been rather well explored in literature. On the tragic side, Racine probably carried the study of them as far as it will go, in tragedies whose point is always the hopeless clash between characters each ruled by a single motive—vengeance, honour, possessive love, maternal affection—and therefore totally unable to respond to one another. And the wide range of writing which goes under the name of Comedy of Humours runs wholly on such characters. They are often named to ram the point home—Joseph Surface, Lady Teazle, Morose. (Many of the names, interestingly enough, are just references to animals—Fang, Kitely, Moth, and all the villains in *Volpone*. The same symbolic use of animals emerges from innumerable caricatures.) All this, however, proceeds at rather a special distance from life. It is not that there are no people like Racine's, or like Dickens's or Ben Jonson's caricatures. Life is always astonishing us by outdoing art. But the general position is that comic characters like this are simply distant views; when we get to know people better we find much more in their lives, and the varied context emerges.

These characters in books, in fact, simply reflect the amazement we feel when somebody appears to be even partly one-sided. And our amusement at them is connected with a quite genuine relief when the author sanely implies that such one-sidedness is not normal—that we do not have to live our lives like that, or accept their world. For if we find, on knowing someone better, that they really are in the situation of one of these comic characters—really devoid of anything to balance their ruling passion—then we think something is badly wrong with them, and that we are moving into the territory of tragedy. This is not to say that there cannot be reasonable single-minded enthusiasm. That is a very different thing from obsessiveness; the obsessive is helpless. Racine's characters are tragic because they are locked in their mouse-wheels. This is an even more important fact about each of them than which particular motive he is ruled by. They cannot even listen to each other—hence the need for each to have his or her confidant. Disaster inevitably follows. But it would not be tragedy—it would not even catch our attention—if this were the universal human condition. Nor, of course, could it do so if it were something unknown and impossible for us.

Obsession is a possibility for all of us, and a danger to many, because the balance of motives which we normally maintain is incomplete and insecure. But that it should not be a danger— that it should be a normal condition—is unimaginable in such a creature as man. Even the most obsessive characters in life and in literature, of course, have not succeeded in reducing themselves to a single need. Misers still eat and sleep and usually have some idea whom they will leave their money to; they often retain the taste for quarrelling and disinheriting people. They are capable of inner conflict. (If things get past this point, they will soon be dead.) And it always makes sense to ask how they got that way. We do not expect people to be born without the usual complement of tastes. There is too, a difficulty about imagining any of the more complex motives as existing alone. Envious people, for instance, have to want more than others of whatever is going, which means that they have also to want these other things directly in the first place. Ambitious people have to care enough about those around them to value their praise. (This is a real difficulty to Coriolanus. It is not easy to make sense of ambition alone.) And so on. Obsessiveness, in fact, has to be exceptional. We normally take for granted a pretty complex background of familiar needs. Flat characters belong to fiction.

Needs, then, come in sets, because they are not entities on their own but aspects of people. And those sets are structured in a more or less familiar way, typical of the species. For instance, grossly disturbing a person's sexual life will not leave the rest of the personality unchanged. Cultures certainly impose a pattern of their own, organizing those needs in their own definite way. But the cultures are themselves responses to familiar conflicts of needs in the first place, and moreover it is well-known that people often cannot fulfil the demands of their culture. Explaining a motive, then, is placing it on the map of this general order, this comprehensive plan of life, just as explaining a single act is placing it on the map of a smaller area—a partial plan, a motive. And the explanation is adequate if it can fit it in without distorting the normal arrangement beyond the bounds of what is credible.

Iago's envy does not fit in like that. It has taken him over. It swallows up every other motive, including that prudent self-regard which is his official rule of life. It has become crazy, paranoid envy, serving crazy, paranoid pride. The craziness means that all other motives have given way to it, that all attempts at inward balance have ceased. At this point, though causal explanation may go on, explanation by motive becomes impossible, because the background map on which the envy ought to be located has vanished. There are no more conflicts. When this happens, we generally reckon people as in some sense

insane, though this may mean little more than that we have had
to give up the effort to understand them.

This, surely, is why Iago refuses to explain his motives:

Othello: Will you, I pray, demand that demi-devil
            Why he hath thus ensnar'd my soul and body?
Iago: Demand me nothing; what you know, you know
            From this time forth I never will speak word.[13]

It has dawned on him that he has nothing to say. Exposed, he
suddenly sees with a fearful clarity that his blind, obsessed
malice has made him quite careless of his own safety as well as of
everybody else's, that he has forgotten everything else for it, and
has indeed—even if he could escape—nothing left to live for. To
admit any of this would be to make himself not just odious, but
contemptible and ridiculous. The capacity to balance one's life,
to relate one's aims, is essential to sanity and maturity. He would
seem childish and foolish. But pride is the centre of his life. So he
takes the only course which might preserve his dignity.

Two alternative ways of understanding him have been suggested, both interesting and both relevant to our theme. It may
therefore be worth discussing them. (We have no need, I think,
to defend one or other view dogmatically as an interpretation of
Othello. What matters is to grasp fully the kind of range of alternatives which we have before us when we wonder whether a
motive is adequate or not.) The suggestion of insanity is a very
important possible terminus for motive enquiries. But the two
now to be discussed are often brought in, when that terminus
heaves in sight, to put it off for a stage or two. This gives them a
special interest.

One suggestion, with a pure Freudian simplicity, credits Iago
with a sexual passion for Othello. The other sees him as an
existentialist hero, deliberately choosing destruction for its own
sake, unmasking the absurdity of the world by defying it.[14] The

first is by no means as silly as it may look. Iago, like many other persuasive psychopaths, owes much of his success to being extremely disturbed sexually. He continually uses crude and powerful sexual imagery to convince his dupes that those they have to deal with are not *people*, needing to be taken seriously, but things—accessible objects to be instantly manipulated, destroyed, or sexually devoured. He can only do this because it genuinely is his own attitude. In particular, he sees everybody as a potential source of sexual satisfaction, and a sexual apparatus to be manipulated. His 'choice' of sexual intrigue as a way to ruin Othello is not a real choice—due, say, to looking for the most painful or efficient method. He never considers any other means. Nothing else can occur to him. So his relation to everybody, including Othello, does have a very strong sexual element.

But this still cannot supply his motive, in the sense of filling in the missing piece of background and making sense of his life. To do this, as we have seen, you have to produce something which makes his whole scheme of life coherent. And this would mean fitting in the other needs which go to make up a more or less normal human being. Moreover, allotting any other person a supreme place in his life is hopelessly contrary to his official egoism. And, call it hate or love, Othello does occupy that place. This is not just an ordinary conflict of motives. Such a conflict is a branching out of one's life-plan in two directions between which one must choose. It could cause doubt and hesitation, perhaps anguish, but it could be solved. This one, on the other hand, is a total incompatibility, so gross as to make it clear that Iago—who never shows any ordinary self-doubt or hesitation whatever—has simply lost grip on his life-plan and is going to pieces.

The existentialist suggestion is, I think, partly refuted by the element of truth in the Freudian one. It is hard to see how somebody in the grip of a sexual obsession can also be a free agent asserting his autonomy by a heroic gesture. Still, this may seem a minor point. Iago's lonely vigour and persistence certainly are impressive. So is his final silence. And he does make some plausible speeches about the will. These, however, are all directed at Roderigo, are beautifully calculated to overturn his inconvenient streak of caution, and seem likely to be pure propaganda, like nearly everything else Iago says to his victims. Ought he, however, to be taken more seriously as a protester and critic, perhaps even as a moralist? This suggestion would, again, supply a way of answering 'Yes' to the question. 'Has he an adequate motive?' and it is clear that those who make these suggestions feel the need of that positive answer very strongly. His motive, we would then say, is justified scorn of society. His real plan of life, in that case, is not egoism, but the deliberate acceptance of some standards by which he finds the world wanting. But what are these standards? The fit between his act and its supposed motive is terribly loose. Why would this particular little bit of spiteful destruction be a suitable protest? Is it an instalment on the destruction of society? Or a symbol for it? Is the point of that destruction the unworthiness of society? Or the wish for destruction as such? In the second case the logic of Iago's position would be close to that of 'evil be thou my good.' But for Satan that logic, as we have seen, presupposes a personal feud in which destruction is an act of vengeance and self-assertion. It takes us back to the kind of hatred which we already know occupies Iago, instead of supplying a broader, more impersonal background which could give a wider sense to that hatred. No doubt Iago does have spasms of more general Satanic thinking. But to give them effect would call for well-planned and successful revolt—for supplanting one's enemy, as Satan planned to do. Iago, though clever enough, has not thought out his attack at all in this strategic light. As a political insurrection, it is a shambles. Only as destruction can it be seen as successful. Destruction, however, is not an aim which others will accept as even rational and intelligible, let alone honourable. In their eyes, he is irremediably a failure, and of course the logic of hell—his own logic—has no place for failure. Only at destruction is Iago a success. And since he is sane enough, able enough to fit means to ends, to show that this is no accident, only the wish for destruction can supply him with an adequate motive. But can there be such a wish? This must be our next question.

SUMMARY

Since the romantic revival, the idea of the grandeur of evil has been a most powerful one. Its dramatic force is unquestioned. To understand and use it, however, we need to extract its meaning in less colourful form. 'The reason Milton wrote in fetters when he wrote of Angels and God, and at liberty when he wrote of Devils and Hell, is because he was a true poet, and of the Devil's party without knowing it,' remarks the devil smugly in Blake's *Marriage of Heaven and Hell*. But the reason for this is surely something quite different—simply the well-known difficulty in writing about God and angels at all. What Milton wrote about the devil is not—once we drop the purple spotlight of romantic partiality—at all flattering. Satan's personal motives are mostly mean and claustrophobic centring on competitive self-assertion. His grandeur stems from his original nature, which is not of his making, and his daemonic force results merely from his concentrating all his efforts within this narrow circle of aims. The phrase 'Evil be thou my good' is no sublime manifesto of creative immoralism, but a competitive political move to establish a private empire. Milton paints him indeed as a tragic figure—therefore as divided, possessing still many virtues. But these virtues are traditional. He has not invented them. We have no reason to leap from the divine frying-pan into the diabolical fire.

Satan's central motives, like those of other instigators, are negative in two converging ways. They are destructive, and empty of positive content in the sense that they do not subserve any other, more constructive aims (compare Hitler).

This rather startling condition can be seen in extreme form in Iago: 'Motiveless malignity?' Iago has motives—converging envy and pride—which explain his actions in so far as they show the interests they serve. Are these motives *adequate?* Scarcely, because an adequate motive should include a context showing why it prevails over other competing motives. Iago is a covert monomaniac; those around him fail to detect this, which is why he can deceive them. Such one-sidedness is not usually expected in life, though it has been well explored in literature—a proceeding which helps our understanding of life by showing its elements in untypical isolation. But obsessives, such as Iago, really are like this. Their case shows up by contrast how necessary the idea of an ordered set of needs is, as a background, for making motivation intelligible. Iago can give no such explanation in these terms—a realization which is the end of him. (Sexual or existential 'explanations' do not fill this gap.) His driving motive seems to be mere destructiveness, which is something he cannot explain to those around him.

Is this, however, really a possible position? The idea of destructiveness as a motive is a somewhat mysterious one. We must examine it in the next chapter.

8

DEATH-WISH

The goal of all life is death.
Freud[1]

1 THE GAP TO BE FILLED

Here we reach our central psychological problem. Can there be a motive which is a pure wish for destruction—not as a means to any good, nor a part of it, but simply for its own sake?

Up to now we have been deliberately seeking out other motives which can lead to destructive behaviour, motives which are explanatory in a more straightforward way, because they do not themselves seem to need explanation as a purely destructive motive needs it. We have seen that there are plenty of them, and that they are very powerful. Mere obsessive concentration on one's own interests, resulting in neglect of other people's, and in a general failure of sensibility, can do enormous damage. Is anything more needed? If it is not, then wickedness is negative in quite a simple sense. It is just the absence, the failure of other motives which ought normally to balance self-regard.

The trouble with this simple account is that it does not explain the failure of the counteracting motives. And unless we are speaking of psychopaths, strictly and medically so-called, we need a motive to explain this. Also, the behaviour itself seems often to go far beyond what can be explained by any sort of self-regard, because it is visibly self-destructive. People act, sometimes quite gratuitously, in ways which seem as much designed to destroy themselves as their enemies. In private life, gamblers, alcoholics and suicidal people often give this impression. On a political scale, Hitler is a striking example, above all in his sudden and militarily nonsensical invasion of Russia, but also in many other details of his conduct. And cases like Iago's may seem to pose a similar problem. The question 'What makes someone become so full of envy—or revenge or ambition—that they neglect their own interests?' is a real one, and the simple reply 'Envy, or revenge or ambition' does not answer it. Normally people, however much they may be absorbed in one activity, have in them some kind of mechanism which reminds them from time to time of the other elements in their lives—especially of their own safety, and of the interests of those around them—and requires some good reason why these should go on being neglected. An adequate motive has to be one which can supply this reason. Psychopaths seem to lack this reminding mechanism, or to lack the other motives to which it would draw attention. But sane people with obsessive tendencies do not naturally lack these things. They therefore need some extra reason for rejecting other aims and letting their other capacities atrophy. At a conscious level, this reason is usually put in positive terms, and consists simply of the overriding importance of the obsessing concern. The relative unimportance of everything else tends to be taken for granted rather than argued. This is a characteristic feature of obsession. From a non-obsessed point of view, however, the notion that everything else could be unimportant is often so extraordinary that extra motives for accepting this priority-system do seem to be needed. This is where the notion of a positive death-wish becomes most plausible.

If this exists, however, is it really a wish for one's own death, or a wish to destroy others? Do both these exist independently, or is one an inversion of the other? And what is their relation to obsession? We ought not to expect simple and sweeping answers to these questions. A cluster of different tendencies seems to be involved here, and we shall need a rather varied set of suggestions to make sense of the matter. Freud's ideas—which are amazingly sweeping—can certainly help us, both where they seem convincing and where they do not. His power of making enormous, imaginative, useful mistakes has seldom been so well shown as on this subject. Before plunging into his suggestions, however, it is worth while to make a simple point, not specially noted by him, about the link between death and obsession. This seems to be a close and necessary one. Obsession has to carry with it the atrophy and gradual death of all faculties not involved in whatever may be the obsessing occupation. And among these faculties is the power of caring for others, in so far as they are not the objects of obsession. To let an obsession take one over is therefore always to consent, in some degree, both to one's own death and to that of others. Or—to look at it another way—a destructive attitude to others, and to one's own nature, can be satisfied by cultivating an obsession. In general, this point does not seem very controversial. The danger is widely recognized in cases where the obsessing activity is itself one not highly regarded, as with fairly crude misers or collecting fiends. But it may have a wider and more sinister importance for a culture which relies as heavily as ours does on highly specialized activities, needing rigorous training which almost requires obsession. Such a society selects for obsessiveness, and if there is any truth in the suggestion just mentioned, that is a serious matter. We will return to this possibility shortly. What, meanwhile, about Freud?

2 THE ISOLATED INDIVIDUAL

Freud's suggestion is simple and startling. We have, he said, a strong wish to die, a wish which is not just one wish among others but an all-pervasive basic instinct, indeed a natural force, one of the two which are engaged in continuous struggle throughout the living world. Death forever opposes life, whose representative is sex or Eros. More deeply still, however, all instinct is an urge to regress towards an earlier, less active condition, and therefore leads away from life. It is 'a tendency innate in living organic matter impelling it towards the reinstatement of an earlier condition, the manifestation of inertia in organic life.'[2] Accordingly, it is the occurrence of life-instinct—and indeed of life itself—which is anomalous and presents a puzzle. This strange idea was made easier for Freud by the fact that he had always treated the pleasure-principle—the central dynamic of his system—as something negative, an urge towards the release of tension. 'Our recognition that the ruling principle of psychic life, perhaps of nerve-life altogether, is the struggle for reduction ... or removal of the inner stimulus-tension (the Nirvana-principle ...) a struggle which comes to expression in the pleasure-principle, is indeed one of our strongest motives for believing in the existence of death-instincts.'[3] Once these instincts were admitted as an inward lethal force, he used them at once to account for aggression towards others, by simply adding that they could be turned outwards when self-preservation wishes resisted them and forbade them to destroy the self. Thus, sadism should now be regarded as a secondary development, and masochism—which had formerly been seen always as inverted sadism—could sometimes be primary, a direct expression of the death-wish.[4]

The oddness of this suggestion deserves attention. On the face of things, it makes far more sense that a wish to injure others should sometimes exist, and should sometimes be turned inward, than that a wish to die should always exist and should be turned outward. Freud's arrangement is obscure, not just because the idea of a pervasive death-wish is itself puzzling, but because this death-wish, even if it existed, seems too passive a motive to generate the lively activity of attack. If there were indeed a constant duel between deathly inertia and self-preservative instincts, we might expect it to result in a compromise—a moderate effort to survive. Why should it ever involve others? If it could do this, would it not be just as plausible to suggest that the self-preservative instincts might find vicarious satisfaction in preserving others—or that the sexual instincts might find it in giving them sexual satisfaction—as that the regressive, inertial ones might find it in causing their death?

Freud's reversal of the most natural interpretation here is very significant, not only for his thought, but for that of his age and our own. The reason why the notion of positive, direct aggression towards others could scarcely occur to him was not the moral objection which people feel to it today, but something much deeper. It was his view of individuality. This made it seem virtually impossible that anybody should directly care about others at all—even sufficiently to aim at their destruction. The point of the pleasure principle was to show all interpersonal dealings as transactions for private gain, means to changing one's own state of consciousness. Freud explicitly repeats this idea at this stage of his thought to give a reductive analysis of love. People who seem to feel disinterested affection are (he says) 'using love to produce an inner feeling of happiness', but this 'love with an inhibited aim was indeed originally full sensual love, and in men's unconscious minds is so still.'[5]

Again, in explaining the origins of the family, he decides that it was only when sexuality ceased to be periodic that 'the male acquired a motive for keeping the female, *or rather his sexual objects*, near him', (my italics) while the female 'kept near her that part of herself which had become detached from her, her child.'[6]

Aggression, however, would need just the same sort of reduction. Anger genuinely directed towards others has to be outgoing, just as real love is. Its aim must be to produce a change in their state, not in that of the angry individual.

The possibility that feeling might really be outgoing in this way was ruled out, not only by Freud, but by enlightenment individualism generally. And since that way of thinking remains very influential, outgoingness is still often hard to grasp today. The kind of individual who is posited by Social Contract Theory is essentially solitary, involved in society only by his need for protection. In *Civilisation and its Discontents*, Freud gives exactly this Hobbesian account of the reasons for the development of cultures, wistfully remarking that, for the individual himself, 'it would perhaps be better' if he could somehow achieve happiness without going through the alien process of socialization, which usually makes happiness impossible.[7] He sees civilization not as a natural expression of human powers and wishes, but as a brutal, though unfortunately necessary, restraint imposed on instincts from without. He never allows that it might itself have any instinctual basis—whether emotionally, in natural affection and gregariousness, or cognitively, in our very striking repertory of social capacities—speech, play, ritual, curiosity, the arts. The transaction appears entirely hostile. 'Culture behaves towards sexuality in this respect like a tribe or a section of the population which has gained the upper hand and is exploiting the rest of its own advantage. Fear of a revolt among the oppressed then becomes a motive for even stricter regulations.' This oppression centres round 'the prohibition against incestuous object-choice, *perhaps the most maiming wound ever inflicted throughout the ages on the erotic life of man.*'[8] We do not know what Freud would have said on this topic if he had been presented with the evidence now available for incest-avoidance in other species: in particular, with the fact that young male chimpanzees and other primates do not seem to show sexual interest in their mothers.[9] He did not have this evidence, any more than he had before him the equally relevant facts that gregariousness is far older than man, and that pair-formation is far older than the change in human sexual period-icity, occurring in many species both of birds and primates as a permanent affectional bond, independent for most of the year of sexual interaction. Unless we suppose our species to have run an evolutionary course quite contrary to that of other social species, we ought to conclude from this evidence, and a mass of similar data, that culture is the fruit of exceptionally well-developed social instincts, not that it is a kind of weed-killer put down to control those few which we possess. Outgoingness—the habit-ual direction of emotion to others—is ancient and natural, not a desperately contrived resort when our inner transactions are hopelessly blocked.[10] Culture channels and directs this outgoingness; it does not have to invent it.

It is too late now to bring Freud up-to-date on these consider-ations from ethology and evolution, tantalizing though the pro-ject may be. He was certainly not one of those who would have ruled them out in advance on the grounds of human dignity. But he did not have them, and accordingly the picture he has left us is one of stark, unrelieved confrontations, both without and within. The individual faces an alien and overbearing society as its victim, just as, within him, his oppressed sexual instincts face society's representative, the overbearing super-ego. There are nowhere any neutrals, any conciliators, any hopes of understand-ing. It is, as Freud cheerfully remarks, an 'exquisitely dualistic conception of the instinctive life.'[11]

3 THE PASSIVENESS OF THE MEDICAL MODEL

It is striking how subtly at this point the medical model deepens the limitations of the individualistic political one. A doctor is expected to treat his or her clients as patients, not agents, to isolate them to some extent in a social vacuum. Their dealings with other people are not supposed to concern medicine, except in so far as those others may act on the patient, especially to do harm. Doctors are not called on to judge patients, except perhaps on the one point of requiring that they should pay proper attention to their own interests. They may, however, well be called on to defend them against the claims of others, and against their own conscientious response to those claims. And if society makes unreasonable demands on patients, demands based on ignorance or humbug, it may well be a doctor's business to protest. Patients, for their part, unless they actually reject their doctors, are expected to be more or less passive towards them and accept what they say without much question. Medicine, in fact, does not stand outside morals, as is sometimes supposed, but imposes a very specific set of duties, adjusted to the special helplessness of patients and the special skill and responsibility of doctors. When this relation is suddenly universalized—as it is by the claim that everybody is sick or neurotic, and by the idea that the medical view of others is the only truly humane one—these duties seem to become the whole of morality. But when we are talking about the whole human condition, things which the medical model deliberately leaves out may well be crucial. We have then to think about at least some people as agents and interactors as well as patients.

Freud, throughout his early work, had operated without much question within the limits of the passive medical model. He had taken traditional morality for granted. He chiefly noticed its defects, and often enjoyed debunking it. Even more than Nietzsche, he concentrated his disapproval against the hypocritical vices—humbug, dishonesty, self-deception, and above all the cowardice which underlay them—making people unable to acknowledge their own sexual nature. The change of tone in *Beyond the Pleasure Principle* (1922) is striking, and becomes still more impressive in its successor *Civilization and its Discontents* (1930). Freud was not one to evade seeing the full implications of the First World War. He saw plainly that motivation was involved here of which his theories could say nothing. With his usual courage, he turned his attention to the breadth and depth of human destructiveness, and tried to extend his ideas to take account of people as responsible agents and instigators, not just as patients. He admitted the size of the gap in his previous thinking ('I can no longer understand how we could have overlooked the universality of non-erotic aggression and destruction') and concluded firmly that 'the tendency to aggression is an innate, independent, instinctual disposition in man', one which 'constitutes the most powerful obstacle to culture', and is 'the derivative and main representative of the death-instinct.'[12]

4 THE COSMIC MOVE

What change could best accommodate this admission with his previous insights? Freud saw it must be deep, affecting even the central pleasure principle itself, and made that clear in his title. But how should that principle be altered? There were two main possibilities—to admit that the pleasure principle had proved too general, or to say that it had not been general enough, and must be brought, along with its exceptions, under some concept still wider and more sweeping. Freud chose this second course. He followed his general formal preference for reductive simplicity, for bringing phenomena under as few headings as possible, because he thought that this was required for scientific parsimony, and so for rationality. He sacrificed to this tidy-minded principle another belief which he had so far thought equally necessary for rationality—namely, the belief that people can only act for their own advantage or pleasure. He now conceded that they can also act to bring about their own deaths—a concession which still preserved the central egoistic feature that action was always essentially directed towards the self. The need to invoke two egoistic aims instead of one was, in his view, certainly a misfortune for scientific parsimony. It showed the world to be less intelligible than it had so far seemed, as well as more alarming. But this concession was not fatal so long as it went no further. Underlying unity was still provided by the notion that in the long run even the life-instincts were regressive and inertial as well as the death ones; they only provided 'circuitous paths to death'[13]—an aim for whose universality he quoted Schopenhauer. Moreover, this duality could be used to bring forward into a still more prominent position that emphasis on inner conflict which had always been central to his psychology, and which is indeed one of his most valuable ideas. The result is not just metapsychology—as it is sometimes called—but metaphysics, and that of a fairly primitive kind, closely recalling preSocratic systems like that of Empedocles (who explained the world as governed by a timeless, cosmic conflict between love and strife), or indeed Manichaean dualism. It is a powerful myth, not just aesthetically 'exquisite', as Freud said, but expressive and influential, a model capable of deeply affecting our view of our problems. It is interesting that T. H. Huxley, expounding a view in many ways similar to Freud's of a fundamental war between ethical man and nature, explicitly invoked a similar preSocratic model, that of Heraclitus. These myths are good servants but bad masters. Where phenomena have not yet been understood properly, their intoxicating effect can be disastrous. It is worth while looking at the evidence which started Freud out in this direction to see whether we can find other, less dramatic but more helpful, ways of understanding it.

5 RADICAL DUALISM

Freud's new views arose from his work on traumatic neuroses produced by the First World War. He found that traumatized patients' dreams continually took them back to the scenes of their disasters, reviving 'experiences of the past that contain no potentiality of pleasure, and which could at no time have been satisfactions, even of impulses since repressed.'[14] He saw that these cases really did break his rule that all dreams must be wish-fulfilments serving the pleasure principle. He connected them with the more general phenomenon of compulsive repetitions of painful experience, which he must already have suspected of breaking that rule. He concluded that 'there really exists in psychic life a repetition compulsion, which goes beyond the pleasure principle', and that, in order to explain this, the drastic, though admittedly only speculative, hypothesis of a general death-wish was needed.

The gap between this vast, mystifying solution and the limited question it answers shows that two quite different kinds of issue are entangled here. Besides the question of how compulsive repetition is caused, Freud is suddenly trying to solve the problem of evil.[15] Only now has its vastness and urgency come home to him. That is why these two books, in spite of much strangeness and confusion, are still so impressive and have much to tell us. (The confusions are largely due to one of Freud's most unfortunate gifts, his immense, lawyer-like ability to argue that he has not changed his mind, and is still saying what he said before. Combined with his incredible fertility in quite new suggestions, this habit has been a major disaster to thought.) What then could be done about the problem of evil? For practical purposes, Freud's solution to it is Manichaean, positing two tendencies in us which are radically separate and can have no intelligible relation. In our world, death and love, though usually mixed up in their operation, appear as totally distinct forces. The unavoidable compromises between them can be made only by violence. It is true that there is a reconciliation at a deeper level, whereby the pleasure principle turns out to partake of 'the most universal tendency of all living matter . . . to return to the peace of the inorganic world', and life instincts only transiently and half-heartedly 'make their appearance as disturbers of the peace.'[16] But it is not clear what meaning this belief can actually have for us. It sounds at first as if it might be meant to induce resignation and withdrawal of attachment from these transient disturbances. Yet Freud, a born fighter, has certainly not been converted to any such policy. His exhortations are all that we should fight on the side of life, and in spite of his rather vague use of the word 'Nirvana' his occasional references to Buddhism remain hostile and uncomprehending. Moreover, he explicitly repeats at this stage his earlier contemptuous rejection of the consolations of religion generally. No way of coming to terms with the death principle by finding a meaning for death has any place in his thought.

6 THE PROBLEM OF ACCEPTANCE

What, then, is the resignation he is certainly demanding? It is essentially a Stoical realism, an honest admission of the appalling features of human life. This is indeed continuous with his earlier demands, in so far as it still requires honesty. But the things we are to be honest about are now so different that the effect is totally changed. As far as our own inner life is concerned, the impulses which we must honestly admit are now not just sexual and childish; they are murderous. Repressing them no longer appears as merely cowardly vanity, but as an entirely understandable caution in the face of a deadly danger. Making this danger cosmic by placing a universal death-force behind it does not help us to understand it or deal with it. Honesty here will only tell us that we are possessed by a demon which we must somehow control. This is certainly better than being possessed by one and not knowing it, but it is not much help till we gain a better understanding of the demon. And as far as the outside world goes, getting similar information about other people has an equally limited value. We are warned that they are more dangerous than we supposed, but not what we can possibly do about it.

Because of the difficulty which—as we have noticed before—there is in admitting bad things without accepting them, Freud's demand for honesty carries him towards fatalism. He thinks that the need to admit human destructiveness involves positing a vast, alien, destructive force behind people's motives. But this move seems to make it useless to try to understand the destructiveness itself. Our life-embracing motives can only deal with the others externally, that is, by controlling them. There seems no alternative to the more or less blind, uncomprehending self-command which Freud had always rejected. The difference between informed suppression and unconscious repression dwindles away when the motive to be admitted is entirely opaque to our thought. In dealing with sex, Freud had usually proceeded on the basis that greater understanding would make it possible to unblock the path to genuine and suitable gratification, even if neurotic and infantile wishes really did have to be abandoned. This could be seen as a good bargain. But have murderous impulses any such acceptable outlet?

The hydraulic or 'economic' model which he still took for granted as the only one for instinct poses a fearful problem here. 'It is not easy to understand how it can be possible to withhold satisfaction from an instinct. . . . If the deprivation is not made good economically, one may be certain of producing serious disorders.'[17] This puzzle made the problems of responsible agents so obscure to him that—though fully admitting the presence of destructive motives—he scarcely touched on their difficulties, and still devoted most of his space, even in *Civilization and its Discontents*, to what are essentially patients' problems—society's oppression of sexuality and the pathological effects of guilt. He is not asking why people act so badly, but simply why they are so unhappy. And when he notices the first question, the connexion he draws is nearly always 'they act badly because they are unhappy', only occasionally 'they are unhappy because of bad actions and bad choices—both their own and other people's.' Morality still figures nearly always as an oppressor, occasionally as a necessary compromise, but never as a reconciler—a way of working out genuinely accepted priorities. Although he sees its development in the individual as similar to that in the group, Freud explicitly denies that the individual can contribute to it. Outward and inward morality, he says, *always agree* in their demands, which originate in the group, and are therefore easier to study there.[18] This extraordinary neglect of the clashes between individual conscience and the demands of society, and of their effect in producing reform, is part of his whole static, fatalistic attitude to politics and society. The stagnant, conventional society of post-Metternich Central Europe has left its mark on Freud as it did on others who saw the need for enormous changes—Kierkegaard, Marx, Nietzsche. Change did not then appear as something which goes on constantly in any case, and which very resolute people can hope in some degree to influence, but as an apocalyptic dream or a sheer impossibility. Conceptual schemes, built as correctives to this ossified society, took on quite different meanings when the dam burst with the First World War. Freud had the misfortune to survive, as the other nineteenth-century prophets did not, and had to try to adjust to this new situation. How far did he succeed?

7 THE NEED FOR SELF-KNOWLEDGE

I do not think that experience shows him to have made things out actually worse than they are, only to have made them look more mysterious, and therefore harder to handle. Events in the world have been about as bad as he expected. And he was surely right to think that our ignorance of human motives, resting on a deep habit of continuous self-deception, has turned out to be the main danger facing the human race. He was not right in his early—and quite understandable—belief that what this ignorance and self-deception concealed was essentially sexual motivation grounded in a certain narrow range of infant experiences. A much wider range of motives was involved. The need not to be ashamed of sex is the one part of his doctrine which has really got across, and people think that they have complied with it. They have not in fact done so, because his central point is not so much the presence of sexual motives as such, but the childish and distorted form in which they operate. The extent to which we are imprisoned in the emotional patterns of our early lives, and insist on reproducing those patterns repeatedly, while projecting on others the guilt of producing them, is something which still has not really penetrated into the public consciousness. The only element of it which seems to have been fully accepted is the mistaken idea that everything wrong with people is the fault of their parents, particularly of their mothers.

These early patterns involve other motives besides sexual ones, and the implausibility of their being only sexual has been an unfortunate obstacle to people's grasping their real importance. We need to be far more awake than we are to their working, both in ourselves and others, and far less willing to accept explanations of everybody's conduct which rationalize it in terms of alleged self-interest. The world is riven with feuds, quarrels and misunderstandings which are not at all in the interest of most of those engaged in them—unless that interest is defined in terms of giving them the particular kind of emotional excitement and support to which they have become accustomed. It is also full of situations where something new ought to be done, and would in practical terms benefit those who could do it, but is not done because it is emotionally unfamiliar and calls for a change in personal life. An obvious example of the first trouble is found in those areas of political life which are so habitually conducted in terms of violent confrontation that people who dislike this find it hard to enter them at all, however much they may mind about the issues. A malign selection for quarrelsomeness then operates, and the actual issues involved may become entirely transformed by such treatment, so that agreement really does become impossible. An example of the second is the deep alarm and anger which has arisen at every stage of women's emancipation, from early demands for the franchise to contemporary ones for employment. It has often been found—as it was in the case of the franchise—that the actual granting of the contested privilege made very little disturbance in people's lives; once made, the change was harmless. But in advance, the symbolism of changing sex roles was terrifying.

Where strong hidden motives like this lead to conflict, they have to be understood and openly dealt with. If, as often happens, negotiators ignore them and mention only the objective issues which are officially at stake, opposition remains stiff and tends to get more bitter as hopes of agreement are repeatedly frustrated, and each side becomes more convinced of the other's unreasonableness. Malign selection for escalation of conflict naturally follows. Games theory, which deliberately studies the official issues in abstraction from the motives involved, is a very misleading guide here. For its purposes, what matters is only the content of a proposal. In actual life, this cannot be considered at all apart from the earlier personal history and the spirit in which the new proposal is offered. The difference between a self-righteous, domineering approach and an imaginative, conciliatory one is crucial to the very possibility of considering it. Nor is this in any way irrational. Proposals are not isolated natural phenomena, but parts of a continuing relation between bodies of people who are already linked by complex webs of concern, sympathy, fear, regard and hostility. New proposals get their meaning from these attitudes, and particularly from the unacknowledged ones. This is reasonable, because it is the attitudes which will determine how the particular proposal now in question will be understood and followed up, and indeed whether it can be trusted at all.

The crucial importance of this is particularly plain over the use of threats. Against a hostile background, a threat which is officially meant to deter may very well turn out simply to provoke and embitter, so that it actually has just the opposite effect to the one aimed at. This happens because distrust and suspicion of hostility were already strong before it was made, and it has only served to deepen them. Deterrence by threats can only work in two quite special situations—either as a friendly warning between parties who already trust each other, but have sporadic conflicts of interest, or as a serious, immediate menace from an undoubtedly superior power to a weaker one, which really expects action to follow. In the second case, fear, anger and resentment are indeed aroused, but are—at least for the moment—ineffectual. In the first, they are not aroused, because the gesture is understood in a limited and inoffensive sense. Outside these two contexts, they are aroused and will commonly take a course unwelcome to the threatener. The moral—which indeed is well understood in all familiar cases—is that threats are a very tricky coinage, which cannot be relied on to play anything but a background part in negotiations, and that the main business ought always to consist of proposals which presuppose some trust and are meant to create more, because only on such a basis can any further aims be pursued. This is as true in dealing with the wicked as with anyone else, because they too will react badly to pure unmitigated hostility. Penal deterrence as well as the political kind suffers if it is not supported by any positive co-operativeness. But on top of this, especially in politics, the assumption that our enemies are wholly wicked and ourselves wholly virtuous is commonly unrealistic and always violently offensive. Threats accompanied by this kind of self-righteousness cannot fail to provoke. The cycle of trouble is then completed by the threateners' concluding that they have been proved right; their enemies have reacted arrogantly, and the next step must be still stronger threats to bring them to their knees at last.

This picture should be familiar enough to show that threat-behaviour is not entirely 'rational' in the sense of being safely determined by enlightened self-interest. If so, the motivations actually at work here need close attention. In fact, it seems likely that the psychology of aggression and fear—which are closely linked—is every bit as complicated as that of sex, and that no more is done towards explaining it by invoking a general death-wish than would be done for sex by invoking a wish for life. And while it may look plausible to say that sex only affects private life, this plainly cannot be true of fear and aggression. Mass attitudes to groups have very deep instinctual roots, which are exploited every bit as much by left-wing thinkers as by right-wing—for instance in the use of concepts like 'class warfare.' Indeed it is right in some cases to be angry and in some cases to threaten; it may sometimes be right to fight. But unless we become more aware of our underlying, much more general fear, anger and hostility, we cannot properly distinguish these cases. And if we accept Freud's idea that all hostility is a death-wish and effect-ively represents the devil in the cosmic duel of good and evil, we make it even harder to acknowledge these things than it was in the first place.

Freud was absolutely right to want odious truths admitted. But truth cannot be admitted wholesale, in vast abstractions. It is specific. All facts are particular facts, and though they must of course be brought under general descriptions, there is a limit to the generality which makes sense in given situations. All very general explanations of motive, such as hedonism or egoism, are notoriously subject to two alternative drawbacks—vagueness and falsehood. Defined very widely, they tend to become analytically true but trivial. Defined more narrowly, they are interesting but have endless exceptions. Freud's pleasure principle differs from other forms of hedonism in a way which makes it more interesting but less plausible; namely, that he usually rules all pleasure to be sexual. But even if he had been willing to drop this stipulation, the principle would, as he saw, have been stretched to the point of vacuity if it was to account for repetition-compulsion. This however, is true of the death-wish too. Used seriously to explain actual motives, it too becomes either vacuous and formal or specific and unconvincing. On the other hand, used more tentatively, and imaginatively as a signpost to other possibilities, it is suggestive and can be quite helpful.

SUMMARY

The idea of a direct wish for destruction is a puzzling one, because normally the first step in 'explaining' a motive is to name the good at which it aims. We have seen that much evil, much destruction, can indeed be explained in this way, as a by-product of other, more positive wishes. It would be simple and satisfactory to explain it all in this way. But it is hard to see how this would meet the facts. Why does the destruction often go so far beyond what other aims could accidentally produce, or call for? Why do the motives which might be expected to counteract it often fail so resoundingly? Cases of self-destruction make this question specially pressing (Hitler, Iago). Obsession itself seems too, to have a link with destruction.

Many motives, not one, are undoubtedly involved here. Freud's idea of a single, vast, cosmic death-wish is suggestive but not coherent. The difficulties about it are instructive. Freud treats outward aggression as a by-product of a frustrated wish for one's own death (not vice versa). He does this partly because he conceives the self as essentially solitary rather than social. Its deepest wishes must therefore always be self-directed. This extreme enlightenment individualism makes him see culture as an alien system, imposed on people from without by their need for protection, not as a natural outgrowth of their interacting faculties.

Individuals starkly confront society without, and their own super-egos within, as alien, oppressive forces. In his early work, the medical model, isolating them as 'patients' from their ordinary social context, deepened this isolation. All desires, at this stage, seemed directed to either one's own pleasure or survival.

The First World War shattered this simple system, convincing him that there was independent destructive motivation. But instead of concluding that motivation might in general be more complex and less solipsistic, Freud invoked a single, still wider and simpler underlying motive—the wish for death, to which pleasure and survival themselves were only 'circuitous paths.' This wish contended, he said, constantly in the universe with its opponent, Eros or love. This suggestion—disproportionately vast for the phenomena it was supposed to explain—seems to be meant as an answer to the Problem of Evil. It is a Manichaean one, invoking two unrelated and irreconcilable forces. What is its moral?

Freud was certainly calling for a more realistic acceptance of the grimness of life. He had always called for honesty. So far this had been honesty about sexual impulses, undignified but not in themselves harmful. Now he required it about death-wishes which—being often turned outwards—were directly murderous. It is not clear how, even with honesty, people could gain control of this independent cosmic force. Demonic possession seems to be back. Freud's recommendation is that we must fight resolutely on the side of Eros. His response to the destructive force which he detects in pugnacity is, as usual, a sharply pugnacious one. The more alarming sides of our nature are simply disowned, not examined to see out of what less lethal things they grow or what other forms they might be induced to take.

The less dramatic view of aggression, which we looked at in Chapter 4, as essentially space-seeking, not destructive, had not been formulated. Nor did it occur to Freud that morality might be a medium for arbitrating, and to some extent resolving, inner and outer conflict by acceptable systems of priority.

Freud was a survivor from the relatively static world—indeed from the stagnant society of Central Europe—in which it made good sense to attack 'morality', simply as such, as an ossified relic curbing individual freedom. After 1918, when disorder was freely available and its joys could be widely tested, he had to adapt his views (as Nietzsche did not). His attempt to do so is well-directed in recognizing the power and independence of destructive human motives, and the likelihood that they would contribute to more wars. It is also good in honestly admitting that some control of them is needed. But by its metaphysical wildness it makes them look fantastic and impossible to control. Accordingly, it discredited the admission that these motives existed with a wide public, in a manner which persists to this day. It is still hard for people who are determined to avoid cynicism and fatalism to admit that Freud could be right about the immense part played by unconscious irrational and destructive personal motivation in promoting large-scale conflicts and obstructing their solution. The tendency to resort to games theory, which abstracts from all such motivation, is disastrous here. Emotional aspects of concepts like threat and deterrence are still largely ignored. The effect of self-righteousness on other parties in dispute is discounted. It is very unfortunate that the slapdash elements in Freud's theory caused his entirely correct attempt to draw attention to such matters to be widely ignored. If death-wishes exist, they cannot be quite like this.

9

EVIL IN EVOLUTION

It is very probable that any animal whatever, endowed with
well-marked social instincts, would inevitably acquire a moral
sense or conscience, as soon as its intellectual powers had
become as well-developed, or nearly as well-developed, as in
man.

Charles Darwin[1]

1 BEYOND THE SELF-PRESERVATION PRINCIPLE

Can we make better sense of the death-wish proposal? What is
there in it which is valuable?

The first service which it surely does for us is to widen our
horizons, freeing us from bondage to an over-tidy, over-simple
model of rationality, centred too narrowly on self-interest.
Official thought has often been amazingly unimaginative about
the range of our natural motives. That is why the early Freudian
account, which set sex up as a rival centre in constant conflict
with self-preservation, remains so influential with us in spite of
much denunciation and endless charges of being unscientific. It

survives for lack of a better. It is, however, itself still much too narrow, ignoring great ranges of motives, good bad and indifferent, which we need to be aware of. Among these are certainly some which supply possible attitudes to death and other disasters, other than sheer blind fear. And fear itself is extremely complex, not just a straightforward device for self-preservation. As we have seen, its addictiveness and its links with aggression need investigating. Like other motives, it is not just a means to an end, but an autonomous emotional pattern with a life of its own, which we must understand if we are to organize our many motives—as we must—into some tolerable degree of harmony.

If we had something as straightforward as a strong, direct natural wish to die, things would no doubt be simpler. But we do not seem to have it. We seem rather to have a great gap in our natural motivation here—a deep general difficulty in even believing in death, in accepting its very existence. We carry on as if we and those around us were immortal. The actual prospect of dying, and the death of others, typically produce in us an astonished and incredulous bewilderment. This is still true even when we have, as they say, 'asked for it' by extreme and obvious rashness. The work of integrating some acceptance of death into our lives is left to culture, which works hard at it, but notoriously usually fails. Culture may make us attend wakes, sacrifice to Hecate, take out life insurance, make our wills and go to church, but it still leaves nearly every individual with a fearful task to perform when the matter is finally forced upon his attention. This is why, as William James put it, 'mankind's common instinct for reality . . . has always held the world to be a theatre for heroism.'[2] That is, for the facing and overcoming of the fear of death. This situation is scarcely compatible—whatever repressive mechanisms we might invoke—with its being the direct object of desire to one half of our nature. The very important element of truth which Freud grasped needs radical restatement. In fact, as Ernest Becker remarks in an absorbing study of modern blindness about death, 'The ambiguities of Freud's legacy were not in the wrong ideas that he had, since it has been relatively easy to lay these aside; the problem has been in his brilliantly true insights, which were stated in such a way that they fell just to one side of reality.'[3] We need, as he says, to give such parts of the truth a new framewok.

2 ROADS TO DESTRUCTION

It is not plausible to present death itself as a direct object of desire, on the pattern of food or sexual satisfaction. But it is necessary to show how, by perversions and recombinations of our natural motives, it actually can come to be sought, and even come—as with Mephistopheles—to be the only thing which is sought. We must sketch out here a process with several stages. The first, I would suggest, is our hostility to other people, which arises normally, and perhaps inevitably, partly from our competition with them for outward benefits, but also, more deeply, as a social response to their mere strangeness and otherness. We all make demands on each other which we all fail to meet. The resulting anger and aggression need not be destructive. If all goes well, it can lead to a deeper mutual understanding and an increased acceptance of each other's independent existence. Personal relations grow and prosper, always containing, but always using, this chronic element of ambivalence. At other times, however, things go wrong, and we refuse to digest the strangeness and otherness of others. Anger then hardens into resentment, envy, bitterness, vindictiveness and hatred. The normal social impulse to assert oneself, to gain recognition and concession from others—which had a positive aim—turns gradually into a demand for their complete submission, their removal from all intrusion on the social space. For a being with an intellectual grasp of the past and future, such as ourselves, this must finally mean their destruction. In two important ways this wish is negative. It originated in a denial—the refusal to accept another's independent existence. And it aims eventually at an absence—the elimination of its object. In between, various positive elements can certainly intervene. The feud can be enjoyed by one side or both as a game, often with sadistic sexual overtones.[4] It can also have valuable bond-forming effects for the parties involved, and be cherished for that reason. Indeed we are much more dependent on these by-products than we realize. They do not yet constitute a death-wish. The trouble with them—which ought to make us far more aware of their dangers—is that they depend for their force on a policy which does.

At what point do the features which make death-wish language appropriate begin? They seem to do so when the issues to which resentment attaches become obsessive—when other considerations no longer balance them and keep them in proportion. At this point the negative aim—destruction of the opponent—ceases to be part of some wider whole and begins to take charge. It is then inevitably matched by a negative motivation—the *lack* of other aims, the creeping incapacity to find any other point for one's own life. Atrophy, leading to self-destruction, follows on the outward destructiveness. Death, as the most thorough form of destruction available, may well now be desired, for oneself or others or both—though not, as we have noticed, because it is fully grasped and imagined. Indeed, a great deal of confusion and concealment sets in here. Guilt may often cause resentment towards others to be denied and directed inward on oneself, producing depression and self-hatred. (Thus, as psychologists have pointed out, neurotic guilt is often not exactly uncalled-for but misdirected—its victims really are guilty of this resentment, which they conceal, but project their guilt busily instead on trifling and often unreal external offences.) The horror attending the whole issue may, moreover, cause a great deal of repression, enabling us to deny it all, and to be left merely wondering why life seems pointless. All this produces unavoidable obscurity. But whatever corrections may still be needed to the kind of account just sketched out, if we are to understand the range and persistence of human destructiveness, some explanation of this kind does seem to be called for.

In *The Screwtape Letters*, a senior devil, instructing his nephew, lays out the negative elements in the situation very clearly:[5]

> You are much more likely to make your man a sound drunkard by pressing drink on him as an anodyne when he is dull and weary than by encouraging him to use it as a means of merriment among his friends when he is happy and expansive. Never forget that when we are dealing with any pleasure in its healthy and normal and satisfying form, we are, in a sense, on the Enemy's ground. I know we have won many a soul through pleasure. All the same, it is his invention, not ours. He made the pleasures; all our research has not so far enabled us to produce one. . . . An ever-increasing craving for an ever-diminishing pleasure is the formula. It is more certain, and it's better *style*. To get the man's soul and give him *nothing* in return—that is what really gladdens our Father's heart.

And again:

> As this condition becomes more fully established, you will be gradually freed from the tiresome business of providing Pleasures as temptations. . . . Habit renders the pleasures of vanity and excitement and flippancy at once less pleasant and harder to forgo (for that is what habit fortunately does to a pleasure). . . . You no longer need a good book, which he really likes, to keep him from his prayers or his work or his sleep; a column of advertisements in yesterday's paper will do. . . . You can keep him up late at night, not roistering but staring at a dead fire in a cold room. All the healthy and outgoing activities which we want him to avoid can be inhibited and *nothing* given in return, so that at last he may say, as one of my own patients said on his

arrival down here, 'I now see that I spent my life in doing *neither* what I ought *nor* what I liked.' The Christians describe the Enemy as one 'without whom Nothing is strong.' And Nothing is very strong. . . .

How it is so strong is certainly still a problem. But *that* it is so is not in doubt. The experience is to some extent common to all of us. And that great crimes often spring out of empty lives is becoming a commonplace of history.

The idea of strong but negative motivation does, then, make some sense, however weird. And it goes some distance to explain some already outstanding weird facts about people's behaviour. This idea, moreover, indicates a firm link between ingoing and outgoing destructiveness. This link—a central theme of Plato's *Republic*[6]—is, it seems, not just a pious platitude, but a psychological fact. We really are not beings so formed as to eat all those around us and pay no price for it. Freud, therefore, was right to make this connexion, though he seems to have made it backwards. What, however, is the relation between this destructiveness and death? Might the motivation indeed be part of some natural adaptation to mortality? At this point it will be worth while to glance at some evolutionary considerations, so as to see what is possible and what is not. Freud did not do this. His notion of sexuality as a kind of hyperdrive, mysteriously outranking all other motives, is most implausible if one remembers to ask how such a tendency could ever develop, and the death-wish seems an even worse candidate for possibility. Are there, however, any indications, on a more modest scale, of positive, natural attitudes towards death?

3 EVOLUTIONARY POSSIBILITIES

Undoubtedly material does exist for such attitudes. Our motivation, after all, is that of an animal which is vulnerable, which can be injured, grow old and die, and which lives among others in that same situation. As Jung pointed out, early Freudian theory did not pay enough attention to this fact, because it concentrated on the lives of comparatively young people who were still occupied with the need to escape their parents. Those who have gone through this phase and become more conscious of age and mortality have (he said) different problems, because they feel the stirring of a further set of faculties. They need to face life as a whole and find meaning in it, without blinking the fact that it will end. The 'mid-life crisis' arises out of the natural structure of human instincts as much as the parent-child interactions which largely shape our early years.[7] (Later psycho-analytic thought has absorbed this insight, though without always thanking Jung for it.) Mortality is not something entirely alien to our motivation.

Does this, however, make it plausible that we might be endowed with an actual death-wish? Scarcely. Evolution, after all, does not need to provide mortal creatures with any actual desire for death, because dying is not an activity like washing or copulating or rearing young, which animals would not perform unless they wanted to. One can die equally well whether one wants to or not, so there could scarcely be a selective pressure to develop such a desire. There is of course a genuine desire for rest, and where a creature is worn out, this can certainly make death easier. There is also something more interesting, a programmed set of tendencies for advancing through the various stages of life, a scheme in which one set of interests and wishes gradually replaces another. In intelligent social species, the influence of wise, experienced old members is often very great. There could therefore well be selection (through the survival of their relatives) for tendencies which develop quite late in life, and these could include a capacity to accept death and other disasters, including one's own, without being overwhelmed or taking one's fears out on others.

Most of the time, however, the pressure is, obviously, the other way, in favour of a strong interest in life and a desire to go on living. Seeing this, people tend to suppose that evolution simply endows all animals with a set of instincts directed neatly to self-preservation, so that a Hobbesian, egoistic account of human natural motivation is correct. Freud himself in his early days, explained all non-sexual instincts in this way. But evolution does not make for this kind of neatness either. Instincts do not at all have to be adapted to secure their owner's survival. They are present because they have, in the past, secured the survival of his or her line, and this has often been done by preserving the next generation, or a large batch of relatives, rather than a single individual. The resulting desires genuinely belong to the individuals who have them, and a bird which sacrifices itself in defence of its young does so of its own will; it has not been deceived or 'manipulated'. Self-preservation is not an all-explanatory aim.

Neither, notoriously, is pleasure. Both pleasure itself and the more general relaxation of tension to which Freud reduced it are aspects of the working of desire, not its objects. It is true that getting what you want gives relief, but that does not make relief itself the desired object. The question of what you actually did want is a distinct and important one, which the mere fact of relief does nothing at all to answer. And, as G. E. Moore pointed out, a pleasant thought need not be the thought of a (future) pleasure.[8] People who are pleased by the thought of helping, or annoying, an acquaintance, and do so, do not at all necessarily aim at producing a special calculated pleasure in themselves by their actions. They are usually concentrating on the effect they want to produce in the outside world. Only when they get this will they be satisfied. Satisfaction, pleasure and relief are internal objects, or aspects, of desire; the external ones are of a quite different kind, and many of them—though of course not all—concern other people and things in the world, right outside the individual. And these do not have to reduce to some clearly statable category. For instance, a liking for some special kind of place, a symbolic importance attached to it, and a wish to preserve it for its own sake even in one's absence, are entirely natural emotions and there is no rule by which they must be deemed 'irrational'. If this seems odd, it is because of special propaganda campaigns in our recent intellectual history. Egoism and hedonism have over-intellectualized our notion of desire, crediting it with a quite unreal degree of organized planning for a limited future, a misleadingly sharp distinction between means and ends, and an arbitrary limiting of future ends to mental states of somebody, preferably ourselves. This pattern comes from the propaganda of individualism, not from impartial observation, and certainly not from the theory of evolution, whose formulations it has gravely distorted.

Since the emotional constitution of human beings, like that of other animals, is much too complex to be explained in this way as directed to a single end, monistic reductions of it to such ends always fail. As far as the problem of evil is concerned, this means that Freud's doctrine of a general, enclosing, all-explaining death-wish makes little sense biologically. It does not mean, however, that the insight which produced it was wasted. Freud was right in thinking that the more cheerful-looking reductions to pleasure and self-preservation are inadequate too, that bad conduct is an area which makes their weakness evident, and that other sorts of explanation were needed. People do act in ways which are meant to injure both others and themselves, and they do not do so always from calculation of pleasure, nor as a means to survival. But that does not mean that their motivation is something cosmic. We need to look, more modestly, for a number of different motives which are destructive in different ways. We have no reason to expect a single culprit, like the monster in Kliban's car. What we are in fact likely to find is often a mixture of two or more motives which in themselves are relatively harmless, but become deadly when combined, as seems to happen with sadism, where aggression combines with sex. Or again, we may find cases where a motive which is harmless when combined with another, and usually is combined with it, becomes deadly when it appears on its own. This seems to happen with ambition, which usually has a strong communal aspect, and involves real attachment to those whom one hopes to rule and impress, but can become selfishly solitary and is then pernicious.[9]

4 THE HUMAN PROBLEM OF CONFLICT: DARWIN'S ANALYSIS

This kind of account lays the main stress on the arrangement of the motives. It does not accept that human beings can invent new motives, or 'invent values' to which those new motives would correspond.[10] Even the most startling innovations do not seem to call for this sort of origin; they can all be seen to be built out of familiar materials. Instead, it takes the main directions of impulse, the general kinds of praise and fear and delight which are open to us, to be given by our constitution. But it stresses that this still leaves enormous scope for reshaping particular motives, and for combining and separating them in different ways. Because humans have much more control over this arrangement than other animals have, the unique features of humanity become crucial here. To say that other animals do not have free will is to say that, in them, innate programming determines the way in which different moods occur and combine and succeed each other. Though their life may well be more complicated than we suppose, in general we take them to be wholly absorbed by the mood of the moment, to have little awareness of other possible moods, and therefore little control over the direction which their changes of mood will follow. They have a sort of emotional tunnel vision.

Increased intelligence, however, widens the view. Our thoughts often remind us that we are capable of something different. The map of other emotional possibilities is to some extent open before us, so that conflicts between various relevant motives become possible on a quite new scale. Darwin, in a most interesting and profound discussion, gives a remarkable example of this, contrasting our situation with that of migratory birds, such as swallows, in whom one mood sharply and completely succeeds another. After caring for their broods assiduously all through the summer, these birds fly off in the autumn, leaving their current nestlings to die:

> At last, at a moment when her young ones are not in sight, she takes flight and deserts them. When arrived at the end of her journey, and the migratory instinct ceases to act, what an agony of remorse each bird would feel, if, from being endowed with great mental activity, she could not prevent the image continually passing before her mind of her young ones perishing in the bleak north from cold and hunger.[11]

In the bird, it seems, this mental activity does not occur. She has no need to find a deeper reconciling principle by which to arbitrate such conflicts. Human beings do have that need. Greater intelligence, being expressed in this much greater imaginative activity, lights up for them the conflicts between successive moods in a way which would (Darwin suggests) cause intolerable confusion and remorse if it were not also used to control their swing and bring them closer to harmony. The bird never learns not to bring up broods in the autumn. Human beings do learn to avoid many conflicts by advance measures of this kind, and the planning which they require is a fertile source of culture. But not all conflicts can be resolved in this practical way with little or no actual loss. There are many clashes which foresight alone cannot avert, for instance, who is to suffer in an unpredictable famine? Or what is to be done when one friend has deeply injured another? Darwin's suggestion is that the remorse attending crude, slapdash solutions to such dilemmas absolutely required the invention of morality—that is, of priority systems acceptable to the stable, underlying personalities of those involved, indicating which motive ought to prevail. He concludes, though with his usual modesty and caution,

> that any animal whatever, endowed with well-marked social instincts, would inevitably acquire a moral sense or conscience, as soon as its intellectual powers had become as well developed, or anything like as well developed, as in man.[12]

This is a world away from Freud's position. Darwin does not see morality as society's army of occupation triumphing over the individual, but as the individual's own necessary remedy for internal conflicts. What puts 'the imperious word *ought*'[13] in the human vocabulary is not (he says) primarily fear of punishment by society or by parents, but horror at one's own conflicting and sometimes destructive motives. Of course a mass of outside fears reinforce this horror, and give it shape, and the content of any particular morality incorporates all sorts of features dictated by the culture. This is to be expected, because the original, underlying conflicts really do not have a single, ready-made, fully satisfactory solution. (If they did we would be paradisal beings and would not need a morality.) A great number of alternative, partial, compromise solutions are therefore possible. But any one of them, once it has been accepted, has the merit of offering some answer to the conflict, of protecting whatever value has been chosen to prevail, and giving reasons why the other must be sacrificed. By contrast, entirely disorganized behaviour will not only frustrate all positive enterprises, but also leave the original conflicts still active, tearing apart the individual character. And the integration of the personality is—on Darwin's suggestion as on Jung's—a primary need, without which nothing else is possible.

Darwin's view may well seem unfamiliar. It has nothing at all to do with what is commonly called 'evolutionary ethics.' And it runs entirely counter to a notion which is deeply ingrained in current thought—the idea of morality as an alien, dead thing like a corset or a set of dentures, manufactured impersonally by society and then 'internalized' by the individual. But if we are ever to bridge the gap between the individual and the social point of view in a way which makes our motivation intelligible, this kind of reason why we accept society, and why we develop it in the first place, has to be grasped. Society is not just an outside device to protect us against disasters; it is itself an expression of preferences. And these preferences can often only be understood by grasping that the choice offered was a choice of evils. That is why all societies are so faulty. The original constitution was not paradisal. A central conflict in it, which gives rise to many others, arises over individuality itself. We need to be continuous beings, harmonious through time, yet we are subject to all kinds of passing impulses, and also to deeper changes of attitude. Hence, as Nietzsche put it in the course of a most penetrating discussion:

> To breed an animal *with the right to make promises*—is not this the paradoxical task which nature has set itself in the case of man? is not this the real problem regarding man? ... This animal which needs to be forgetful, in which forgetfulness represents a force, a form of *robust* health, has bred in itself an opposing faculty, a memory, with the aid of which forgetfulness is abrogated in certain cases—namely, in those cases where promises are made. This involves no mere passive inability to rid oneself of an impression, ... but an active *desire* not to rid oneself, a desire for the continuance of something desired once, a real *memory of the will*.... How many things this

presupposes . . . if he is to be able to stand security for his own future!

. . . The tremendous labour of that which I have called 'morality of mores' (custom) . . . finds in this its meaning, its great justification, notwithstanding the severity, tyranny, stupidity and idiocy involved in it.[14]

It does indeed, and of course the achievement goes far beyond the case of formal promising. It covers all long-term enterprises, solitary as well as social; it applies even to planting a garden or learning the trombone. But its central and crucial field is that of personal relations. We would all like to have other people bound and dependable, while remaining free ourselves. But as Darwin pointed out—following Hume—we have, because of our active imagination, an inconvenient faculty of sympathy, which tells us just what this policy looks like from the other point of view. We can see the need for the Golden Rule, 'Do as you would be done by.'[15] Yet we often have the strongest possible objection to following it. Our motives continually conflict in a way which would pose hard problems even for a disinterested intelligence trying to solve them. And we are so far from being disinterested that we use our intelligence quite as often to cheat and to obscure the solution as to reach it. Is it any wonder that human moralities are themselves very imperfect, and that even their deepest and most widely accepted principles are constantly disobeyed?

5 POSITIVE ELEMENTS

It is time to draw these divergent speculations together and see whether we are getting a better perspective on the problem of evil. The aims which this better perspective ought to meet are those with which we set out. Above all it should be realistic, not under-estimating the depth and extent of evil nor regarding it as a passing accident due to temporary, technical faults in our society. The plain unconvincingness of such a view makes it a futile refuge. We must look for deeper sources for the trouble, in particular for those sources which lie, alarmingly enough, in our own natural motivation. The mere fact that they do lie there, rather than elsewhere, is no reason to be fatalistic about them. We need to study them because they clearly are important, because they are very difficult to understand, and because lately they have been neglected.

In studying them, we need to avoid dismissing bad motives sceptically as something which we simply do not understand. There is indeed a danger of allowing understanding to slide into acceptance. But failure to understand carries the still worse danger of making effective action impossible. Very often—as when an opponent is acting badly out of fear, and an understanding of this makes it possible to stop frightening him—the actual evil is much less than we suppose, and cherishing a mystery about it simply allows us to project our own unjustified hostility. The part which this kind of gratuitous scepticism plays in political attitudes—for instance in the cold war—seems extremely potent and badly needs to be noticed. The whole idea of a 'cold war' seems indeed to be necessarily a corrupting one, since it extends the general excuse for hostility, conveyed by the notion of emergency in wartime, to situations where no war exists. But more generally, the notion that we 'cannot understand' bad conduct is a trap, because it leads us to treat evil unrealistically, as something entirely alien, and so to misunderstand it and to overlook our own contribution to it. Certainly we have to arm ourselves against letting understanding slide into acceptance. But having done that, we need to treat questions about bad motives like any other factual questions, as soluble until they have been proved otherwise.

This policy means that we should commit ourselves to being very persistent in looking for a positive point for bad actions—

very unwilling to suppose, until we are driven to it, that any act is wholly bad, that is, pointless. This persistence does not express any rosy optimism. It is simply a requirement arising from the way understanding works in this kind of case. To grasp a motive just is to come to know what good it aims at. Knowing this is of course quite compatible with seeing how the pursuit of this particular good, in isolation from others which should have corrected it, constitutes in a given case an appalling evil. Aristotle seems to be right in remarking that the existence of 'bad pleasures' cannot prove pleasure itself to be bad. Even in the worst cases, such as cruelty, what is bad is not the fact of pleasure itself. It is something wider—the taking of pleasure in such situations.[16]

So far in the argument, the need to look for a positive point flows from the nature of mutual understanding among conscious subjects. Behind this, however, lies the wider, objective, evolutionary context. Here, understanding an activity or a motive is seeing what advantages it brings which might be strong enough to affect survival, and so to implant hereditary tendencies. From this angle, too, what is innate may be expected to make some sense, and we have a right to resist explanations which label any motive as senseless, or directed merely to death or destruction. Certainly this right must not be overstretched. We must avoid the Panglossian confidence with which some evolutionists today declare everything to have a function. Some features of organisms really are passengers. Selection is nothing like sharp enough to produce a slick machine. Still, the assumption that major features do in general have functions works reasonably well much of the time, and the assumption that they do not, or that they work for death, makes thought impossible. Motives are major features of animals as much as organs are, and we can look for functions for them with the same degree of confidence. The human appendix has no function now, but that does not mean that it got there by mistake, nor that it is a device for producing sudden death. By the careful use of well-informed comparisons we can do better than that for the appendix, and there is no reason why we should not do as much for human aggression and callousness too.

In general, then, we do right to look for a positive purpose behind any human motivation, however peculiar, because finding one is the only possible way of understanding it. We may not get one, but if not there will be no substitute. Both the subjective and the evolutionary modes of interpretation call for this method. And this is just why the notion of evil as negative is a helpful one. By looking for the residual positive point in bad motives, it shows them as still intelligible on the same general principles as good ones—marked somewhere on the same map as it were—unlike dualistic accounts such as Freud's and the Manichee one, which treat them as radically unrelated. In this way the typical analysis of a bad motive will show its badness— without in any way minimizing it—as depending essentially on what it lacks. Thus Bishop Butler, discussing what constitutes the real horror of selfishness, remarks that there is not 'any reason to wish self-love were weaker in the generality of the world than it is. . . . The thing to be lamented is, not that men have so great regard to their own good or interest in the present world, for they have not enough; but that they have so little to the good of others' (italics mine).[17] In the same way possessiveness and ambition are in themselves harmless, even sometimes necessary—but they become pernicious where they are not balanced by respect and affection. And aggression itself—the mere desire to attack and drive off—is neither bad nor good till we know whom it is directed against and why. Each of these motives has its own characteristic point, which gives it a kind of internal justification and makes it intelligible. In animals, so far as they are absorbed in their current mood, this is all that matters. For human beings, however, intelligence raises the much bigger question of relating these moods to the whole context and to other background possibilities. Awkward questions about other motives which might have balanced the current ones can arise, and do not easily go away. This is where things really get intolerably puzzling.

What we most need here is, I think, to distinguish between the two stages of motivation—the many more or less specific natural motives which are, so to speak, our raw material, and the reflective, unifying determinations of the will which attempts to oversee and direct them. As far as the specific motives go, certain sources of evil are clearly provided by their unevenness, rather than by any one of them which could be named as the demon. We find it much easier to care about some things than others, and to control some motives than others. Some issues obsess us; others fail to interest as we know they ought to. Cultures work hard to smooth over this unevenness, but all cultures leave staggering gaps, observable to outsiders and often to their own members too. What we most need here may well be to recognize that the problem is a real one—to believe in the extraordinary fitfulness of our own natural concern, rather than accepting the assurance which cultures tend to offer that everything is really quite all right. Since sheer incredulity about this is often an important part of our difficulty, we may find it helpful to notice how often evolution does produce this kind of unevenness elsewhere. The study of plants and animals presents us continually with dramatic contrasts between beautiful pieces of adaptation and apparent crude failures. When we think about these contrasts—as we cannot help doing—on the pattern of purposive human activity, we seem to be seeing alternatively works of superb craftsmanship and pieces of sheer incompetence and neglect. (Presumably the genetic material for making some kinds of change was present; that for making others simply was not.) The situation of the swallows rearing their autumn broods is thoroughly typical. Our own constitution certainly contains gaps and anomalies of this kind. Intelligence, which makes them visible to us, also imposes the alarming demand that we should somehow resolve them. We have to try and meet that demand. In stressing that some of the difficulties are real ones, not created by culture, I am of course not suggesting that we therefore have to resign ourselves to putting up with them fatalistically, but that we shall need to grasp their seriousness if we are to meet their challenge effectively. They are not our doom, but they are our real problem.

6 THE PLACE OF DUALISM

In discussing these natural motives, the temptation to go dualist—to paint everything as black or white, good or evil—is not yet very strong. There are obviously many colours. Most motives are clearly versatile and capable of playing many parts in life. Most are plainly necessary in one form or another. The ones most likely to be seen as purely menacing and gratuitous are probably aggression and the wish for dominance. In both cases this impression seems to be mistaken. About aggression the mistake is usually the one of confusing it—as Freud did—with a full-scale death-wish. A little thought will show that this must be wrong, because aggression is found in many quite simple animals, while—as has often been pointed out—the concept of death is not really available to any creature other than man. To want somebody really dead is to want them abolished permanently. But the notion of permanence requires a very sophisticated sense of the past and future. By contrast, most aggression—including human aggression—is perfectly well satisfied with getting rid of an opponent. This may mean chasing them out of sight, but often calls only for something much milder, such as making them leave one alone or relinquish some advantage or accept a subordinate position. Of course it is true that where aggression is exceptionally strong, and is returned, death can be the only way of getting rid of them. But that does not show that, even in these extreme cases, the significance of death has been fully grasped, even in humans. With children especially, though they are supposed to have grasped the idea, it is often not clear that 'wishing somebody dead' means more than wanting them out of the way. And there are of course cases where getting someone else out of the way may really be a necessary condition of one's own independent existence or that of those around one, which is a genuine good. Things are rather similar about dominance, which is a necessary feature of many protective relations, and centrally of that between parent and child. Of course with both these motives corruption is easy and can be disastrous. But that is true of many other motives too, including love. In all of them, corruption seems to depend on a special relation between a whole set of motives, rather than on the presence of one essentially pernicious one. These bad relations can occur to some extent in animals, but their full development depends on the richer complexities of human motivation, and especially on our greater conscious control, making much greater corruption possible. Along with the capacity for the virtues, we have gained impressive capacities for vice.

When we turn to this second region—to the will—Freudian dualism is likely to seem much more appropriate. It is true that here we are apparently almost forced to operate with the notion of a binary choice—up or down, better or worse—and that this choice does have some connexion with the antithesis of life and death. This is how it strikes even the most other-worldly of the sages. The Buddha forbids killing. 'I am come that they might have life, and that they might have it more abundantly,' says Jesus.[18] Mephistopheles for his part answers, 'I am the spirit that always says No', and adds, in case we are left in any doubt:

> And rightly too; for all that comes to birth
> Is fit for overthrow as nothing worth;
> Wherefore the world were better sterilized . . .[19]

And though morality must not simplify our dramas—though indeed it must avoid doing this at all cost—it always needs this vertical dimension. In spite of the many complex cases, the real conflicts of value, it demands that we face in the end the choice between these two directions. Great immoralists like Nietzsche are no exception to this. Their bitter anger reveals them as fighters. Their objection is to fighting the wrong battles, and indeed to apathy. They are not going to tell us that the whole drama is unnecessary. Neither are great champions of liberty and toleration like Mill. They value liberty and tolerance as paths to greater fullness of life, not as ways of evading the choice. Neither are great psychologists like Freud. They too point out where past moralists have mistrusted choice, and in particular where self-deception has allowed people to claim that they were moving upward when they were merely gyrating, locked in an inner conflict. But the very force of their objection to this is itself a commitment to fullness of life, and once they grasp the social context as well as the inner one, they are forced—as Freud eventually found—to see the function of ordinary morality, as an essential one with its whole range of ideals, as well as the medical ideals of health and normality. None of these modern ways of thinking gives any support for the notion so naively expressed by the journalists we noticed in Chapter 1—that the whole vertical dimension has vanished, and the idea of sin is out of date. For the reasons Darwin gave, it is probably impossible for human life to go on at all without that dimension, at least without losing everything that makes it human. The impression that it could do so could only arise briefly in a period of extraordinary security and privilege, and then only in response to certain passing quirks of intellectual fashion.

Morality, then, is our way of dealing with the up-and-down dimension which everybody who thinks seriously about human life must see as our central problem. What makes this dealing so hard, however, is the constant ambivalence, the way in which nearly every feature of human life can be described and thought of either more or less favourably. The relation of any particular possibility to the up-down dimension is never simply given; it may always be made to look different by changing the background. Because all our motivation is riddled with this ambivalence, we are always liable to waste our efforts, or even do damage. This is what gets morality a bad name. It is one main function of cultures to accumulate insights on this matter, to express them in clear ways as far as possible, and so to maintain a rich treasury of past thought and experience which will save us the trouble of continually starting again from scratch. In this work, as we have mentioned, an enormously important part is played by what we call the arts, especially (because words are more informative than pictures or music) by great works of literature. Any notion of 'art' which plays down this function betrays its subject matter disastrously. From the earliest myths to the most recent novel, all writing (including comic writing) that is not fundamentally cheap and frivolous is meant to throw light on the difficulties of the human situation, and if, in tribute to arbitrary theories of aesthetics, we refuse to use that light, we sign up for death and darkness. Where the refusal extends to teaching students not to use it, the responsibility is particularly grave.

Besides the arts, however, many theoretical studies also play their part in making morality possible, in saving it from the blindness and narrowness which have so often limited its use. They make the facts intelligible to us; they help us to interpret the world in which we must move. This is plainly true of history, of anthropology and the other social sciences. But most of all it is true of psychology, which can have a central function. I have argued throughout this book for greater attention to the psychology of motive, and shall say no more on the matter now. Instead, I shall end by simply considering an example of the kind of work which continually needs doing here, and which is especially vital in our rapidly changing world—namely, the investigation of new dangers, new and unsuspected psychological traps which some recent shift in our lives is setting for us. It is typical of human morality that we are always fighting the last war—concentrating our attention on dangers which are no longer pressing, and overlooking those which lie in front of our feet.

The example I would like to mention—obviously just as a pointer for investigation, not as a completed case-history—is Erich Fromm's discussion of modern machine-symbolism in *The Anatomy of Human Destructiveness*.[20] Officially, our attitude to machines is a prosaic and practical one. They are supposed to exist only as means to our ends. Plainly, however, they often get a strong grip on our imagination and are treated as ends in themselves. How does this work? What do they stand for? Fromm traces the literature which has celebrated machines, showing how steadily it leans to the glorification of death. Thus, in that potent and venerated source of the Modern Movement, the First Futurist Manifesto of 1909, Marinetti declared:

1. We intend to sing the love of danger, the habit of energy and fearlessness. . . .

4. We say that the world's magnificence has been enriched by a new beauty, the beauty of speed. A racing car whose hood is adorned with great pipes, like serpents of explosive breath—a roaring car that seems to ride on grapeshot—is more beautiful than the 'Victory of Samothrace'. . . .

7. Except in struggle, there is no more beauty. No work without an aggressive character can be a masterpiece. Poetry must be conceived as a violent attack on unknown forces, to reduce and postrate them before man. . . .

9. We will glorify war—the world's only hygiene—militarism, patriotism, the destructive gesture of freedom-bringers, beautiful ideas worth dying for, and scorn for women.

10. We will destroy the museums, libraries, academies of every kind, will fight moralism, feminism, every opportunistic or utilitarian cowardice.

In his Second Futurist Manifesto (1916) a still more remarkable religious tone becomes evident:

If prayer means communication with the divinity, running at high speed is a prayer. Holiness of wheels and rails. One must kneel on the tracks to pray to the divine velocity. One must kneel before the whirling speed of a gyroscope compass; 20,000 revolutions per minute, the highest mechanical speed reached by man.

The intoxication of great speeds in cars is nothing but the joy of feeling oneself fused with the only divinity. Sportsmen are the first catechumens of this religion. Forthcoming destruction of houses and cities, to make way for great meeting-places for cars and planes.[21]

There is not much doubt about the importance of death here. The references to women are specially striking, because they seem like a sudden digression from the main theme of the manifesto, and they chime so closely with the views of Gnostics and Manichees on this subject. Apart from feminism, everything which the Futurists opposed was traditional. In principle they welcomed every new movement. If they drew the line at this one, it has surely to be because women stand for life.

This is not, of course, the only reason why Marinetti's manifesto sounds distinctly embarrassing today. He lets many other cats out of bags. He is alarmingly open, naive and gushing about attitudes on which our civilization habitually acts, but which it is now a good deal more cautious about expressing. Since the Futurists' day, we have behaved very much as he advised us to, but we do not like to give such simple reasons for it. We prefer to show that all our technology is useful, is designed soberly for sane and defensible ends, not just for pathological intoxication produced by rapid travel. No doubt a great deal of it is. But what about the rest? Fromm is uncompromising—'Necrophilia, the attraction to what is dead, decaying, lifeless and purely mechanical, is increasing throughout cybernetic industrial society.'[22] He thinks the obsession with machines and the material goods they produce central, but it does not stand alone. 'The call for "law and order" (rather than for life and structure) and for stricter punishment of criminals, as well as the obsession with death and violence among some "revolutionaries" are only further instances of the powerful attraction of necrophilia in the contemporary world.'[23] He sees destructiveness not as a basic drive, but as 'one of the possible answers to psychic needs which are rooted in the existence of man.'[24] He traces various paths by which individuals can come to see their salvation in it. I cannot attempt to do justice to his discussion here. But among these paths, the direct, unthinking veneration of technology for its own sake still seems to need particular emphasis, because it still is not sufficiently conscious and suspected. Norman O. Brown, in his forceful and impressive book *Life Against Death; The Psycho-Analytical Meaning of History*, had earlier given an alarming, and often convincing, account of much of this symbolism in more directly traditional Freudian terms. The problem which he and Fromm share—the problem of *why* machines exercise such fascination—is a real one, and those who want altogether to reject Freudian and Jungian explanations have a responsibility to produce something better. As it is, neither of these books has had half the attention it deserves, because of the disastrous barrier which for a long time divided the study of personal motives from that of politically significant behaviour. Social scientists did their best to keep psycho-analysis in a kind of intellectual purdah, resorting to it only in private life, while analysts often failed to take public concerns sufficiently seriously, and exposed themselves by reductive over-confidence in alluding to them. There is no longer any excuse for this tribalism, which indeed is becoming less fashionable.

The kind of analysis of evil suggested in this book need not tread on any departmental toes, any more than it need involve fatalism. The inevitability of conflict does not imply the impossibility of solution; it merely means hard work. But we need to locate the conflict somewhat differently from where tradition has put it. St Paul said: 'The flesh lusteth against the spirit and the spirit against the flesh, so that ye cannot do the things that ye would.'[25] This declaration—or a simple interpretation of it—has led certain hopeful humanists to think that if we could just get rid of the spirit—which they identified with a kind of moral pretentiousness—conflicts would cease. Darwin, however, was surely right to dissent. As he argued, all the indications are that sharp conflict is already present within the flesh, calling for positive reconciling efforts at all levels if it is not to result in general destruction. We resort to the spirit—in all the forms in which it presents itself—because without it we could not deal with our conflicts at all. From those conflicts arises the consciousness of diverging possibilities which is our freedom. We need to understand them if we are to use it.

SUMMARY

Freud's death-wish idea has its pros and cons. Pro. It does something to correct the common, narrow idea of motives as direct, simple paths to self-interest. Freud's earlier view of sex as warring with self-preservation had already loosened this somewhat. The death-wish proposal allows further progress towards acknowledging the variety of natural motives and their inevitable tendency to conflict. Con. However, the idea of a direct desire for death is too crude and implausible a form for this insight. Destruction, both for oneself and others, can indeed become an aim, even a dominant aim, but only through perversion, recombination and narrowing of natural desires. The raw materials for this process are mainly our natural, but naturally passing, hostilities towards others. Their perversion, which is in principle avoidable, consists in retaining and cherishing them as obsessions, which become partially autonomous. These feed on the rest of the character, which atrophies, so that the individual disintegrates, though his detached desires retain their force. Self-destruction is thus a secondary, but seemingly inevitable, consequence of indulged resentment. Plato was therefore not being silly when he said that it is indeed in the end *even* worse to commit great injustice than to suffer it. The impression that this is a pious invention results from failing to attend properly to this horn of the dilemma. The Fall of Man appears to consist in choosing to follow this path.

To see how this possibility arises, some evolutionary considerations will be helpful. From this angle, the death-wish is not plausible. It does make sense to suppose that our species can have developed some power of *accepting* death, and indeed of aging without resentment. (In any advanced social species, wise and experienced members can be of great value to a group and can help its survival. Since their wisdom preserves their relatives, selection is possible even for qualities which they develop late in life. Tendencies making for realistic resignation could therefore well be favoured.) But a direct desire for death seems to be something for which selection is impossible.

So obvious is this that many people think of evolution simply as an egoist's rat-race, which can only allow self-serving qualities to develop—a view which Freud himself originally took of non-sexual instincts. This is wrong, because inherited traits are not passed on through individual survival, but through the survival of relatives. Evolution is not a single-purpose device for self-preservation nor for anything else. On the contrary, it seems to be a process which makes it inevitable that our natural desires must conflict. As Darwin pointed out, social instincts do not evolve to a neat blueprint ensuring their convergence, but only in a rough, approximate balance. When increasing intelligence brings to consciousness conflicts which in other animals seem to pass unnoticed, human beings are forced, on pain of disintegration, to form some kind of policies for reconciling their contrary impulses. This makes some kind of morality necessary, and the nature of the contending motives lays limits on what kind it can be.

Thus, when moral questions puzzle us, we need to grasp both the original motives involved and the kind of perversion to which they are liable. The same proceeding is necessary when we want to understand bad conduct. For particular cases, this means spotting particular motives. For humanity as a whole, it means looking for general tendencies, and for historical and evolutionary considerations which make them intelligible. In both kinds of case, we have to look for the characteristic *advantage* involved—for the personal or evolutionary pay-off. If we cannot find that positive pay-off, we are left with the radical incomprehension of evil which belongs to dualist views (Freud and the Manichees). We shall find bad conduct simply incredible. Finding the pay-off does not, however, commit us to thinking it an adequate motive. Where a personality has begun to disintegrate, motives will no longer need to be adequate, since adequacy is a notion adapted to judgment by a complete, integrated personality. They need only be obsessive or addictive. And at this point we characteristically think that the badness of a bad motive does centre on what it lacks, e.g. selfishness is not centrally excessive self-love, but indifference to others (Butler).

Perhaps the hardest point for us to grasp in this analysis is the real unevenness and conflict of our natural motives. Culture, in striving to correct these discrepancies, tends also to obscure them. Here evolutionary considerations are helpful, since they show many similar discrepancies elsewhere between systems which are individually well-formed. Life is an unpredictable mixture of the amazingly well-adapted and the crude.

What, now, of the *value* of dualistic thought? This becomes clear when we turn from our raw material—the natural motives—to deliberate policies and the will which forms them. In order to choose, we do need a map with an up-and-down dimension, oriented to light and darkness, backward and forward, life and death. However complex all else may be on this map, it still has to show this duality for all of us, including immoralists. It is, however, very hard to relate the confusions of life realistically to this up/down dimension. A good understanding of the psychology of motives is a great help here. This understanding needs constant adaptation to changes in the world, if we are to conquer our habit of always fighting the last war rather than the present one—as in the current way of treating Victorian conventionality and cosiness as still the prime enemy.

An example of the kind of thing needed is Erich Fromm's investigation of the significance of machine-symbolism in contemporary life. He suggests that what is officially just a practical interest in useful devices is really an obsessive glorification of death. Objects—things—are systematically exalted over people, sterile, gleaming metal over vulnerable flesh, means over ends, thought over feeling, and calculative, impersonal thought over the imagination. He diagnoses obsessive necrophilia. It is quite wrong for social scientists to dismiss such enquiries as irrelevant to the social scene because they concern individuals. Personal and social life are intertwined; no quarantine can divide the disciplines which study them.

NOTES

1 THE PROBLEM OF NATURAL EVIL

1 *The Anatomy of Human Destructiveness* by Erich Fromm (Jonathan Cape, London, 1974), p.432. Italics mine.

2 *Purity and Danger: An Analysis of the Concepts of Pollution and Taboo* by Mary Douglas (Routledge & Kegan Paul, London, 1966), p.36.

3 I have argued this case at length in my book *Beast and Man* (Harvester Press, Sussex, 1979; Methuen, London, 1980) and shall try to avoid repeating much of it here.

4 Thus for instance C. B. Moss: 'The Church, following St Paul's teaching, has always maintained that everybody is born with a tendency to sin, a weakness of the will which, if not checked, will result in sin. This weakness was called by the Latin Fathers "original sin" (*originale peccatum*); it is not a good name, because, strictly speaking, original sin is not sin at all, but a weakness leading to sin, just as a weak chest is not consumption' (*The Christian Faith* SPCK, London, 1943), pp.149–50.

5 See for instance his *Modern Man in Search of a Soul* (Kegan Paul, Trench, Trubner, London, 1945, translated Dell and Baynes), p.46–8 and 234, and *Answer to Job* (Routledge & Kegan Paul, London, 1954, translated R. F. C. Hull), p.133–5 and 154.

6 Aristotle's notion that the vices are essentially just excesses or defects of the tendencies which, at a right level, produce the virtues is a typical expression of this approach. No doubt it is too schematic, but it can be very useful as a starting-point for bringing this problem in focus. See the *Nicomachean Ethics*, Book II.

7 Preface to the *Sermons*, section 40 (p.24 of the edition of *Fifteen Sermons* published by G. Bell, London, 1969).

8 *Faust*, part 1, scene 2, translated by Philip Wayne (Penguin, Harmondsworth, 1949), p.73.

2 INTELLIGIBILITY AND IMMORALISM

1 Translated by Walter Kaufmann (Vintage Books, New York, 1969).

2 See a very interesting discussion by C. G. Jung in 'Psycho-Analysis and the Cure of Souls', *Collected Works*, vol.11 (Routledge & Kegan Paul, London, 1958).

3 For an interesting account of these views, see Richard Cavendish, *The Powers of Evil in Western Religion, Magic and Folk Belief* (Routledge & Kegan Paul, London, 1975), pp.220–2.

4 So did Plotinus, in an impressive essay 'Against the Gnostics', (*Enneads*, book II, chapter 9). Though his Neo-Platonism agreed with them in advising withdrawal from practical life ('flee alone to the Alone'), it sharply rejected the idea that the world was alien or impenetrable to reason.

5 His very interesting vicissitudes may be traced in Cavendish, *The Powers of Evil*, chapter 8.

6 Plato, great rationalist though he was, retained at all stages of his thought a dualistic element which limited his confidence in the intelligibility of the world. Even in the *Timaeus*, which presents the physical world as much less alien and chaotic than the *Phaedo*, he shows matter as pervaded by the Wandering Cause (*Timaeus*, 48 and 69), an element foreign to thought, which renders exact physical science impossible and is also the source of evil. This idea is of course related to his deep conviction that the human soul was radically divided, having an irrational element, akin to matter, which is the source of all its troubles. (See *Republic*, book IV, 435 and book IX, 588, also *Phaedrus*, 245–50.) It was Aristotle who, by getting rid of the Wandering Cause, made exact physical science again a serious possibility.

7 Well traced by Brian Easlea in *Witch-Hunting, Magic and the New Philosophy* (Harvester Press, Sussex, 1980), p.33–4.

8 See an interesting discussion of Luther's views in Norman O. Brown, *Life against Death; The Psycho-Analytical Meaning of History* (Wesleyan University Press, Connecticut, 1970), p.211. Brown quotes from Luther, 'We are servants in a hostelry, where Satan is the householder, the

world his wife, and our affections his children.' We shall come back to this topic in Chapter 7.

9 Reported by Plato (*Protagoras*, 352a) and also by Xenophon (*Memorabilia of Socrates*, book III, chapter 9).

10 David Hume, *Treatise of Human Nature* (1739), book II, part III, section 3.

11 *Enquiry Concerning Human Understanding* (1951), sections V–VIII.

12 The great advantages of his undogmatic, non-Procrustean conceptual scheme are well set out by Anthony Stevens in *Archetype; A Natural History of the Self* (Routledge & Kegan Paul, London, 1982). Stevens brings out particularly well what good evolutionary sense Jung makes—an advantage not shared by Freud.

13 *Beyond Good and Evil* (translated by Marianne Cowan, Gateway Edition, Chicago, 1955), section 36.

14 See *Beyond the Pleasure Principle*, p.51, in vol.XVIII of Freud's *Complete Works* (Hogarth Press, London 1951). I have discussed the various reductive principles involved here in my *Heart and Mind; The Varieties of Moral Experience* (Harvester Press, Sussex, 1981), pp.158–66. See also the last three chapters of the present book.

15 See Thrasymachus in Plato's *Republic*, book 1, and Glaucon and Adeimantus at the beginning of book 2. More impressive still is Callicles in the Gorgias (481–522) who is a striking precursor of Nietzsche. Plato clearly took the position very seriously, though he thought it could be answered.

16 See his thought-provoking paper. Peter Strawson, 'Social Morality and Individual Ideal' in *Freedom and Resentment and Other Essays* (Methuen, London, 1974), p.44.

17 Ibid., pp.28–9.

18 Ibid.

19 I have given my own view on the plurality of human needs—which I think extremely important—and its relation to personal identity in *Beast and Man*, pp.189–94 and throughout chapter 11. It will also be a persistent theme in the present book.

20 Originally an article in *Proceedings of the Aristotelian Society*, supplementary volume L (1976), pp.115–35, reprinted in his collection: Bernard Williams, *Moral Luck* (Cambridge University Press, 1981). My comments refer to this version.

21 Ibid., p.37. Though Williams does not treat this as an argument for Gauguin himself to use, he seems quite satisfied with this wording of it for the spectator, both here and on p.23 where it first occurs.

22 In my article 'Is "Moral" a Dirty Word?' in *Heart and Mind*, reprinted from *Philosophy*, vol.47, no.181, July 1972.

23 Williams, *Moral Luck*, p.22. Later, on p.38, where he points out that the argument is only a spectator's one, he seems to return to a wider sense of moral, saying that the spectator must consider, not a casual Gauguin, but one who 'shares the same world of moral concerns. The risk these agents run is a risk within morality, a risk which amoral versions of these agents would not run at all.' Oscillation in the scope of 'morality' between these senses seems to play a considerable part in generating his paradoxes, including that of 'moral luck.'

The rather vague sketch of 'Kantian' views given on this page makes things harder. We need a specific modern opponent. We do not get one on p.24 either. Williams deals there only with 'the narrower question whether there could be a prior justification for Gauguin's choice in terms of moral rules,' and concludes that there could not, because his own suggested formulations for such rules all look fatuous—at least in the isolation where he presents them. Since rules normally only make sense as part of a system, this is not surprising. He adds that 'Utilitarian formulations' will be no better, because they must leave out a great deal of what could count as justification for a painter. This, however, results from treating 'Utilitarianism' as a rootless abstraction, isolated from the background of subsidiary concepts which any such sweeping theory must grow out of and presuppose. As Mill reasonably remarked, 'there is no difficulty in proving any ethical system whatever to work ill, if we suppose universal idiocy to be conjoined with it' (*Utilitarianism*, Everyman, London, 1936, p.22). Mill himself had plenty to say, notably in the *Liberty*, on the reasons why art is valuable. G.E. Moore in chapter 6 of *Principia Ethica* was one of many taking the matter further. It seems strange to post a notice of bankruptcy on this, one of the most fertile, if confused, areas of modern thought about values.

24 J. P. Sartre, *Existentialism and Humanism* (trans. Mairet, Eyre Methuen, London, 1948), p.35.

25 Williams produces some good arguments against over-emphasizing one's continuity through time, and also against an unrealistic, Rawlsian attempt at temporal impartiality. But he does not give—what his full case surely calls for—a sufficient objection to *all* attempts at such continuity and integration. We shall come back to this crucial point in Chapter 6. I return to Williams's discussion in the next chapter, though there is much in it (and in Strawson's) to which I cannot do any

sort of justice here. Their emphasis can be extremely valuable; I am only concerned here to point out that it must not stand alone.

26 In Isaiah Berlin, *Against the Current: Essays in the History of Ideas* (Hogarth Press, London, 1979). The article is called 'The Originality of Machiavelli' and was previously published in Myron P. Gilmore (ed.), *Studies on Machiavelli* (Samsoni, Florence, 1972).

27 *Ecce Homo*, translated and edited by Walter Kaufmann with *On the Genealogy of Morals* (Vintage Books, New York, 1969), pp.328 and 334.

28 Ibid., chapter on *Thus Spake Zarathustra*, section 6, p.306.

29 Bishop Butler, Sermon V (in his *Fifteen Sermons*) 'Upon Compassion' section II—'The Stoics ... appear to have had better success in eradicating the affections of tenderness and compassion, than they had with the passions of envy, pride and resentment; these latter, at best, were but concealed, and that imperfectly too.' I have discussed this point in my *Beast and Man* (Harvester Press, Sussex, 1978) p.191.

30 *Ecce Homo*, chapter on *The Birth of Tragedy*, section 3, Kaufmann (ed.), p.273.

31 Notably in 'Ethical Consistency' and 'Consistency and Realism,' both in *Problems of the Self and Other Essays* (Cambridge University Press, 1973) and in 'Conflicts of Values' also in *Moral Luck*. The comparison with theoretical knowledge is mentioned in *Moral Luck*, p.39, note, with a useful reference to Williams's book *Descartes, The Project of Pure Enquiry* (Penguin, Harmondsworth, 1978), p.37 *et seq.*

32 In his article 'On Forgetting the Difference Between Right and Wrong' in *Essays in Moral Philosophy*, ed. A. I. Melden (Seattle, 1958).

33 See Wittgenstein, *Philosophical Investigations*, p.293.

34 In Jenny Teichman, 'Conflicts of Obligation' (forthcoming).

35 A crucial point made by Philippa Foot in several seminal articles, notably in 'Moral Beliefs,' *Proceedings of the Aristotelian Society*, vol.59 (1958–9), pp.83–104, reprinted in her collection *Virtues and Vices and other Essays in Moral Philosophy* (Blackwell, Oxford, 1978) and also in *Theories of Ethics*, ed. P. Foot (Oxford University Press, 1967).

36 What he did mean varied greatly from time to time (as with all his terms) but the account given in *On the Genealogy of Morals*, preface, section 6, is typical in being thoroughly one-sided.

There is no serious attempt to question *all* values simultaneously— nor does it seem likely that there could be. The new priority system is assumed before the questioning ever starts.

37 *Beyond Good and Evil*, sections 260–76 (Gateway edn, p.202).

38 *Thus Spake Zarathustra*, part two, section on 'Of Self-Overcoming' (trans. R. J. Hollingdale, Penguin, Harmondsworth, 1961).

39 This is a guiding idea in Jung's *Answer to Job* (trans. R. F. C. Hull, Routledge & Kegan Paul, London, 1954).

40 A point strongly put by Nietzsche in the Madman's Speech in *The Gay Science*, as following from the death of God.

41 An issue sensibly discussed by I. Eibl-Eibesfeldt in *Love and Hate: On the Natural History of Basic Behaviour Patterns* (trans. Geoffrey Strachan, Methuen, London, 1971), pp.101–2.

42 I have dealt with it directly in 'On Trying Out One's New Sword' in *Heart and Mind*.

3 THE ELUSIVENESS OF RESPONSIBILITY

1 Hannah Arendt, *Eichmann in Jerusalem*, rev. ed. (Penguin, Harmondsworth, 1963), p.296.

2 That they cannot be made, morality being essentially a private matter, is a view which has some influence today, having been clearly expressed by Reinhold Niebuhr in his book *Moral Man and Immoral Society* (Charles Scribner's Sons, New York, 1948). The problems he raised are real ones, but this simple solution to them has grave drawbacks. It is one of a number of ways of limiting the term *morality* to narrow spheres, which seem bound to bring it into contempt. See 'Is "Moral" a Dirty Word?' in my *Heart and Mind*.

3 We would not wish never to have any opinion, good or bad, formed about us,—so 'judge not that ye be not judged' cannot forbid the forming of such opinions. The tag 'to understand all is to forgive all' cannot do so either, since forgiveness is in place only for acknowledged offences. See 'On Trying Out One's New Sword' in my *Heart and Mind*.

4 As Strawson pointed out in his admirable paper 'Freedom and Resentment' in the volume with that name.

5 *Eichmann in Jerusalem*, p.298.

6 It is admirably discussed by John Benson in an article called 'Who is the Autonomous Man?' in *Philosophy*, January (1983), vol.58, no.223.

7 I cannot do much to correct this here. Kant wrote the whole *Critique of Practical Reason* to explore the connexion between morality and happiness, and the *Critique of Judgment* to explore that between feeling, purpose and thought. He also wrote a short preliminary book to make certain distinctions needed for this work. Significantly, he called it the *Groundwork to the Metaphysic of Morals*, not suggesting that it was his

last word on the matter. (Its title in Paton's translation, *The Moral Law*, obscures this.) British philosophers, who in many other cases have now relaxed their rule of reading only one book by each philosopher, sternly adhere to it in Kant's case, and treat a few quotations from the rather dramatic opening sections of the *Groundwork* as his last words on both individuality and freedom. Both Williams and Nagel take as their chief opponent the resulting shadowy figure, who is supposed to be Kant, but to whom they amazingly attribute 'a very simple image of rationality' (Williams, *Moral Luck*, p.22). Kant himself spent most of his life emphasizing and studying the complexities of this concept. Unless one means to deploy his view as a whole, it is surely better to deal directly with contemporary autonomy-worship, which is our real headache today. (For Kant on free-will, see Chapter 5, note 4.)

8 Sartre, *Existentialism and Humanism*, p.28.

9 Nagel's article (also called 'Moral Luck') was originally a reply to Williams's and appeared along with it in the *Proceedings of the Aristotelian Society*, supplementary vol. L (1976), pp.115–35. It is reprinted in his collection *Mortal Questions* (Cambridge University Press, 1979) and I shall refer here to this version.

10 *Mortal Questions*, p.35.

11 Ibid., p.27.

12 p.22. This language is considerably stronger than that which he uses at the end of the article ('scepticism about the freedom of morality from luck cannot leave the concept of morality where it was' it will become 'less important' (p.39)). But both remain so vague that there is real difficulty in seeing how the change is meant to affect our lives. The change proposed in our attitude to the blaming (and presumably praising) of others is, up to a point, clear enough; we are meant to become far less confident about it. But—unless one *means* by morality merely a tendency to blame, or, as a Shaw character put it, 'morality consists in suspecting other people of not being legally married',—this is only a tiny segment of the work our notion of morality does in our lives. Are we also meant to become less confident about trusting our judgment in our own decisions, or perhaps *more* confident, if there are no right answers and the whole thing is a gamble anyway? And how are we to build up any principles at all if—as seems to be suggested—our judgment of other people's cases is not just often over-confident, but an altogether impossible enterprise?

If the point of the sceptical argument was to avoid the paradoxes arising round traditional moral judgment, something will surely have to be done to sort out its own practical consequences in a paradox-free manner.

13 Barbara Wootton, *Social Science and Social Pathology* (Allen & Unwin, London, 1959) p.251. Her argument, though much less subtle, seems to be essentially the same as Williams's—if an argument cannot handle every kind of case, it was a bad argument, and cannot be used anywhere. This is a quick way to empty the tool-kit in any department of thought. And did anyone ever see reason to suppose that morality was likely to be a specially simple area—one where a single way of thinking would always do the whole job? It is an enormous merit in Williams's discussion that he does justice to the complexity of life. But this makes it hard for him to draw any such simple, sweeping sceptical conclusions.

14 Notably, of course, in affectation of the Nietzschean virtues—courage and honesty.

15 *Nicomachean Ethics*, book VII.

16 Quoted by Konrad Heiden, *Der Fuehrer: Hitler's Rise to Power* (trans. Ralph Mannheim, Gollancz, London, 1944), p.30.

17 *Nicomachean Ethics*, book VII, chapter 8. Plato makes the same point, *Republic*, book III, 409.

18 *Eichmann in Jerusalem*, p.175.

19 A matter checked by R. J. Hollingdale and reported in his biography *Nietzsche* (Routledge & Kegan Paul, London, 1973), p.201.

20 *Eichmann in Jerusalem*, pp.287, 289.

21 Ibid.

22 *Das Sogenannte Böse* (trans. by Marjorie Latzke, Methuen, London, 1966).

4 UNDERSTANDING AGGRESSION

1 I have discussed this point more fully in a paper on 'The Notion of Instinct' in *Heart and Mind*, and throughout my book *Beast and Man*. A classic statement of it may be found in Theodosius Dobzhansky's book *Mankind Evolving: The Evolution of the Human Species* (Yale University Press, New Haven, 1962). That admirably humane and balanced book ought to have stopped the debate. The fact that it did not testifies to the incredible inertia of conflict.

2 See for instance John Harris's chapter called 'A Defence of non-"Violent" Violence' in his *Violence and Responsibility* (Routledge & Kegan Paul, London, 1980).

3 See Niko Tinbergen, *The Study of Instinct* (Oxford University Press, 1951; new introduction 1969), chapter V, 'An Attempt at a Synthesis.'

4 Extremely calm, sensible and serious discussions of the vexed question of human aggression can be found in I. Eibl-Eibesfeldt's two books, *Love and Hate* (Methuen, London, 1971) and *The Biology of Peace and War: Men, Animals and Aggression* (trans. Eric Mosbacher, Viking, New York, 1979). Eibl-Eibesfeldt has gone to great trouble to work out Lorenz's basic insights without making the moves which caused Lorenz's book *On Aggression* to infuriate some social scientists. Both he and another anthropologist, Melvin Konner in *The Tangled Wing: Biological Constraints on the Human Spirit* (Heinemann, London, 1982) spell out a very formidable case against the view, still popular with some anthropologists, that it makes any sense to think of human beings as creatures devoid of innate tendencies to aggression.

5 *Nicomachean Ethics*, book II, esp. chapter 5, and book III, chapters 6–9.

6 In *Patterns of Culture* (Routledge & Kegan Paul, London, 1935) chapter IV.

7 *The Biology of Peace and War*, pp.150–8.

8 Ibid., pp.129–50. Both Eibl-Eibesfeldt and Konner, who has also lived and worked among Bushmen, esteem them very highly, but none the less think it essential to resist the projection on to them of misleading fantasies. A survey has found, incidentally, that the murder rate among !Kung bushmen is higher than that in the United States (see R. B. Lee, '!Kung Bushmen Violence' in *Hunters and Gatherers To-Day*, ed. M. G. Bicchieri (Holt, Rinehart & Winston, New York, 1972). Konner reports a similar situation for the San Bushmen (*The Tangled Wing*, p.9).

5 FATES, CAUSES AND FREE-WILL

1 These phrases have become standard ammunition in the attacks made by social scientists, first on ethologists and more lately on sociobiologists. They have the very serious weakness that they may express either a general objection to all determinism—to all causal explanation of human affairs—or a much more limited one to the use of *biological* causes in explanation rather than economic or social or historical ones. The latter use is the natural one for Marxists, who accept economic determinism. It makes a totally different case, which I shall not discuss here, because it has nothing to do with free-will and I have dealt with it elsewhere repeatedly— by insisting that one kind of explanation does not exclude another.

The way in which these phrases are currently used can be seen, e.g. in *The Use and Abuse of Biology* by Marshall Sahlins (Tavistock, London, 1977), p.11 onwards, and in the attacks collected in A. Caplan's collection, *The Sociobiology Debate* (Harper & Row, New York, 1978). The appalling confusion of sociobiological writing itself of course adds to the chaos. Roger Trigg has lately made a commendable attempt to arbitrate the main issues in *The Shaping of Man: Philosophical Aspects of Sociobiology* (Blackwell, Oxford, 1982). I said a good deal about it in *Beast and Man*, dealing with the meaning of 'determinism' briefly on pp.62–8. I do so more fully in 'Rival Fatalisms: The Hollowness of the Sociobiology Debate in *Sociobiology Examined*, ed. Ashley Montagu (Oxford University Press, 1980).

2 *The Duchess of Malfi*, Act V, Scene 4.

3 See his *Behind the Mirror: A Search for a Natural History of Human Knowledge* (trans. Ronald Taylor, Harcourt Brace Jovanovich, New York, 1977), 'Epistemological Prolegomena,' pp. 1–20. This is a very important argument, strangely neglected.

4 Kant's idea was not that the will was a peculiar part of people which—like a specially hard rock—was impervious to causes. He thought that notion useless; its failure was the starting-point of his whole project, as the introduction to the *Critique of Pure Reason* shows. (Williams's phrase 'immune to luck' is I think a little unlucky in suggesting this rejected model.) Instead he distinguished between two radically different ways of thinking about people—the theoretical and the practical. Causality belonged to the first; terms like will, freedom, responsibility and morality to the second. The first concerns the hand dealt us; the second, what we try to do with it. They do not compete. Neither is supreme, both are necessary, both are incomplete. When Williams reproves Kant for 'trying to make morality immune to luck,' he seems to be treating the first framework as the only proper one, and practical thinking as an anomaly within it. Before Kant's time, this was treated as the only possibility. Kant, however, was far more sceptical than is often noticed in not only distinguishing the two, but seriously accepting that the connexion between them could never be made fully intelligible. (See the closing section of the *Groundwork*.) With great care, which sometimes produces great obscurity, he explained the need for the division and how to use it without destroying our general confidence in thought. Whatever mistakes he made here, the distinction itself has surely enormous value. To Spinoza, as to Plato, it had seemed plausible to treat morality as a more exalted relative of geometry. The result

had been to shake confidence in the whole possibility of using reason practically at all. Kant pointed towards a quite different way of doing so. The modern distinction between fact and value derives from him. But it has been distorted—on the one hand by the attempt to exclude thought again entirely from the sphere of value (emotivism and existentialism) and on the other by various attempts (oddly described as 'naturalism') to get value back into the domain of fact.

Both these devices can make moral judgment seem a much easier, less painful affair than it actually is, and can seem to provide infallible, sure-fire ways of performing it which can insure us against future self-reproach. That Kant did not suppose this possible is clear from many sceptical passages, e.g. that which opens the second chapter of the *Groundwork*. Williams and Strawson are right to protest against such distortion. But scepticism which does not mark its limits produces only another over-simplification—'we can never judge.' The grimness of many real choices—which Kant never doubted—must be firmly accepted. But it is not the only datum.

Metaphysically, it seems far easier for us today than it was for Kant to accept that thought has a number of branches which can legitimately be used together, even though we have no neat enclosing system for them, and that the joints of every conceptual scheme—including those of science—are certain to be marked by paradoxes.

5 Personifying fatalism rages here unchecked, 'We are survival machines—robot vehicles blindly programmed to preserve the selfish molecules known as genes' (Richard Dawkins, *The Selfish Gene*, Oxford University Press, 1976, p.x). 'The individual organism is only the vehicle of genes ... the organism is only DNA's way of making more DNA' (Edward O. Wilson, *Sociobiology; The New Synthesis*, Harvard University Press, Cambridge, Mass., 1975, p.3). Complaints are met by the claim that this is just a metaphor. But a chronic, unvarying metaphor cannot fail to be part of the meaning.

6 *Capital*, vol.I, chapter 24, section 5 (trans. Ben Fowkes, Penguin, Harmondsworth, 1976), pp.758–9 footnote. Somewhat mysteriously, this passage does not appear in full in all translations, nor even in all editions of the same translation. But it does appear in the first official English translation (by Moore and Aveling) of 1887, which was checked and edited by Engels in person, so there is no doubt of its authenticity.

7 *Enquiry Concerning Human Understanding*, part 1, section viii, 65.

6 SELVES AND SHADOWS

1 It appears on the cover of his collection of cartoons, appropriately called *Well, There's your Problem*, published by Penguin, Harmondsworth, 1980.

2 Bishop Butler, *Fifteen Sermons*, Sermon X 'Upon Self-Deceit', section 16.

3 *Nicomachean Ethics* book VII, chapters 1–10.

4 R. L. Stevenson, *The Strange Case of Dr Jekyll and Mr Hyde*, Chapter 1 (Nelson, London, 1956), p.6.

5 *Enquiry Concerning the Principles of Morals*, part ii, section V, 183.

6 Stevenson, chapter 10, p.86.

7 Ibid., pp.94–5, 96–7.

8 Ibid., chapter 2, p.25.

9 Ibid., p.75.

10 Ibid., p.21.

11 Ibid., p.25.

12 These and other cases are well discussed by Ralph Timms in *Doubles in Literary Psychology* (Bowes & Bowes, Cambridge, 1949).

13 James Hogg, *The Confessions of a Justified Sinner*, 1824, reprinted with an introduction by André Gide, Panther Books, London, 1970.

14 Ibid., p.111.

15 Ibid., pp.121–2.

16 Stevenson, chapter 10, p.90.

17 C. G. Jung, *Modern Man in Search of a Soul*, p.40.

18 A remarkable story, well traced by Charles Williams in his *Witchcraft* (Faber, London, 1941).

19 For this extremely strange business, see Konrad Heiden, *Der Fuehrer: Hitler's Rise to Power* (trans. Ralph Mannheim, Gollancz, 1944), chapter 1.

20 Ibid., p.118.

7 THE INSTIGATORS

1 *Paradise Lost*, book 1, ll.589–612.

2 Ibid., book 2, 481–98.

3 Ibid., book 4, ll.73–83.

4 Ibid., book 4, ll.108–13. Italics mine.

5 Ibid., book 1, ll.159–162.

6 William Styron, *Sophie's Choice* (Corgi Books, London, 1980), p.201.

7 Elizabeth Anscombe, *Intention* (Blackwell, Oxford, 1957), p.79.

8 *Paradise Lost*, book 1, l.263.

9 Hannah Arendt, *Eichmann in Jerusalem*, pp.115, 139, 153, 213.
10 Ibid., p.287.
11 S. T. Coleridge, *Notes on the Tragedies of Shakespeare: Othello*.
12 *Othello*, Act II, Scene 1, 1.208; Act II, Scene III, 1.102.
13 *Othello*, Act V, Scene II, 1.300.
14 The first is discussed by F. L. Lucas in *Literature and Psychology* (Cassell, London, 1951), p.76, and J. I. M. Stewart, *Character and Motive in Shakespeare* (Haskell, New York, 1977), p.143, S. E. Hyman in *Iago: Some Approaches (Atheneum, New York, 1970)* discusses both.

8 DEATH-WISH

1 From *Beyond the Pleasure Principle* (trans. C. J. M. Hubback, International Psycho-Analytical Press, London, 1922, p.47. Hereafter referred to as *BPP*.
2 *BPP*, pp.44–5.
3 *BPP*, p.71.
4 Ibid.
5 *Civilization and its Discontents* (trans. Joan Riviere, Hogarth Press, London, 1930), pp.70–71. Hereafter referred to as *CD*.
6 *CD*, pp.66 and 68.
7 *CD*, p.135.
8 *CD*, p.74.
9 See Jane van Lawick-Goodall, *In the Shadow of Man* (Collins, London, 1971), p.168.
10 A criticism of Freud well argued by Victoria Hamilton in *Narcissus and Oedipus: The Children of Psycho-analysis* (Routledge & Kegan Paul, London, 1982).
11 *BPP*, p.62.
12 *CD*, p.99 and p.102.
13 *BPP*, pp.48 and 63.
14 *BPP*, pp.20 and 24.
15 Explicitly mentioned at *CD*, p.100, and clearly a pervasive interest throughout that book.
16 *BPP*, pp.81–2.
17 *CD*, p.64.
18 *CD*, p.137.

9 EVIL IN EVOLUTION

1 *The Descent of Man* (1st edition, reprinted Princeton University Press, 1981), pp.71–2. The word *instinct* may give us trouble here. Darwin used it in the traditional sense for any inherited tendency to a particular kind of behaviour. Since his day, the whole idea of such tendencies in man has come under political attack, and the word instinct in particular has been used distortedly, to stand for a specially narrow, automatic kind of tendency whose presence in man was easy to deny. Its proper use, which seems as suitable for man as for any other species, may be seen in *The Study of Instinct* by N. Tinbergen (Oxford University Press, 1951, see especially chapter 5). I have discussed this point in *Beast and Man*, chapter 3, using the distinction of open and closed instincts, and more fully in 'The Notion of Instinct' in *Heart and Mind*. Since Tinbergen wrote, zoologists themselves have, for quite different reasons, turned to a different terminology which allows of making further distinctions, and 'instinct' is not currently a technical term with them. (It does not, for instance, figure at all in the index of Robert Hinde's *Ethology* (Fontana, Glasgow, 1982) though Tinbergen's views are constantly discussed throughout.) The reasons for this change are admirably explained by Adolf Portmann in *Animals as Social Beings* (trans. Oliver Coburn, Viking, New York, 1961). I do not think that these technical considerations need affect ordinary usage, and I have continued to use the word in Tinbergen's sense, which is fully compatible with Darwin's, though more developed. The cause of intelligibility is, I think, best served by keeping such continuities where possible.

   The attempts of Freud's followers to expel instinct from his thought have been vigorous but not very successful.

2 *Varieties of Religious Experience* (Mentor, New York, 1958), p.281.

3 *The Denial of Death* (Free Press Macmillan, New York, 1973), p.30.

4 Eric Berne, in *Games People Play* (Penguin, Harmondsworth, 1964) has brought out well the power and deadly seriousness which such games can have. He is especially interesting on the game he calls *Cops and Robbers*—showing how the mutual obsession of opponents leads them to become alike, and eventually indistinguishable.

5 By C. S. Lewis (Geoffrey Bles, London, 1942), see pp.49–50 and 64. Aristotle's discussions of bad pleasures are very relevant here. See his *Nicomachean Ethics*, book VII, chapter 12 and book X, chapters 3 and 5.

6 Its central question is whether it is better to do injustice or to suffer it— a question posed at the opening of book two and answered by Socrates

in book nine (588B) by the conclusion that thorough injustice cannot fail to destroy its owner inwardly.

7 See for instance papers V and VI in his *Modern Man in Search of a Soul* (trans. Dell and Baynes, Routledge & Kegan Paul, London, 1945) and chapter 2 of *The Integration of the Personality* (trans. Dell and Baynes, Routledge & Kegan Paul, 1940). Anthony Storr in his book *Jung* (Fontana, Glasgow, 1973) rates Jung's grasp of the mid-life crisis as a particularly valuable achievement.

8 *Principia Ethica* (Cambridge University Press, 1948), pp.68–70.

9 Aristotle's doctrine of virtue as a mean is often useful here. (See *Nicomachean Ethics*, books II, IV and V.) He was not, as is sometimes thought, recommending a cautious mediocrity, but pointing out how many good attitudes can turn out vicious if allowed to develop without limit at the expense of others, which are needed to correct them.

10 The idea of creating or inventing values was put forward by Nietzsche (see for instance *Thus Spake Zarathustra* part 3, 'Of Old and New Tables') and strongly supported by Sartre (see *Existentialism and Humanism*, p.49). I have discussed the serious difficulties attending such concepts in 'Creation and Originality' in my *Heart and Mind*.

11 Darwin, *The Descent of Man*, pp. 84 and 91.

12 Ibid., pp.71–2.

13 Ibid., p.92.

14 *On The Genealogy of Morals* (trans. W. Kaufmann and R. J. Hollingdale, Vintage Books, New York, 1969), pp.57–8.

15 'The social instincts—the prime principle of man's moral constitution—with the aid of active intellectual powers and the effects of habit, naturally lead to the golden rule, "As ye would that men should do to you, do ye to them likewise" and this lies at the foundation of morality' (Darwin, *The Descent of Man*, p.106).

16 *Nicomachean Ethics*, book VII, chapters 12–14; book X, chapters 2–5.

17 Preface to Butler's *Sermons*, section 40.

18 St John, X. 10.

19 Goethe, *Faust*, Part 1 (trans. Philip Wayne, Penguin, Harmondsworth, 1980), p.71. On this whole issue, see Norman O. Brown, *Life Against Death: The Psycho-Analytic Meaning of History* (Wesleyan University Press, Connecticut, 1959).

20 Erich Fromm, *The Anatomy of Human Destructiveness* (Jonathan Cape, 1974).

21 Quoted in *The Anatomy of Human Destructiveness*, pp. 344 and 345

from *Selected Writings of F. T. Marinetti*, ed. R. W. Flint, Farrar, Strauss & Giroux, New York, 1971.

22 *The Anatomy of Human Destructiveness*, p.10.

23 Ibid.

24 Ibid., p.218.

25 Epistle to the Galatians, V: 17.

INDEX

acceptance, problem of 169–71
Adler, A. 7
ageing 185
aggression 3, 4, 7–8, 195, 216;
    anger and 78, 81–2, 85–6, 91,
    93–4; in animals 78, 197; in
    children 84, 90–1, 94; death-
    wish and 163, 166, 176–8, 197;
    destructiveness and 87–90; fear
    and 80–4, 175; functions of 90–3;
    innateness of 66–7, 73, 74–7,
    94, 96; non-aggression 74–9,
    82–3, 85–6, 93; physical basis of
    84–6; repressed 131;
    understanding 74–94; see also
    anger
alien being, evil as 116–17,133–4
ambition 8, 7, 152, 159, 195
Andersen, H. 123
anger 77–8, 81, 85, 91, 93–4,
    128–30, 135; see also aggression
animals: aggression 78, 197;
    'instincts' 8; intelligence, lack
    of 188–90, 191; sexuality
    163–4; symbolic 122
Anscombe, E. 141
anthropology 39, 91
anti-semitism see Jews
apathy 40
appeasement 6
approval 51
Aquinas, St T. 20
Arendt, H. 49–51, 52, 63, 65,
    144
argument 88, 90
Aristotle: on mean 81, 222; on
    motives 23; on pleasure 194;
    on unconscious vice 60–1,
    118; on weak will 69
arts 200
attack and aggression 77–8
Augustine, St 102–3
autonomy versus continuity
    55–6

balance of vice and virtue 3, 14, 95, 140
banality of evil 65
Becker, E. 180
Belgium 11
Benedict, R. 92
Bentham, J. 109
Berlin, I. 31, 212
birth 18–20
Blake, W. 74, 156
blame 10, 51–2, 70, 97
boredom 84
Brown, N. O. 203
Browning, R. 1
Buddhism 169, 198
bureaucracy 66, 72
Buridan's ass 30
Bushmen 92, 216
Butler, Bishop J. 14, 33, 117–18, 195, 206

callousness 121
Calvin, J. 103, 124
Cathar heresy 19
causes: fates and free-will 95–115; as hostile beings 97; of wickedness 2–4, 9, 14
celibacy 20
centrality of thought 20–1
centre, empty 143–4
chance see luck
change, personal 105–6
children 198; play and aggression 84, 90, 94
choice, optimism about 28–9
Christianity: and Manichaeans 18–20; and negativity of evil 13, 19–20; Satan 136–143, 155–7, 184; and sin 2; and slave morality 41; see also God
Coleridge, S. T. 144, 149
comic characters 150–1

communal crimes 131
competitiveness 7
compulsive repetition 168
conflict, inner 119–35; Darwin's analysis of 189–92
continuity 106; autonomy versus 55–6; of motives 42
co-operation 110
Copernicus, N. 42–3
Coriolanus 152
corporate views 53, 54, 73
cosmic move 166–7
courage 14, 43
cowardice 38, 40, 43, 80, 165
creativity 112, 115
cruelty 121, 149
cultural: differences 44–5; relativism 21; scepticism 38–40

darkness 1–7
Darwin, C. 99, 179, 199, 204, 206; analysis of conflict 187–192
death 98–9; fear of 180
death-wish 158–78, 204–5; acceptance, problem of 169–71; aggression and 163, 166, 176–8, 197; ambition and 159; cosmic move 166–7; dualism, radical 167–9; gap to be filled 158–61; individual, isolated 161–4; medical model, passiveness of 164–6; negative motivation and 182–4; self- knowledge, need for 171–6; self-preservation and 179–81
dehumanization 108
deity, chance seen as 99; see also God
denial of innate causes 96
Denmark 10–11
Descartes, R. 21, 35, 112

destruction, roads to, in evolution 181–4

destructiveness 15, 34, 58, 93–4, 143, 155–7, 203

distinguished from aggression 87–9; *see also* death-wish

determinism 53, 96–7, 100–3, 110–15

deterrence 174

devil 4, 10, 19, 124, 137; *see also* Satan

dialogue, inner and duality 119–22

Dickens, C. 112, 150

differences, cultural 44–5

dirt 6

disapproval 51

dishonesty 165

dogmatism 38

dominance 7, 197

doubt *see* scepticism

Douglas, M. 6

drama 119

dreams 167–8

dualism 206–7; and Christianity 19–20; in evolution 197–204; Freudian 167–9, 195, 197–9, 206; Manichaean 18–20, 46, 167–8, 177; Platonic 209; and self-deception 116–17

Durkheim, E. 3

Eden, A. 6

Eibl-Eibesfeldt, I. 92

Eichmann, A. 50, 65, 135, 144

emancipation of women 173

emotions 21, 82, 85, 94, 146

Empedocles 167

empiricism 22

Engels, F. 26

Enlightenment 70

envy 146–8, 152, 157, 159

epiphenomenalism 115

Eros 161, 177

Euripides 150

evil: and aggression 67, 74–94, 197; as independent force 17–19, 46; as negative 13–18, 38, 120, 135, 183; banality of 64; beyond good and evil 40, 63; choice of evils 29–30; problem of evil 1–16, 64–5, 177, 192

evolution, evil in 179–207

excitement, need for 84–5, 94

excuse for negligence 64

existentialism 21, 57, 153–4

external: being, evil as 116–17, 133; causes of wickedness 2–4, 9

Fall and Atonement 69, 70, 73, 205; *see also* Satan

fatalism 29, 74–5; death-wish and 170; determinism and 99–100, 110–15; fear of 8; menace of 95–100

fates, causes and free-will 95–115

'fault-finding' 97

Faust 15, 87, 222

fear 8, 193; aggression and 80–4, 175; courage and 43; of death 180; evil, avoiding 40; innateness of 79–85, 93–4; need for 84–6, 90–1, 94; obsessive 87

feelings *see* emotions

followers and leaders 131–3

foreknowledge 102–3, 114

forgetfulness 191

France 11, 130

freedom 105, 106; to sin 124–6

free-will 53, 95–115 passim 188

Freud, S., and Freudianism 22, 57, 70, 107–8; on aggression 67, 90, 94; on death-wish 158–71, 175–6,

184–5, 187, 203–4; on dualism 167–9, 195, 197–9, 206; followers 67; on motives 114; on Othello 153 reductiveness of 23
Fromm, E. 4, 201, 203, 207
functions of aggression 90–3
Futurists 201–2

gambling option 27–31
games theory 173, 178
Garibaldi, G. 143
Gauguin, P. 27–9, 37
generosity 14
Germany see Jews; Nazism
Gnostics 18–20
God: blaming 1–2, 15, 19, 69; evolution and 99; existence of 7; foreknowledge 102–3, 114; punitive 70; prayer and 202; reversal and 138–43; see also Christianity
Goethe, J. W. von 15, 33
good 14, 18, 38, 40, 139–41
grandeur, sources of 136–8, 156
gratitude, argument from 28
Gray, Dorian 123–4
Greek thought 13, 69
groups 174–5
guilt 52, 170, 172, 182

habit and pleasure 183
hatred 87–8, 155
Heiden, K. 131–2
hell 10; see also Satan
Heraclitus 33, 167
heresy 19, 134
Hinduism 69
Hitler, A. 60–3, 131,143, 157, 159, 176; see also Nazism
Hobbes, T. 7, 163, 186
Hogg, J. 123
honesty 169–70, 177

Höss, R. 139
hostility see aggression; anger
Housman, A. E. 98
human nature, notion of 107–9, 114
humbug 40, 165
Hume, D. 22, 109, 121, 192
Huxley, T. H. 167
hypocrisy 24, 27–8, 59, 165

Iago 144–7, 152–7 passim 176
ideals and practice 108
identity, personal 119
illusion 107
imaginary evil 140
immoralism 24, 31–2, 47; see also intelligibility and immoralism
incest-avoidance 163
individual 162–3; autonomy and continuity 55–6; invisible 53; isolated 161–4; judgment and 50, 54; loss of 52–4
'individualism, methodological' 54
inertia 40
innateness: of aggression 66–7, 73, 74–7, 93–4, 96; denial of 96; of fear 79–85, 93–4; of norms 43
insanity 60–3, 153; psychopathy 58, 80, 132, 154, 159
instigators 136–57
instincts 8, 190, 221
intelligence 189, 192
intelligibility: and immoralism 17–48; of moral judgments 141
internal causes of wickedness 2–4, 14–15
isolated individual 161–4
Italy 11

James, W. 180
Jekyll, Dr, and Mr Hyde 120–6, 134
Jesus 198; see also Christianity

Jews, attitudes to 50, 63, 135, 143–4
Jonson, B. 150
judgment 54, 56–7, 71–2, 140; fear
    of 49–53
Jung, C. G. 41, 108, 126, 185, 191,
    203
justification 27, 75–6

Kant I. 28, 55, 102, 114
Karenina, Anna 26–7, 29
Kierkegaard, S. 171
Kliban, E. 116, 187
knowledge: concept of 35–6;
    disagreeable 107; Gnostic 18;
    theoretical 35
Konner, M. 216

law, natural 98
Lawrence, D. H. 25–6
leaders and led 131–3, 135
Leibniz, G. W. 21
liberty 141–2
life-instinct 161, 186; see also death-
    wish
Lorenz, K. 67, 102
love 162–3; and death 168, 177
luck/chance 27, 56–7, 99, 211, 217
Luther, Martin 209

McCarthy, J. 132
Macbeth 86, 144
Machiavelli, N. 31
machine-symbolism 201–3, 207
madness see insanity
Mani 18
Manichaeans 18–20, 46, 167–8,
    177, 195, 206
Marinetti, F. T. 201–2
Marx, K. and Marxism 3, 26, 53,
    108–9, 114, 171
masochism 161
master-morality 40

meanness 38
medical model 61–2, 164–6, 176
Mephistopheles 13–15, 20, 33, 69,
    87, 181, 198
'methodological individualism'
    54
Mill, J. S. 25, 199
Milton, J. 136–7, 140, 156
misfortune 62
misogyny 19, 202
monomania 150–7
Moore, G. E. 186
moral: evil 12; luck 27, 56–7, 58,
    211; vacuum 63
morality 199–201, 213–15, 217;
    meaning of 27–32; phantom
    62–3; as vampirism 32
motives 7–9, 21–2, 193–200, 207;
    adequacy of 148–50, 157;
    arrangement of 188; continuity
    of 42; hidden 173; lack of 65–6;
    Nazis 4–5; negative 75, 143,
    156–7, 182–4; power-related 8,
    15; unrecognizable 127–8
mystification 24
myth 11–12, 167; see also Satan

Nagel, T. 56–7, 214
natural: evil, problem of 1–16; law
    98
Nazism 5–6, 30, 60, 139;
    Eichmann 50, 65–6, 135, 144;
    Hitler 60, 63, 131, 143, 157, 159,
    176; ideology undefended 63;
    Jews and 50, 63, 135, 143–4; as
    moral vacuum 63; motives
    4–5
necrophilia 203; see also death-
    wish
negativity 33, 198; of evil 7–10, 13–
    20, 38, 64, 72, 135, 195; of
    motives 76, 143, 157, 182–4; and

Nietzsche 32–3; views of human nature 107
negligence 64–6
Nietzsche, F. 31, 47, 59–60, 107–8, 165, 178, 199; on going beyond good and evil 40–2; Hitler, effect on 63; on immoralism 31–2; on 'morality of mores' 191–2; negativity 33; on power 7, 23–4; revaluation 39; on Zarathustra 17, 33
Nirvana-principle 161, 169
no, saying see negativity
non-aggression 74–9; see also Nongs
Nongs (non-aggressive creatures), 79, 82–3, 85–6, 93
norms, innate 43
Norsemen 69
Nuremburg trials 63

obsession 86, 150–7, 160, 182
Oedipus 98, 100, 111, 114
omnipotence, psychological 70
optimism about choice 29
Orwell, G. 128
Othello 145, 153–4

pain 82
pair-formation 164
paradox 24, 39, 46, 55–6, 64–6
passivity: of herd 131, of medical model 164–6, 177
Paul, St 204, 208
Pelagius 102
persecution 130
personality 106, 190
Persia see Manichaeans
phantom moralities 62–3
physical: basis of aggression 84–6; sciences 53, 104–5; things, bad 19

Plato 21, 140, 184, 205, 209, 210
play and aggression 84, 90, 94
pleasure-principle 161–2, 176, 183, 186
pluralism 25–6, 30
politics 45, 172
positivity 7–9, 46, 133, 192–7; see also negativity
possession 117, 133
possessiveness 7, 195
power 7–8, 15, 23–4
practical thought 54
praise 38–9, 141
prediction: and determinism 110–12, 113–14; limited role in thought 100–4
preferences, society as expression of 191
pride 137, 139, 146, 148, 157
projection 127–30
propaganda 131
Protestants 20; see also Christianity
psychopaths 58, 80, 132, 154; death-wish and 159; see also insanity
Pythagoras 111–12

Racine, J. 150–1
radical dualism 167–9
randomness 105–14
rationalism 21–2, 46, 55, 102
realism, difficulty of 67–73
reductiveness 23–4; death-wish theory and 161–2, 166
regularity 105
relativism, cultural 21
religion see Christianity; Manichaeans
remorse 69, 189–90
repetition, compulsive 167
repression 131

reproduction 18–20, 85
resentment 10
responsibility, elusiveness of 30, 49–73
revenge 159
reversal, meaning of 138–43
risk 149
Röhm, E. 60
Romantic Movement 142
Rousseau, J.-J. 22
Russell, B. 25–6
Russia 130
Ryle, G. 36

sadism 161
Sartre, J.-P. 29–30, 37, 55–6, 211
Satan 136–42, 155–6, 183–4
scepticism 34–9, 45, 56–60
Schlemihl, P. 123, 134
Schopenhauer, A. 167
sciences 52–3, 94, 96–97, 104–5, 109–10
self: -deception 40, 116–19, 134, 165; -destruction see death-wish; -divisions in 118–19; -knowledge, need for 171–6; -preservation 162, 179–81
selves and shadows 116–35
sentimentality 40
sexuality: of animals 163–4; culture and 163; denial of 165, 170; disturbed 154; and emotion 85, 94; family and 162; Freudian view of 172, 177, 184; as instinct 79, 85, 162; and life 161; as motive 8; not sinful 11, 16; pleasure and 176; as sin 18–20
shadows 41; see also selves and shadows
Siegfried 80
simplicity 23–5

sin 199; belief in 10–11, 16; concept of 2, 11; original 9, 12, 70
slave morality 40–1
slavery 104
social: conditions 2–4; Darwinism 114; sciences 53, 96, 104–5
socialization 163–4
society 53–4, 96, 191
sociobiology 218
Socrates 20, 23, 24, 46, 55, 64–5, 67–8, 71–2
Spinoza, B. 26
splendour, sources of 136–8, 156
Stevenson, R. L. 120, 126
Stoics 33, 169
Stoppard, T. 34
Strawson, P. 25, 26–7, 30, 36
Styron, W. 139–40
Suez expedition 6
symbolic animals 122
sympathy 192

Teichman, J. 36
temptation 70–1
territoriality 7
theoretical: knowledge 35; thought 54
thought: centrality of 21; and prediction 100–4; types of 54, 72
threats 174–5
Tinbergen, N. 221
totalitarianism 66
tragedy 37, 137, 150–1
traumas 167–8
trivialization 67
truth 35–6, 176

unconscious vice 60–1, 118
understanding aggression 74–94

unreality of vices without virtues 3,
14
utilitarianism 211
Utopia 82–3, 92

vacuum: evil as 120; moral 33–7,
63
vampirism, morality as 32
vanity 125
vice *see* virtues; wickedness
vicious people 59–62
vindictiveness 10
violence, justification of 76
virtues, balanced by vice 3, 14, 95,
140
Voltaire 70

Wagner, R. 63
wars 131; cold 193; (1870) 130;
glorified 201; World, First 64,
68, 75, 127, 166, 171, 177; World,
Second 6, 82

Webster, J. 99
weightlessness 42–4
Weil, S. 140
will 55, 217; free- 53, 95–115; weak
60–2, 69
Williams, B. 27–30, 35, 37, 56, 58,
210, 214, 217–18
Williams, C. 219
witch-hunting 129–31, 134, 219
Wittgenstein, L. 212
women: attitudes to 18–20, 201–2;
emancipation 173
Wootton, B. 58–9
Wringhim, R. 123–4, 134
wrong, not doing it willingly 20–2,
46, 55, 64

yes, need to say 33

Zarathustra/Zoroaster 17–18; *see
also* Manichaeans
Zuni Indians 92